SPORTING GUNS

SPORTING GUNS

A GUIDE TO THE WORLD'S RIFLES AND SHOTGUNS

Chris McNab

amber
BOOKS

First published in 2007 by
Amber Books Ltd
Bradley's Close
74–77 White Lion Street
London N1 9PF
United Kingdom
www.amberbooks.co.uk

ISBN 978-1-905704-47-7

Project Editor: Michael Spilling
Designer: Jerry Williams
Picture Research: Kate Green

Printed and bound in Dubai

10 9 8 7 6 5 4 3 2 1

CONTENTS

INTRODUCTION

Shooting is an intense, absorbing pastime. The gun, however, is only part of the equation. Any good shooter will also understand fieldcraft, ballistics, basic animal anatomy, the climate and environment, gun mechanics, the law, and a host of other topics and issues. All this knowledge and interest should be channelled into that single moment when aim is taken and the trigger is pulled.

This book is, admittedly, only a partial view of sporting guns. Here are listed 166 of the latest shotguns and rifles, the main purposes of which are hunting and shooting at targets. Only long guns are featured here, not handguns.

This is mainly to give the book a greater focus within what are the most popular categories of sporting weapons (a predominant number of handguns are purchased for personal or home defence rather than sport).

The book aims to give the rifle or shotgun buyer some grounding in what is out there, whether it is intended to be a first gun or an addition to an already well-filled gun cabinet.

Safety

The first duty of any gun book is to reiterate the principles of firearms safety. Like the safety briefing aboard an aircraft, these can often be treated casually. Thousands of people die every year in shooting accidents, yet almost every incident could be prevented with basic safety measures.

These are:

- Treat every gun as if it was loaded. On picking up any weapon make sure that it is empty by breaking open the action or opening the bolt.
- Never point the muzzle at anything you wouldn't be prepared to shoot.
- Keep the safety on at all times, and your finger off the trigger, until you are ready to shoot.
- Understand how your gun works. Spend time with the user guide and also, vitally, be clear about what ammunition type your gun will take. Keep the gun clean and well maintained.
- If you pull the trigger and the gun doesn't go off, point it at a safe place and do nothing for up to 30 seconds. Then unload the gun.
- Check the barrel of the gun for obstructions before you shoot, and the same if the barrel of the gun has come into contact with mud or earth.
- Don't load the weapon until you are ready to shoot. Keep the gun safely stored so that unauthorized people cannot get access to it. This is particularly important if there are children in the house.
- Be aware of what is beyond your target. Remember that you can miss and that some bullets can pass through prey and continue their flight for a long distance. Make sure your shot has a solid stop in the background.
- When hunting in a pair or group, be continually aware of where everyone else is, and set generous margins of error for how much swing you will allow yourself before abandoning the shot because other people are too close.

It is crucial that every shooter understands the basic workings of his or her weapon to avoid unnecessary accidents.

• Never use anything that impairs your mental focus while shooting, particularly alcohol or drugs (prescription or otherwise).

Responsibility and the law

Following these rules strictly will ensure your shooting experience is safe and enjoyable. Shooters must be models of responsibility if the sport is to survive. This is particularly important in hunting. Hunters should only shoot another living species if a) it is lawful (read up on national, state and local legislation); b) there is a legitimate purpose, such as pest control, authorized culls, or for food; and c) if they have the skill to do so. If you hunt, try to eat or use everything you kill. Hunters should find out as much about nature as they can, because, despite the frequent public perception, most good shooters are passionately interested in conservation.

Responsible shooting also means owning and using firearms within the limits of the law. Check out all district, state and national laws before purchasing a firearm, and ensure that all the correct paperwork is filed promptly with the authorities. Remember that gun laws vary dramatically between states and countries, particularly with regard to transportation and storage of firearms and the places guns can be used, so find out about legal variations prior to making a journey with your gun. Be particularly careful if taking your gun abroad on a sporting trip – it may be best to hire guns abroad to avoid the complex mass of paperwork it requires to transport firearms. Be aware that falling foul of a gun law can result in serious penalties, including imprisonment, so take legal issues very seriously.

NOTE ON PRICING:

Gun prices change every year, shifting with factors such as inflation, marketing strategies, retail offers, new lines, and upgrades.

In this book a simple system of pricing symbols is used to give the reader a general idea of the price band each particular weapon belongs in. This is:

$ – up to $1000 (£550/€800)

$$ – from $1000 to $2000 (£550–1100/€800–1600)

$$$ – from $2000 to $5000 (£1100–2750/€1600–4000)

$$$$ – from $5000 to $10,000 (£2750–5500/€4000–8000)

$$$$$ – $10,000+ (£5500/€8000)

These price bands are a general guideline only, and the reader should clarify pricing before any purchase. Furthermore, all data in this book is based on current information sources. The reader is therefore advised to consult with gunshop staff or the relevant gunmaker before purchasing a firearm to make sure that it truly meets their requirements and budget.

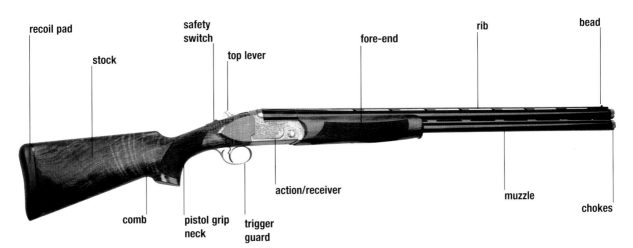

recoil pad · stock · safety switch · top lever · fore-end · rib · bead · comb · pistol grip neck · trigger guard · action/receiver · muzzle · chokes

CHAPTER 1

BREECH-LOADING SHOTGUNS & RIFLES

From .410s to 12 gauges, shotguns vary in size and weight. If possible, try a variety of guns before you purchase one. Although some adjustments can be made, it is best to get a gun that 'feels right' if you can.

The over-and-under layout is the most popular format for clay-target shooting, and accounts for many field shotgun sales. An over-and-under recoils in a 'straight in line' manner, whereas a side-by-side gun produces more of a lateral kick when fired.

For those wanting to buy a breech-loading shotgun, the choice is initially bewildering. The majority of shotguns are either side-by-sides (where the barrels are side-by-side) or over-and-unders, so choosing between the two formats is often the first, and simplest, decision. Side-by-sides tend to be light, have a very different sight plane to over-and-unders (which are flatter, with the rib set only a short distance from the front hand), recoil in a lateral manner, and also, many feel, bring with them the older traditions and aesthetics of shotgunning. Over-and-unders, by stacking the barrels on top of one another, give a much slimmer view down the barrel, recoil straight in line with the shoulder, interfere less with the peripheral vision, and, generally, seem to take the lion's share of innovation. (The over-and-under's recoil makes it better for rapid shooting, hence it is almost universally standard for clay shooting.) Arguments roll on about the relative advantages of the two, but buying any shotgun really centres on two criteria – what do you want the gun for, and how does it fit?

The gauge of the weapon is one of the first choices that determine a shotgun's purpose. The main shotgun gauges,

Rifled break-action guns tend to be used for hunting sports where the quarry is fast-moving, like boar or light deer. The scope here will give the gun accuracy out past 100m (328ft).

working from smallest to largest, are .410, 28, 16, 20, and 12, with 10-bore, 8-bore, and even larger, shotguns also available.

Both .410 and 28-bore shotguns are principally suited to shooting small, light game, especially when the shooter wants no recoil, while the 16- and 20-bore guns are good for a wider range of bird shooting, such as pigeon, quail and pheasant, and ground animals like rabbits and hares. The 20-gauge is also an enjoyable clay gun for sporting disciplines.

An advantage of the small-calibre guns is that they tend to be light, which means they can be comfortably carried around on a day's shoot. Disadvantages can be limited killing power, particularly at range, and expensive shells. This is especially true of more rare gauges such as the 28 and 16.

The 12-gauge shotgun is by far and away the most popular. Depending on the cartridge type selected (an important consideration for any of the gauges), a 12-gauge shotgun will serve the shooter from hunting small ground game up to large wildfowl, and is the definitive clay-shooting gauge. The heavier bores are much more rarely used, and tend to be for those who specialize in long-range wildfowling, where they need to project a great deal of shot up to an unusually high altitude.

Layout and fit

Once the shooter has decided on a gauge, many other variables come into play. Here are some general guidelines. Barrel length is important. The longer the barrel the tighter will be the spread of shot at range, hence long-barrelled 81cm (32in) guns tend to be used more for distance clay disciplines such as trap shooting. A 76cm (30in) gun is a good clay all-rounder and a workable field gun, while the 71cm (28in) barrel serves well for walked-up game and bird shooting and for clay disciplines like skeet and sporting. If you want a gun purely for field shooting, stray towards lighter guns of up to 3.4kg (7.5lb) – you have to carry one around all day – while for clays my personal preference is for a slightly heavier gun. Weightier guns give a more controlled swing, ideal for moving smoothly with a crossing clay, while a lighter gun swings much faster, hence is useful for those snap-shot movements that present themselves in the field.

Chokes

All barrels have a choke, where the barrel narrows to concentrate the shot. Most barrels are fixed choke. A multichoke gun (i.e. one where the choke constriction can be changed via interchangeable choke tubes) is fairly essential for clay shooting, it giving you some control over the spread of shot depending on the layout and even stand (although it is easy to become unnecessarily obsessive about choke changing).

However, for heavy field use a good fixed-choke gun has much to recommend it – there are a few less parts to worry about in terms of corrosion and maintenance. Remember that the choke constrictions can have different terminology depending where you are. In the United States, the standard chokes (from most open to tightest) are Cylinder, Improved Cylinder, Modified, Improved Modified and Full, whereas in the UK the terminology is Cylinder, ¼, ½, ¾ and Full.

Barrel length, gauge, chokes and other variables are unimportant if the gun doesn't fit properly. Have a gun fitted properly for drop (the distance between the top line of the barrels and the comb – the cheek piece – of the gun), cast (the position of the stock in relation to the gun's centreline), and length of pull (the distance between the butt plate and the trigger). Some shotguns come with adjustable stocks to control these dimensions, while others will require professional adjustment by a gunsmith.

The shotgun should mount easily into a shooter's shoulder, the eye seeing a few millimetres of rib incline, straight in line down the barrels. Once a shotgun is fitted properly, and the mount is perfected, the shooter can be confident of shooting where he or she is looking, which is the essence of using a shotgun well.

Gauge Chart

Most non-shooters are not aware that shotguns are available in different sizes of barrel, or gauges. Here is a guide to the most popular gauge sizes.

	10	**12**	**16**
Bore Diameter:			
Inches	.775"	.729"	.662"
Millimeters	19.685	18.516	16.814

	20	**28**	**.410***
Bore Diameter:			
Inches	.615"	.550"	.410"
Millimeters	15.621	13.970	10.414

Aya Model No.2

$$$

The Aya No.2 is a classic side-by-side shotgun from Spain. It is available in many gauges, and has a high-quality sidelock mechanism with fine receiver finishing.

SPECIFICATIONS: **Aya Model No.2**
GAUGE/CALIBRE: 12, 16, 20, 28, .410
BARREL LENGTH: 71cm (28in)
WEIGHT: up to 3.8kg (8.5lb)
EJECTOR TYPE: automatic ejectors
CHOKES: fixed
FEATURES: chopper-lump barrels; sidelock mechanism

Sidelock guns, as their name implies, have the firearm's lockwork mounted on plates on the side of the action. Simply remove the holding pins from the side of each plate, and the gun's main mechanical parts drop out attached to the plate, providing easy maintenance access. While the common boxlock mechanism is stronger and less complicated, sidelocks are generally more prestigious, partly through the standard of engineering that goes into a high-quality sidelock, and partly through the larger expanse of metal on which the engraver can apply his art. (Be careful to distinguish a gun with mere sideplates from an actual sidelock.)

The Aya No.2 looks similar to the No.1, although it is far more common than the latter. It is available in the full spectrum of bores commonly used in field shooting: 12, 16, 20, 28 and .410, and the chamber lengths are either 70mm (2.75in) or 76mm (3in). Chopper-lump barrels give the No.2 a dependably solid connection between barrels and action (the barrels come in one length – 71cm/28in). The action itself is made from forged steel and has a double-locking mechanism.

Classic styling

Although the No.2 is made using the latest production techniques, it is a traditional double-trigger gun (the barrels have fixed chokes, the chokes to order), even when the gun is mounted. The grain of the high-quality walnut and also the superb standard of engraving on the receiver define the look of the gun, which is available in either colour-hardened, old silver or a bright metallic finish.

The No.2 pays special attention to safety. Intercepting safety sears dramatically reduce the possibility of accidental discharge, and the safety switch itself is of an automatic type.

The Aya No.2 is a well-balanced gun, with a slim fore-end that nestles neatly in the hand. Note the shooter's extended finger, a typical method of improving accuracy.

Aya Model No.4

$$$

The Aya Model No.4 is a boxlock shotgun from the prestigious Aya firm, a solid field-shooting weapon from a company with nearly 100 years of gunmaking expertise.

SPECIFICATIONS: Aya Model No.4

GAUGE/CALIBRE: 12, 16, 20, 28, .410

BARREL LENGTH: to order

WEIGHT: from 3.1kg (6.8lb)

EJECTOR TYPE: extractors

CHOKES: fixed – to order

FEATURES: automatic safety; double triggers

Aya is a company that embodies a long and prestigious history of Spanish gunmaking. Founded in 1917 by Nicolás Aranzábal and Miguel Aguirre, Aya is based in Eibar in the Basque region, and has established an international reputation for first-class double guns, particularly its sidelock side-by-side weapons.

These include the Models No.1 and No.2, both twin-trigger weapons featuring double-barrel block locking. The Model No.4 adds a boxlock weapon to the Aya catalogue. It is available in 12, 16, 20, 28 or .410 gauges, thereby covering most requirements for field shooting. Standard barrel length is 71cm (28in) with other barrel lengths available to order (76cm/30in being the most popular alternative).

Chamber length is 70 or 76mm (2.75 or 3in), the latter accommodating magnum loads for longer-range field shooting. The 12-bore model with 71cm (28in) barrels weighs in at around 3.1kg (6.8lb). Its light weight gives the weapon a fast swing and an easy portability.

The Model No.4 is a fixed-choke gun, the chokes being set to order – ¼ and ½ or ½ and Full are typical combinations (these are equivalent to Improved Cylinder and Modified or Modified and Full in the United States).

Doubler trigger

Many Aya shotguns have double triggers. Unlike a single-trigger shotgun, a double-trigger weapon allows the shooter to make an instant selection of barrel when a shot presents itself. Thus a high pheasant can be taken with the more tightly choked barrel, which will give a tighter pattern of shot at distance, whereas a close-range woodcock bursting from cover can be taken with the more open barrel. The No.4 has an automatic safety, although many shooters choose to have this modified to a manual safety to allow quicker field responses.

Aya side-by-sides tend to be fixed-choke guns. Fixed chokes are a good option for a field gun destined for hard use, as there are less parts to attract rust.

Baikal IZH-27/Remington SPR-310 $

The Russian gunmaker Baikal is known primarily for its range of budget shotguns. The IZH-27 is one of its most popular models, and in the United States Remington has repackaged it as the SPR-310.

SPECIFICATIONS: Remington SPR-310
GAUGE/CALIBRE: 12, 16, 20, 28, .410
BARREL LENGTH: 66cm (26in), 71cm (28in)
WEIGHT: 3.4kg (7.5lb)
EJECTOR TYPE: automatic ejectors
CHOKES: fixed or interchangeable depending on model
FEATURES: chromium-lined barrels and chambers; walnut furniture

Baikal/Izhevsky Mekhanichesky Zavod introduced the IZH-27/SPR-310 in 1973. It is a basic over-and-under double-barrel shotgun, available in many gauges, including 12, 16, 20, 28 and .410. These budget weapons can often have a rudimentary quality of barrel blacking and finish, but their reliability and

Baikal guns are superb choices for those who will give their field gun some hard abuse, which they can take.

performance are not in doubt. Barrel bores and chambers are all lined with chromium to ward off corrosion from either weather or propellants, and the locking mechanism meets international guidelines for strength. (Indeed, Baikal shotguns are known for their near-indestructible qualities.) Safety is also a primary feature, with the safety mechanism locking the sears while hammer interceptors provide more reassurance.

Variants

The SPR-310 has several variant types, differences between the models centring round cartridge-extraction and barrel-selection features. Chokes are of the interchangeable variety on the 12-, 16- and 20-gauge guns, with the 28 gauge and .410 having fixed chokes. The 28 typically has Improved Cylinder and Modified chokes, while the .410 has Improved Modified and Full. Remington has also brought out the SPR-310S Sporting model, designed specifically for the clay-shooting market. This not only comes with screw-in multichokes, but also has sophisticated features such as a ported barrel (to reduce muzzle flip) and a palm swell on the right side of the pistol grip.

The key feature of the SPR range, however, is not necessarily the features, but the price. A basic 310 can cost less than $500, and yet the guns are reliable work tools. An SPR is particularly useful for those who give their guns hard use, such as agricultural workers or rough shooters, and demand that their gun works well and without complaint.

The SPR-310 is a 'no-frills' gun, yet despite its budget price it still features a ventilated rib, recoil pad and multichokes.

Beretta 471 Silver Hawk

$$$

Although Beretta is primarily known to shotgunners for its over-and-under and semi-automatic weapons, it also offers a prestigious side-by-side gun in the 471 Silver Hawk.

SPECIFICATIONS: **Beretta 471 Silver Hawk**

GAUGE/CALIBRE: 12, 20

BARREL LENGTH: 66cm (26in) and 72cm (28in)

WEIGHT: (12-gauge, 72cm/28in barrels) 2.95kg (6.5lb)

EJECTOR TYPE: selectable automatic ejectors/manual extraction

CHOKES: Mobilchoke® or Optima-Choke® interchangeable

FEATURES: excellent safety systems; anticorrosion treatments

As is typically the case with side-by-side weapons, weight is kept to a minimum, partly through the availability of only two short barrel lengths – 66cm (26in) and 72cm (28in). The 12-gauge 72cm (28in) weapon weighs in at 2.95kg (6.5lb) while the 20-gauge with 66cm (26in) barrel drops the weight to 2.68kg (5.9lb).

Light gun

The lightness makes the Silver Hawk an ideal rough-shooting gun, where having a fast-swinging gun is more important than having the long and steady swing commonly used with heavier guns in clay shooting. Furthermore, a heavy gun can be a burden

This side view of the Silver Hawk shows off the gun's great elegance. It is a tough gun, however, and all metal parts are corrosion-proofed for field use.

on a long session of field shooting, where every extra half-pound is felt by the end of the day.

Modern technology

Although the Silver Hawk has a traditional look, its construction benefits from the latest in Beretta's technological innovations. The monobloc – the solid block of metal into which the chambers are machined – is fused to the barrels with laser rather than traditional brazing to give the gun an exceptional strength.

In profile the Silver Hawk has a very slender and elegant look to it. The stock is a classic straight English type and the low-profile receiver contributes to the gun's overall slenderness. A useful innovation is the gun's provision for either automatic ejection or manual extraction of the spent shells (the selector switch is located on the fore-end iron). The former is useful when there is no issue about the fall of shell cases, such as on a pegged pheasant shoot where all spent cases will be picked up later. Switching to manual extraction, however, is practical for farmland or wilderness shooting, where spent shells should be removed manually from the gun and placed in a bag or pocket for proper disposal.

While the Silver Hawk is available in fixed-choke configurations (typically Improved Cylinder/Improved Modified), multichoke tubes are standard. The Optima-Choke® and Mobilechoke® tubes are options.

Beretta 682

$$–$$$

Beretta is a giant company in gunmaking history, established by Bartolomeo Beretta in Gardone, Italy, in the fifteenth century. Today it produces a massive array of high-quality weapons, both military and civilian, and its shotguns are amongst the most popular sporting models.

SPECIFICATIONS: **Beretta 682 Gold E Sporting**

GAUGE/CALIBRE:	12
BARREL LENGTH:	72cm (28in), 76cm (30in), 81cm (32in)
WEIGHT:	3.45kg (7.6lb)
EJECTOR TYPE:	automatic ejectors
CHOKES:	Optima-Choke® multichokes
FEATURES:	adjustable trigger pull; adjustable stock optional; Optima-Bore® barrels

This Beretta 682 is fitted with extended chokes, which are standard features now of many Beretta guns.

The Beretta 682 is an out-and-out clay gun, and it has taken many international trophies in the hands of professionals. It evolved from the 680 in the early 1980s, and is mechanically very similar to its predecessor. It uses the Beretta system of pin-locking, the barrels being locked prior to firing by conical pins engaging with two corresponding holes set either side of the barrel. This system produces a highly reliable slim receiver. Its self-adjusting nature means that locking remains solid even if the holes have become worn.

Competition gun

The modern incarnation of the 682 is the 682 Gold E. Gun fit is all-important to clay shooters, and the Gold E can be fitted with an adjustable comb on the stock that can reconfigure drop, cast-on and cast-off. (Many other models of Beretta have the adjustable stock as an option.) A shooter's personal stock settings are fixed with a 'memory system' that allows him or her to retain the right configuration even after the gun has been dismantled. Optima-Choke® multichokes come as standard and Beretta also states that 'Some models of the new 682 Gold E feature the Optima-Bore® barrel profile that reduces felt recoil and improves shot distribution'. This consists of elongated forcing cones that lead into barrels bored out to wider than normal dimensions. Taken with Beretta's generally good after-sales service, the 682 is an excellent model for the aspiring clay shot, and there are different versions for trap, skeet and sporting shooters.

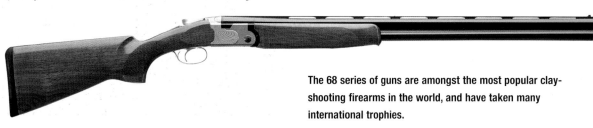

The 68 series of guns are amongst the most popular clay-shooting firearms in the world, and have taken many international trophies.

Beretta 687 Silver Pigeon Series $$$

The Silver Pigeon series of shotguns has been one of Beretta's most successful ranges of 'competition-grade guns', and they have an established popularity with clay and field shooters alike.

SPECIFICATIONS: **Beretta 687 Silver Pigeon II 12 gauge**

GAUGE/CALIBRE:	12
BARREL LENGTH:	72cm (28in), 76cm (30in), 81cm (32in)
WEIGHT:	3.5kg (7.7lb)
EJECTOR TYPE:	automatic ejectors
CHOKES:	Mobilchoke® multichokes
FEATURES:	deep-relief engraving; 76mm (3in) chambers

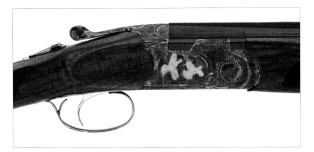

The quality of finish on the Silver Pigeon is high – here the engraved action is accented with gold birds.

Current basic models of the 687 Silver Pigeon include the II and III models, with sideplate premium versions being the EL Gold Pigeon II and the EELL Diamond Pigeon.

The Silver Pigeons use Beretta's time-proven pin-locking system, and are available in 12, 20 or 28 gauges. The first two gauges can take 76mm (3in) magnum cartridges. Even though the additional power of the magnum loads is prohibited from many clay grounds, they provide a useful extension of range and killing force when shooting high-flying game birds (magnum loads tend to be very popular amongst wildfowlers).

Silver Pigeons use the Mobilchoke® System of multichokes, although a wide range of other choke types – particularly extended chokes – are available for Beretta guns, both Beretta branded or produced by other companies such as Teague. The advantage of using extended chokes is that they can often be changed simply using finger strength – no dedicated wrench is required – and many claim the patterns they produce are improved over the shorter flush-fitting chokes.

Dimensions and appearance

Barrel lengths of the Silver Pigeon weapons are 72cm (28in), 76cm (30in) and 81cm (32in) – the most popular barrel lengths for clay shooting – and the gun weights range from around 2.4kg (5.3lb) to 3.1kg (6.8lb) depending on gauge and barrel length. Attractive deep-relief engraving and scrollwork on the receiver is a defining feature of the Silver Pigeons, often depicting hunting scenes on contrasting left and right sides. The metallic parts are treated with a nickel-based anticorrosion treatment, and the walnut stock and fore-end are matte-lacquered or oil-finished to enhance the grain of the wood.

The Silver Pigeon series weapons are good clay guns, being well balanced and having the versatility of multichokes.

Beretta DT10 Trident

$$$$

Pushing up over the $7000 mark, the DT10 is a premium-grade competition gun for clay shooting. Many world champions have claimed their titles with a DT10, which is known for its sturdy construction and fast trigger responses.

SPECIFICATIONS: Beretta DT10 Trident
GAUGE/CALIBRE: 12
BARREL LENGTH: 76cm (30in), 81cm (32in)
WEIGHT: approx 4kg (8.8lb)
EJECTOR TYPE: automatic ejectors
CHOKES: Optima-Choke® multichokes
FEATURES: adjustable, quick-remove trigger; cross-bolt locking; Optima-Bore® barrels

The DT10 was designed specifically for clay-target shooting, and different barrel groups are available for the main disciplines within the sport – sporting, skeet, and trap. (The trap barrels in particular are configured for a high point of impact, so the shooter can keep the barrels beneath the rising trap clay.) DT10s are also weighted with the centre of mass concentrated around the bottom barrel, thus reducing muzzle flip on the first shot of a pair and technically giving the shooter better acquisition of the second shot. Adjustable 'memory system' stocks are available on many models of the DT10, and Beretta's 'sporting fore-end' provides a wide and solid front grip.

Trigger unit

The 'DT' of the DT10's name means 'Detachable Trigger'. Trigger-group removal is performed with the gun broken and in three straightforward steps – a useful facility for cleaning and maintenance – and the trigger position is also adjustable using a provided screwdriver.

Different from shotguns such as the 68 series, which have a pin-locking mechanism – the DT10 has a powerful cross-bolt locking system for very dependable locking even after tens of thousands of rounds have passed through the gun, and the sides of the receiver are noticeably thick. Lock times are particularly quick on the DT10, the hammers being powered by V-shaped springs, and standard multichokes are of Beretta's Optima-Choke® System.

In addition, the DT10's barrels have Beretta's Optima-Bore® barrel profile to produce excellent patterns with no competition-losing holes and which also further reduce recoil to make possible a better second-shot acquisition.

The DT10 is a true competition clay gun. Note the broad fore-end on the gun pictured here; this gives the user a very stable and controlled grip, which in turn translates to the smoother swing essential for good clay-shooting technique.

Beretta SO9

$$$$$

Firmly in Beretta's 'Premium Grade' category of field guns, the SO9 represents, according to the firm's publicity, 'a melding of the world's most popular gauges … with the world's most prized engraving'.

SPECIFICATIONS: **Beretta SO9**

GAUGE/CALIBRE: 12, 20, 28, .410	
BARREL LENGTH: 66cm (26in), 71cm (28in), 76cm (30in)	
WEIGHT: (12-gauge) 3.25kg (7.16lb)	
EJECTOR TYPE: automatic ejectors	
CHOKES: fixed or interchangeable	
FEATURES: sidelock mechanism; hand-engraving; thumbscrew sideplates	

Beretta's SO series contains some of the finest over-and-under shotguns available on the market. A sidelock gun with multiple Olympic gold medals and world championship titles to its credit, the SO5 is particularly well regarded. The SO9 is another sidelock shotgun, the sideplates being treated to scenes that are hand-engraved by master craftsmen and which can be customized to order. Stocks and fore-ends are taken from the finest quality European walnut, the checkering being hand-cut and the oil finish lifting out the wood's grain.

Such is the beauty of these weapons that they are serious collector's pieces – the singer Madonna paid around $100,000 for a matching pair for her husband Guy Ritchie. However, the SO9's interior mechanism matches the quality of its exterior aesthetics. The locking system is a double longitudinal bolt that secures the barrel by engaging internal monobloc lugs in the receiver body.

The sidelocks are mounted on pins on the sideplate, and Beretta gives the option of removable thumbscrews so that the sideplates can be taken off by hand for ease of inspection. A further level of customization is the option of a double trigger instead of the single, non-selective trigger fitted as standard.

Barrel technology

Beretta barrels are of pre-bored Boehler Antinit steel and are cold-hammer forged. The light weight of the barrels puts the centre of gravity around the receiver, which, combined with an overall gun weight of 3.25kg (7.16lb) for the 12-gauge model, gives the SO9 a fast but balanced swing. The rib is either solid or ventilated, the ventilated rib improving gun cooling. Chokes are either fixed or multichoke depending on needs.

The standard of engraving on an SO9 is the best available. The engravings are done by some of the world's master engravers, who will also sign their work and so add to the value of the gun.

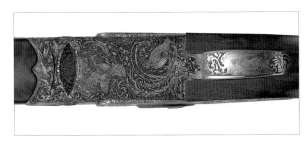

Although the SO9 is of the highest quality, it is instantly recognizable as being a Beretta, with the low-profile action and the visible hinge pin just behind the fore-end.

Beretta SS06

$$$$$

The Beretta SS06 utilizes Beretta's SO shotgun action to produce a heavy-duty break-action over-and-under rifle, and demonstrates how breech-loading guns are well suited to the most powerful rifled rounds.

SPECIFICATIONS: **Beretta SS06**

GAUGE/CALIBRE: 12/.458 Winchester Mag., .375 H&H Mag., 9.3x74R

BARREL LENGTH: 61cm (24in), 76cm (28in)

WEIGHT: 5kg (11lb)

EJECTOR TYPE: automatic ejectors

CHOKES: interchangeable, fixed or rifled barrels

FEATURES: optional Zeiss scope; spare cartridge holder in stock

The SS06 has a prominent cheek swelling on the stock and a rubber recoil pad to soak up some of the punch from the heavy-calibre rounds. Note the simple notch-and-post sight configuration, ideal for quick target acquisition.

The SS06 is derived from the action of the SO shotguns, and indeed the SS06 can take a set of shotgun barrels to give the shooter true versatility on a long hunting trip. Typical of many double-barrelled rifles, the SS06 is designed to fire large-calibre, heavy-charge shells during big-game hunting.

Calibre

The rifle calibres are .458 Winchester Mag., .375 H&H Mag., and the 9.3x74R. These are all venerable big-game calibres (the .375 H&H Mag., for example, was developed in 1912) and the recoil generated on firing the 270- or 300-grain bullet is extremely heavy. The .458 round is even heavier at around 500 grains, and both will stop the largest of land animals. The 9.3x74R is not quite as forceful as the other calibres, and has less muzzle energy (hence it is often found in light double guns), so is not used for the largest game animals, but is still a powerful round for hoofed creatures. A trapdoor for additional cartridges is fitted in the stock.

Short-barrelled accuracy

The SS06's rifled barrel is 61cm (24in), and comes with a simple blade front sight and a corresponding V-notch rear sight. However, an optical Zeiss scope can also be fitted, the sight attaching to the top barrel via claw mounts.

The sight is set out to 100m (328ft), and the relatively short range is practical, as the movement of breaking open and closing the barrels can cause more disruption to the sight than on a fixed-barrel gun, although the gun will be accurate well out beyond this range.

Requisite solidity also makes the SS06 a weighty firearm at around 5kg (11lb). The SS06 is an attractive-looking weapon, but for those wanting exquisite receiver decoration the SS06 EELL offers a more expensive option.

Beretta Ultralight

$$$

A light gun can be a blessing after a long day out field shooting. Beretta has produced the Ultralight as one of the lightest 12-gauge guns on the market, weighing in at only 2.7kg (5.9lb).

SPECIFICATIONS: **Beretta Ultralight**

GAUGE/CALIBRE: 12

BARREL LENGTH: 71cm (28in)

WEIGHT: 2.7kg (5.9lb)

EJECTOR TYPE: automatic ejectors

CHOKES: Mobilchoke® System interchangeable

FEATURES: very light; optional barrel set with rifled bottom barrel

It is not simply the case that the lighter the gun, the better. Light guns fly very quickly on the swing, and this can make them difficult to control when the shooter needs to move smoothly with the target – such as on a long crossing pheasant. However, Beretta's Ultralight combines pared-down weight with a very manageable layout to make a high-comfort field gun.

Such an amazingly light weight, which also makes the weapon ideal for some young, disabled or physically smaller shots, has been achieved through the use of, according to Beretta, 'a light but remarkably strong aircraft aluminium alloy, specially heat-treated to deliver the strength and durability of steel – but with 65% less weight'.

Although the alloy is strong in itself, Beretta has still built a titanium insert into the breech face to guarantee that there is no deformation under the force of the cartridge heads being driven backwards on firing. Further titanium inserts in the receiver walls prevent wear around the ejectors.

Barrel options

The Ultralight's barrels come with a narrow 6mm (0.23in) wide ventilated rib on the upper barrel. Ribs on field guns tend to be narrower than ribs on clay guns, because the field shooter wants an unhindered view of his target as it suddenly bursts from cover. (The slimmer ribs also help to keep the overall weight of the gun down.)

Inside the bores, a chrome lining protects against corrosion from both propellant and climate and allows the use of steel shot. (Steel shot is preferred, and often mandatory, for many types of game shooting, particularly shooting over wetlands.) Mobilchoke® multichokes allow the shooter to configure the shot spread for the type of target.

The Ultralight also has the option of a combination gun-barrel set, featuring a smoothbore top barrel and a rifled bottom barrel. Beretta says the rifled barrel is designed 'to increase dispersion of shot pattern'. This gun, known as the Ultralight SR, has a ramped foresight and no rib.

Although it is an extremely light gun, the Beretta Ultralight still has the full Beretta dimensions in the stock. The fore-end is of a classic design typical of many Beretta models.

Bernardelli Express 2000

$$$$

Bernardelli is another veteran Italian gunmaker, having originated in Gardone in 1721 under the directorships of the Bernardelli brothers (although the company was not registered until 1865).

SPECIFICATIONS: **Bernardelli Express 2000**

GAUGE/CALIBRE: 30-06 Spr., 7x65R, 8x57JRS or 9.3x74R, .357 H&H Mag

BARREL LENGTH: 55cm (21.7in), 60cm (23.6in)

WEIGHT: up to 3.3kg (7.3lb)

EJECTOR TYPE: automatic ejectors

CHOKES: rifled barrel

FEATURES: twin triggers; scope mountings

Today Bernardelli specializes in a range of different firearms types, including handguns (automatics and revolvers) and break-barrel shotguns and rifles. Its side-by-side range includes the Hemingway, S. Uberto 2 boxlock, and its Roma series guns, the latter having sideplates (not sidelocks). Bernardelli even makes a side-by-side hammer gun (the Italia) for the more traditionally minded. (Hammer guns are actually making something of a comeback in recent times, appealing to those who want to explore something of shooting's more distant history.) The company's over-and-under range, however, includes the Saturno 200 and the Express 2000 double rifle.

The Express barrels have a range of calibres – .30-06 Spr., 7x65R, 8x57JRS or 9.3x74R, and .357 H&H Mag. The broad selection of calibres offers a useful selection for hunting, ideally for hoofed animals. Twin triggers are fitted, allowing for the selection of different barrels according to the target presentation and range. The barrels themselves are available in two lengths: 55 or 60cm (21.7 or 23.6in). Furniture is of walnut, and the receiver metalwork is either of plain metal or is blued to match the barrels.

Express operation

The Express 2000 comes with a range of mountings for telescopic sights. These – depending upon both the magnification and the talent of the shooter – can give confident kill predictions over a range of 400m (1312ft) and beyond. The standard open sights are of the rack and bead variety, and in competent hands these will give accurate performance up to 200m (656ft).

The neck of the stock on the Express 2000 features a sliding safety switch, operated by the thumb, and the ejectors are of the automatic type.

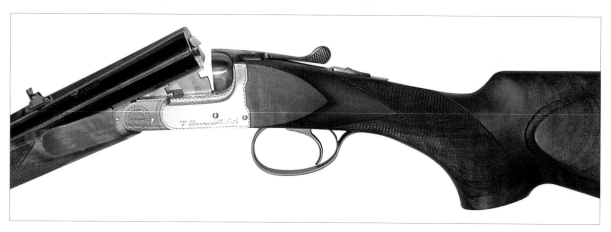

Blaser 97

$$$

Breech-loading combination guns offer the versatility of a rifle and a shotgun barrel in one weapon. Many shooters appreciate this versatility when hunting unknown quarry in close-in woodland environments.

SPECIFICATIONS: **Blaser BBF 97**

GAUGE/CALIBRE: upper barrel: 12, 16, 20; lower barrel: approx 19 calibres between .22 Hornet and 9.3 x 74R

BARREL LENGTH: 52cm (20.5in), 60cm (23.6in)

WEIGHT: approx 2.8kg (6.2lb)

EJECTOR TYPE: automatic ejectors

CHOKES: fixed/rifled barrel

FEATURES: option for scope mounting

Blaser guns are known for their robust build quality. Here two hunters are seen in the field with their Blasers, the hunter on the right using the 97's sling attachment.

The Blaser 97 is a combination gun, with several possibilities for what combination the shooter selects. He can either have a combination of shotgun and rifle barrel, two different calibres of rifle or shotgun, a pure over-and-under shotgun, or a pure breech-loading rifle. All these options are available through fitting different barrel types to the Model 97 action.

The Model 97 action has a strong underlug locking system to cope with the power of cartridges available within the series. It has a manual cocking system in which the two firing-pin springs are cocked at the same time by pushing the safety forward, with the second shot ready to fire without re-cocking, producing a very fast second shot.

Looking at the BBF 97 combination rifle/shotgun, the upper shotgun barrel is available in three gauges: 12, 16 and 20. The 12- and 20-gauge barrels have 76mm (3in) chambers, while the 16-gauge gun has 70mm (2.75in) chambers. Two barrel lengths, 60cm (23.6in) and 52cm (20.5in), are available. In the long version of the gun, the rifled barrel is available in up to 19 different calibres. These run from .22 Hornet and .223 Rem up to 8x75RS and 9.3x74R. The upper barrel of the guns can take a scope.

Quality

Blaser is known for the high standards of its guns, and the 97 range is no exception. The basic Grade 1 level of finishing has high-quality walnut woodwork and a plain-metal action.

Beyond this the quality of finish can rise very high indeed. The BB97 Classic model not only has a slightly slimmer profile, but also has very elegant engraving on the receiver body. (It also comes with a Zeiss Varipoint riflescope as part of the standard package.) Options include a filigree top lever, an engraved trigger guard and even an ammunition storage section in the stock.

Blaser F3

$$$

Better known for its rifles, the German Blaser Company has had a significant impact on the clay-shooting market with a revolutionary new over-and-under shotgun.

SPECIFICATIONS: **Blaser F3 Competition Sporting**

GAUGE/CALIBRE: 12

BARREL LENGTH: 71cm (28in), 76cm (30in), 81cm (32in)

WEIGHT: up to 3.8kg (8.4 lb)

EJECTOR TYPE: automatic ejectors

CHOKES: Briley interchangeable

FEATURES: ultrafast lock time; Blaser 'balancer' in stock

The F3 features several different grades and styles of finish, from an almost unadorned metal to detailed game scenes.

The Blaser F3 has superb balance and seems to drop into the pocket of the shoulder for a well-aligned mount.

The F3 design process involved the input of John Bidwell from the United Kingdom, five-time FITASC Sporting World Champion and the winner of numerous other international trophies. An essential requirement for the new gun was a very fast time between pulling the trigger and the cartridge detonating, known as the lock time. Reducing this time to the absolute minimum helps guard against the shooter 'hanging on' to the clay, and thus missing behind. The Blaser achieves the fast lock through an inline design of firing pin and hammer: the hammer drives forward in a straight line rather than swinging through an arc. The result is an exceptionally fast shot, which combined with a crisp trigger pull makes the F3 a pleasure to shoot. 'Triplex' bore design ensures consistent patterns of shot. To give the gun perfect balance, Blaser has installed a 'balancer' in the stock, this consisting of a threaded rod with two adjustable weight cylinders. The shooter can adjust the weights until perfect balance is achieved. Briley flush-fitting multichokes are provided as standard.

Advanced features

Safety has also been central to the Blaser design. The hammers are restrained by the safety system regardless of whether the safety catch is engaged, hence protecting against accidental knock discharges. The locking system is also extremely robust. Blaser weapons are highly customizable. Two different fore-ends and stocks (for trap or sporting disciplines) are available, the fore-ends being Schnabel and semi-Beavertail. The Blaser Ejection Ball System ejectors set the ejector springs only when the shot is fired and the gun is opened, eliminating ejector-spring fatigue when the gun is in storage.

Despite its advanced features, the Blaser F3 is very competitively priced, attacking the $5000 price bracket in the United States, while costing around £2100 in the United Kingdom.

Blaser S2

$$$$$

While over-and-under combination guns are common, side-by-side versions are less so. The S2, however, is a modern and highly sophisticated example from the Blaser Company.

SPECIFICATIONS: **Blaser S2**

GAUGE/CALIBRE: left barrel: 20; right barrel: approx 19 calibres between .222 Rem and 9.3 x 74R

BARREL LENGTH: 57.5cm (22.6in)

WEIGHT: approx 3.2kg (7lb)

EJECTOR TYPE: automatic ejectors

CHOKES: fixed/rifled barrel

FEATURES: option for scope mounting; safety-catch firing-pin cocking

The S2 provides the hunter with useful hunting options. A sudden flight of birds or some light ground game can be taken with the shotgun barrel, while the rifled barrel handles deer or even larger creatures, depending on calibre.

The S2 in its standard format is a combination rifle/shotgun, with options for having two rifled barrels instead of just one. Blaser presents the S2 for those wanting a gun that will handle either straightforward stalking through to big-game hunting, and has even produced a special edition S2 Safari gun. This awesome double rifle takes the true big-game calibres – these include the .375 H&H Mag, the .470 Nitro Express and the .500 Nitro Express. Firing such a relatively short and light gun – the barrel length is 62cm (24.5in) and the weight is approximately 5.3kg (11.7lb) – with such powerful rounds must be an awesome experience, and Blaser has fitted the S2 with a Pachmayr® Decelerator® rubber gunstock recoil pad to provide extra cushioning.

S2 setup

If the S2 Safari is a special edition, what are the basic characteristics of a standard S2? For the combination shotgun/rifle, a 20-gauge shotgun barrel is paired with a rifled barrel in a selection of popular calibres from .222 Rem to 9.3x74R. The double rifle comes with the same calibres, and the shooter has the option of having different rifle calibres set side by side. Like

the 97, the S2 cocks the firing-pin springs by pushing forward the safety catch (Blaser emphasizes that this is a completely silent procedure so as not to scare off the target). This system also makes the S2 a very safe gun to use. The shooter can select either single or double triggers. The action on all Blaser guns is anodized and the barrels are nitrated for durability.

Various options are available at purchase for the shooter to customize his S2. These include a left-handed stock, half-beavertail fore-end, a rubber recoil pad and a filigree top lever. Scope options offered by Blaser include the HitPoint Pro red dot sight and various riflescopes made by Carl Zeiss, Swarovski and Schmidt & Bender. The saddle-mount fittings allow the user to remove the zeroed sight and replace it without loss of zero.

BRNO 800

$$

The Czech arms manufacturer Zbrojovka Brno was founded in 1918 and specialized in military-grade weapons from rifles to machine guns. Today it is also a significant producer of sporting firearms for international civilian markets.

SPECIFICATIONS:
Combination Rifle/Shotgun Model BRNO 800

GAUGE/CALIBRE:	12/8 x 57JRS, 7 x 65R, .308 Win, .30-06, 9.3 x 74
BARREL LENGTH:	60cm (24in)
WEIGHT:	3.65kg (8lb)
EJECTOR TYPE:	automatic ejectors
CHOKES:	fixed/rifled barrel
FEATURES:	double triggers

Depending on the barrel configuration chosen, the BRNO 800 is several different firearms in one. Pure shotgun, combination gun (one barrel smoothbore, the other barrel rifled), or rifle only are options. This makes the 800 a versatile weapon for a single owner looking to engage in a broad range of hunting sports, from pigeon shooting through to wild boar hunts.

Configurations

The Combination Rifle/Shotgun Model BRNO 800 consists of a 12-gauge shotgun barrel combined with a rifled barrel for the following calibres: 8x57JRS, 7x65R, .308 Win., .30-06, and 9.3x74R. Barrel length is 60cm (24in). The shotgun barrel is chambered for the standard 70mm (2.75in) cartridges. Double triggers are standard and safety is automatic, this being preferable for a gun purely intended for shooting game.

The BRNO 800 can also be fitted with a set of shotgun barrels or rifled barrels only. In its pure double-barrelled shotgun form the barrels are 70cm (27.5in) long and are chambered for the magnum 76mm (3in) cartridges. A single trigger is standard. To make the shotgun suited to clay as well as field shooting, a set of four interchangeable screw-in chokes are provided. For fixed chokes, the muzzles are usually bored to Improved Cylinder and Full, although different chokes can be ordered depending on the clay discipline, such as skeet, where the standard configuration might be considered too tight by some shooters.

The BRNO 800 can be ordered in left-hand versions, and its walnut woodwork is of good quality. Total weight for the combination gun is around 3.65kg (8lb), and the same as a standard competition-grade clay gun.

Left: The barrel groups of the BRNO 800 series can be easily switched over to change the combination of rifled/smoothbore barrels.

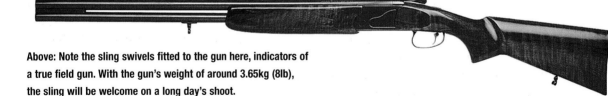

Above: Note the sling swivels fitted to the gun here, indicators of a true field gun. With the gun's weight of around 3.65kg (8lb), the sling will be welcome on a long day's shoot.

Browning B425

$$$

In the shotgun market Browning is Beretta's greatest competitor. The B425 has an ancestry reaching back to John Moses Browning's B25 shotgun of 1925, and is one of the most respected amongst mid-priced guns.

The classic B425 sporting model has a high ventilated rib to promote barrel cooling during heavy shoots.

The option of purchasing the B425 in photo-realistic camouflage is ideal for wildfowlers or woodland hunters.

SPECIFICATIONS: **Browning B425 Sporting**

GAUGE/CALIBRE: 12, 20

BARREL LENGTH: 71cm (28in), 76cm (30in), 81cm (32in)

WEIGHT: 3.5kg (7.75lb)

EJECTOR TYPE: automatic ejectors

CHOKES: Invector-Plus interchangeable

FEATURES: chrome-lined barrels; barrel compensator vents on some models

Launched in the mid-1990s, the B425, as with many of Browning's weapons, is a series rather than an individual firearm. Members of the B425 family include the B425 Light Hunter (itself separated into two guns, one fitted with Invector multichokes, the other with fixed chokes), the B425 Sporting Clays, the B425 Privilege Hunting and the B425 Waterfowl. Various grades of gun also denote the quality of the design, wood quality and aesthetic finish, Grade 1 being the most basic, followed by Grades 3, 5 and 6.

The B425 signalled an important shift in Browning gun manufacture. Earlier weapons, such as

the 325, had 'chopper-lump' barrels, meaning that the lumps (the pieces of metal that hinge the barrels to the action) were actually part of the barrel forging, rather than separate pieces brazed on. With the B425, Browning shifted to the monobloc-construction system, where a single block of steel is machined to form the barrel breech end, including the lugs, and then the block is brazed to the barrels (most shotguns are now made by this method).

Internal mechanism

Brownings are well known for their reliability, and the B425 is a straightforward boxlock ejector with a proven inertia-block system of switching between barrels. Barrels – which come in 72cm (28in), 76cm (30in) and 81cm (32in) lengths, depending on model and purpose – are lined with chrome to protect against corrosion. Chambers are standard 76mm (3in), although the B425 Waterfowl has 89mm (3.5in) chambers to accommodate the very heavy loads often felt as essential by wildfowlers. Many shooters would argue, however, that 76mm (3in) cartridges are able to handle all situations with the right shot and chokes.

Browning B525

$$$

Browning's B525 is the latest incarnation of a long series of -25 shotguns. Differences from guns like the B425 are subtle rather than striking, but the B525 is a competitively priced firearm ideal for those looking for competition performance.

SPECIFICATIONS: **Browning B525 Sporting**

GAUGE/CALIBRE: 12, 20

BARREL LENGTH: 71cm (28in), 76cm (30in), 81cm (32in)

WEIGHT: (12-gauge, 76cm/30in barrels) 3.5kg (7.75lb)

EJECTOR TYPE: automatic ejectors

CHOKES: Invector interchangeable

FEATURES: double-bead sights on top rib

The Browning B525 is the fifth generation of Browning over-and-unders. The guns will take steel shot, which is becoming more common because of environmental legislation.

The B525 has the recognizable Browning shape, although in the US version the rear edge of the receiver slopes towards the back, unlike the straight lines of earlier Brownings. A basic Grade 1 Sporting is available in either 12- or 20-gauge versions, with the typical 72cm (28in), 76cm (30in) and 81cm (32in) barrel lengths. Both the Sporting and the Light Hunter models are supplied with Invector multichokes. The five-choke set of screw-in tubes consists of Cylinder, Improved Cylinder, Modified, Improved Modified and Full. By contrast, the Trap Advance versions of the B525 are fitted with Briley chokes or have fixed chokes set at Improved Modified and Full.

Multipurpose gun

The B525, like its predecessors, denotes a family rather than a single gun. The Light Hunter model, as its name suggests, is a lightweight field model, and the 20-gauge Hunter model with 71cm (28in) barrels drops the weight down to 2.9kg (6.38lb). The 81cm (32in) barrel Trap Advance, by contrast, weighs in at 3.5kg (7.75lb). On all models the rib is vented, as is the mid rib. The pistol grip has a very pronounced downward curve that fits comfortably in the hand.

The top rib of the B525 features a front bead sight and a white centre bead. The centre bead is particularly useful for trap shooting – the two beads stacked up in a figure-of-eight shape with the clay just above the top of the barrel signals a potential hit. However, many sporting shooters also like the double-bead configuration, particularly if they have been brought up with Brownings.

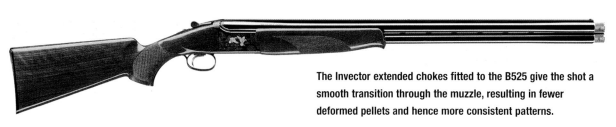

The Invector extended chokes fitted to the B525 give the shot a smooth transition through the muzzle, resulting in fewer deformed pellets and hence more consistent patterns.

Browning Cynergy

$$$

The Cynergy marks a futuristic departure from Browning's past shotgun styles and technologies. Billed by the company as 'the future of over and unders', the Cynergy has a strikingly modern, even controversial, appearance.

SPECIFICATIONS: **Browning Cynergy Sporting, Composite**

GAUGE/CALIBRE: 12

BARREL LENGTH: 71cm (28in), 76cm (30in), 81cm (32in)

WEIGHT: approx 3.4kg (7.48lb)

EJECTOR TYPE: automatic ejectors

CHOKES: Invector-Plus interchangeable

FEATURES: MonoLock Hinge; ported barrel; adjustable stock; back-bored barrels

The Browning Cynergy is a radical departure from traditional Browning designs, from the stock to the muzzle.

The visually defining features of the Cynergy are its very pronounced top rib, ramped up at the back, angular woodwork, a shallow receiver profile, and (in the Composite Sporting and Composite Field models) a fully adjustable stock. Cynergy Sporting models also have ported barrels, these venting off some of the firing gases to reduce muzzle flip, an advantage when a clay shooter needs to make a fast switch to the second of a pair. The futuristic look, however, is not just superficial. Indeed, the Cynergy is a totally new design for Browning, inside and out.

State-of-the-art

The extremely low receiver profile is the result of Browning's new MonoLock Hinge, which integrates the monobloc and the hinge as one and so avoids the need for trunnions and stub pins. Square-section pins are used for locking and these, in a similar manner to Beretta's pin-locking, adjust themselves according to wear and tear.

Another internal revolution inside the Browning is the Reverse Striker ignition system. When the trigger is pulled the coil springs travel backwards, striking rockers that then drive the firing pins forwards. The effect is a crisp trigger pull and a fast lock time. Cartridge ejection is very brisk and, again unlike previous Brownings, the ejectors are set between the barrels rather than in the fore-end.

Cynergy shotguns are available in 12 or 20 gauges, and in barrel lengths ranging from 71cm (28in) to 81cm (32in). The barrels are also 'back-bored', meaning they are bored out to the maximum specifications for the cartridge, thereby alleviating friction on the shot as it travels down the barrel and reducing the number of pellet deformations (a principal cause of poor patterning).

Browning's shotguns have traditionally been deeper in the action than those of its arch-rivals, Beretta. The Cynergy, however, is fractionally shallower than the Beretta 682.

Fabarm Axis 20M

$$

Fabarm's range of 20-bore guns plugs into the international shooting community's growing interest in the 20 gauge. The physical lightness of the 20 bore makes it an ideal weapon for a day's field shooting.

SPECIFICATIONS: **Fabarm Axis 20M**

GAUGE/CALIBRE: 20	
BARREL LENGTH: 61cm (24in), 66cm (26in), 71cm (28in), 76cm (30in)	
WEIGHT: 3.6kg (8lb)	
EJECTOR TYPE: automatic ejectors	
CHOKES: InnerHP interchangeable	
FEATURES: Tribore barrels; Triwood waterproof finish	

Although 20-gauge guns are not as popular as 12-gauge firearms, they can still be just as good for both clay and field.

The Axis 20 gauge is just one of a range of Fabarm firearms to have received good press. Like the STL VS 12- and 20-gauge shotguns, the Axis has Tribore technology, with extended forcing cones, a 20cm (8in) tapering section and the lengthy Fabarm multichokes. The gun also incorporates the Triwood process, a satin-acrylic varnish that dramatically enhances the grain of the wood.

Internally the Axis is fairly conventional, with a solid locking action using a full-width bolt that slots into a bite beneath the bottom chamber.

Titanium finish

Many of the metal parts of the Axis are treated with a protective coating known as PVD titanium. This is applied to the receiver, trigger guard, top lever and metallic parts of the fore-end, and provides a heavy-duty level of protection against corrosives such as sweat and cleaning solvents. The Axis comes in barrel lengths of 61cm (24in), 66cm (26in), 71cm (28in) and 76cm (30in). The weighting of barrel sizes towards shorter lengths shows that the Axis is mainly intended as a field rather than a clay gun, and would be good for a long day's rough shooting. Typically for a field gun, the rib is fairly narrow, tapering from 8mm (0.31in) down to 5mm (0.19in).

A small rod-type transparent sight sits at the end of the ventilated rib (there is also a ventilated mid rib). The chambers are 76mm (3in). Safety is provided in a single switch mounted on the neck of the stock, with the safety switch and the barrel selector combined in a single unit. All in all the Fabarm Axis is a good entry-level 20-bore. A lightweight version is also produced, called the Axis AL 20M.

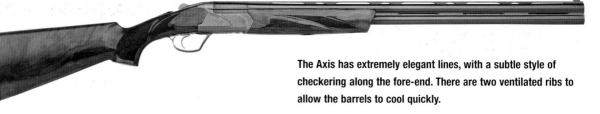

The Axis has extremely elegant lines, with a subtle style of checkering along the fore-end. There are two ventilated ribs to allow the barrels to cool quickly.

Fabarm Beta

$$

The Fabarm Beta range is one of a new breed of side-by-side shotguns coming out of Europe. Based in the town of Travagliato near Milan, Fabarm has developed the traditional side-by-side using ultramodern technology.

SPECIFICATIONS: **Fabarm Beta Grade IV**

GAUGE/CALIBRE: 12	
BARREL LENGTH: 66cm (26in), 71cm (28in), 76cm (30in)	
WEIGHT: 3.3kg (7.2lb)	
EJECTOR TYPE: automatic ejectors	
CHOKES: interchangeable or fixed	
FEATURES: Tribore barrels; patented four-lug locking	

The Fabarm Beta has its weight distributed slightly more towards the front, giving it a steady swing.

The Beta shotguns are available in four general models: the Beta Lux Paradox, Beta 3T, Beta Europe and Beta Grade IV, the differences lying in the aesthetics rather than the design. Beta guns come in four different barrel lengths, ranging from the 66cm (26in) weapon, ideal for close-range field use, through to the 76cm (30in) model. The Beta's barrels benefit from the same Tribore barrel process as Fabarm's competition over-and-unders.

Heavy duty

The Beta has been designed for robust and prolonged use. While the Beta is mainly intended for shooting game in tough conditions, the massive and Fabarm-patented four-lug locking system means that it can also be used in the burgeoning sport of side-by-side clay shooting. Such is the strength of the locking system that tens of thousands of rounds could be put through the gun without any loosening. To make the

Beta even more suitable for clay shooting, the rib is raised to give a better sight picture (the rib is 10mm/0.38in along its length) and the trigger is single, selective. Weight is also quite manageable at around 3.4kg (7.5lb) for the 76cm (30in) models, but the weight is heavy enough to enable the guns to more comfortably handle 76mm (3in) magnum loads.

The Beta Grade IV is the high-end of the Beta range. Depending on the model, Betas also come with either fixed chokes or multichokes. When the chokes are fixed they are Improved Cylinder/Improved Modified or Modified/Full.

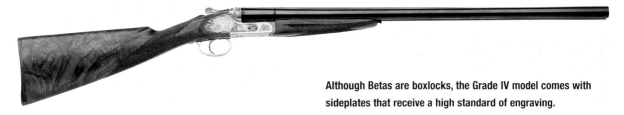

Although Betas are boxlocks, the Grade IV model comes with sideplates that receive a high standard of engraving.

Fabarm STL VS

$$$

In price and quality, the Fabarm STL VS Sport squares up to the likes of the Beretta 682 and Browning XS. It successfully melds a solid action with Italian styling in a practical range of competition and field guns.

SPECIFICATIONS: **Fabarm STL VS Sport Exis 76 AS**

GAUGE/CALIBRE:	12
BARREL LENGTH:	71cm (28in), 76cm (30in), 81cm (32in)
WEIGHT:	3.6kg (8lb)
EJECTOR TYPE:	automatic ejectors
CHOKES:	Exis interchangeable
FEATURES:	Tribore barrels; Triwood waterproof finish

The history of the Fabbrica Bresciana Armi (Fabarm) is not as venerable as that of a Beretta or Bernardelli, but the company has already established a respectable reputation for its over-and-under and semi-automatic shotguns (it also produces some side-by-side models). Over the past 20 years the over-and-under models, primarily 12 and 20 bores, have included the Gamma Lux Competition Sporting, the Gamma Lux Hunter and the Max Luxus, all featuring barrel-block locking and the basics of modern competition guns (such as a single trigger, ventilated rib, interchangeable chokes and so on).

The new STL VS range puts three new weapons into the Fabarm stable: the Sport Exis 76 AS, the Trap AS and the Trap Exis AS.

Modern specifications

Looking at the Sport model, the STL VS comes in the usual 71cm (28in), 76cm (30in) and 81cm (32in)

barrel lengths with 76mm (3in) chambers. A set of eight titanium-coated Exis interchangeable chokes is provided – an unusually generous allocation of chokes – and these can be changed without a key. A ventilated rib that narrows down from 10mm (0.4in) to 8mm (0.31in) tops the barrels. The muzzles feature a Hi Viz luminous sight as standard, this standing out strongly in the peripheral vision when the gun is mounted for a shot.

Barrels

The barrels are central to the STL VS's marketing, as they use what Fabarm calls the 'Tribore' system. Here the bore moves through three stages: an over-bored section in front of the chamber, a narrow section lower down the barrel and finally the choke section. Fabarm claims that this system improves recoil, patterning and velocity.

The STL VS has a high standard of exterior finish. The woodwork is treated with Triwood, a waterproof synthetic that seals the walnut in an extremely durable weatherproof finish. Both the Sport and Trap models are fitted with adjustable combs on the stock for precision fitting, these being adjustable for both drop and cast.

Shooting with the STL VS is, as with many Fabarm guns, a pleasure. It contentedly soaks up the recoil of some substantial loads without discomfort to the user and the patterns from the choke cleanly break targets.

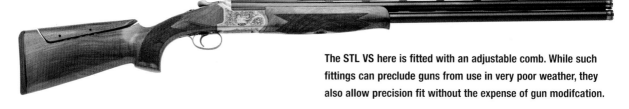

The STL VS here is fitted with an adjustable comb. While such fittings can preclude guns from use in very poor weather, they also allow precision fit without the expense of gun modifcation.

FAIR Jubilee Prestige

$$

The FAIR Jubilee guns are high-quality over-and-unders that offer reliability and performance for both clay and field use, with styling that makes an impression on any shooting gun.

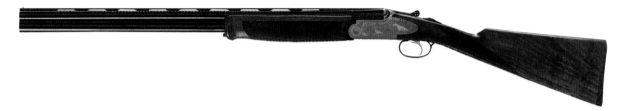

SPECIFICATIONS: **FAIR Jubilee Prestige**

GAUGE/CALIBRE: 12, 16, 20, 28 and 36

BARREL LENGTH: 66cm (26in), 71cm (28in), 76cm (30in)

WEIGHT: 3.2kg (7lb)

EJECTOR TYPE: automatic ejectors

CHOKES: interchangeable or fixed

FEATURES: chrome-lined barrels; action specific to gauge

The Jubilee range balances up FAIR's budget guns by demonstrating subtle attention to aesthetics and refinements in shooting performance. It runs from the standard Jubilee 702 through to the Jubilee Prestige guns.

Jubilee shotguns are new weapons amongst the FAIR catalogue, and demonstrate, as stated in FAIR company literature, the desire 'to create an over-and-under shotgun combining a classic design and the most modern technologies'. A buyer is immediately struck by the choice of gauges with the Jubilee range – 12, 16, 20, 28 and 36. FAIR is quick to point out that the selection is not simply a matter of dropping different barrels onto the same action, but that the action bodies for the 12-, 16-, 20- and 28-gauge weapons actually have different configurations of action unique to each gauge. Three different barrel lengths are available for the guns – 66cm (26in), 71cm

The Jubilee Prestige is visually centred on its striking sideplates, which features an excellent standard of engraving set between the dark lines of the woodwork. The raised, straight comb alludes to the classic English shotgun style, and other accents include the gold trigger and fret-worked top lever.

(28in) or 76cm (30in) – and the chamber lengths are either 70mm (2.75in) or 76mm (3in) depending on the model (the 12-, 20- and 36-gauge models all come with the 76mm/3in chambers).

All guns are fitted with automatic ejectors and single selective triggers. Weight for a 12-gauge gun is around 3.2kg (7lb), dropping to some 2.7kg (5.94lb) for the 36-gauge gun.

Outer details

The Jubilee range has a transparent quality in its design. The trigger is gold-plated and the fret-worked top lever also has gold details. The walnut stock and fore-end have a deep and luxurious grain and thin-cut laser checkering, and the fore-end has a release button set immediately in front of the Schnabel-type front. Receiver work on the 702 is colour-hardened for an attractive and durable finish.

The Prestige gun differs from the 702 in having sideplates, and these receive even more attention from the engraver, including gold animal motifs. Using FAIR's Technichoke multichoke system, the Jubilee guns offer a very attractive series of firearms for both clays and field.

FAIR Premier

$$

FAIR (marketed as Lincoln in the UK) have established a strong foothold in the budget first-gun market with an excellent range of multichoke shotguns perfect for sporting clays or shooting game.

SPECIFICATIONS: **FAIR Premier**

GAUGE/CALIBRE: 12, 16, 20, 28, .410	
BARREL LENGTH: 71cm (28in)	
WEIGHT: 3.4kg (7.4lb)	
EJECTOR TYPE: automatic ejectors	
CHOKES: interchangeable	
FEATURES: chrome-lined barrels	

The whole action of the Premier has a reassuringly solid feel that is ideal for sporting clays.

The Premier multichoke falls into the busy sub-$1000 category, and so it is a wise consideration for anyone looking at his or her first serious shotgun for clay or field shooting. The overall style of the Sporting model is that of a conventional sporting gun. A generous beavertail fore-end wraps around the lower barrel and features deep checkering for a substantial grip. Similar checkering is found on the pistol grip of the stock, and the nose of the stock is recessed to make a comfortable fit for the heel of the thumb.

All wood is walnut, and the grain is brought out with a matt varnish finish. A deep rubber recoil pad is fitted as standard and this provides a comfortable cushion against impact. However, the rubber can be fairly 'sticky' and many shooters may want to replace it with a more sophisticated sporting pad.

Clay performance

Being a sporter, the Premier is supplied with five flush-fitting multichokes, these being inserted or extracted with a supplied choke wrench. Barrel length is 71cm (28in). Although there appears to be a vogue for shooters preferring longer barrels when it comes to sporters – particularly 76cm (30in) – the 71cm (28in) is a good length for anyone wanting to take a clay gun between disciplines, such as switching from sporting to skeet. The only incongruity with the Premier Sporting as a clay gun is its automatic safety, but this could be easily modified to a manual.

The barrels themselves have chrome-lined bores, ventilated top and mid ribs and a simple red-bead sight. Locking is performed in two lugs set beneath the bottom barrel. Furthermore, for a budget gun the action is attractively decorated, with laser engraving depicting hunting scenes and acanthus scrollwork decorating both sides of the receiver and the underside as well.

Falco SO27A

$

Based in Marcheno, Italy, Falco is a specialist in the production of small-gauge shotguns. With over 40 years of experience, Falco's range is popular with those wanting light, dependable field guns.

SPECIFICATIONS: Falco SO27A

GAUGE/CALIBRE: .410	
BARREL LENGTH: 70cm (27.5in)	
WEIGHT: 2.7kg (6lb)	
EJECTOR TYPE: extractors	
CHOKES: fixed	
FEATURES: double triggers; light weight	

Falco's output is not only confined to small-gauge shotguns. Its Palombe range of standard boxlock over-and-unders and its single-barrelled Monocanna guns come in the full range of popular calibres, including 12, 20 and 28.

It also produces an innovative selection of folding single-barrel weapons, ideally suited to those wanting maximum portability from their field arm. These include the Overtop rifle, available in calibres from .22H through to .308 Win. However, it is Falco's selection of .410 shotguns that is the centre of the company's catalogue.

Small gauges

Falco makes .410s in both single- and double-barrelled versions, the latter including the SO27A. The SO27A is an over-and-under weapon fitted with 70cm (27.5in) barrels. These are choked at Modified and Full, the tight chokes being essential for making decent killing patterns at distance from the small loads of the .410 cartridges. Chambers are set for 76mm (3in) magnum cartridges, and using the SO27A with no.6 shot makes the weapon suitable for a range of vermin and game, such as rabbits, rats, crows and squirrels, depending on the range and the shot presentation.

In terms of operating features, the SO27A has double triggers and the safety switch is manual. Automatic safety switches tend to be more common on field guns, so extra care is needed when using the SO27A in company. As with most .410s, the SO27A is a light weapon, weighing only 2.7kg (6lb).

For those wanting a side-by-side .410 gun, Falco's basic SO27 model fills the gap. In many ways specifications are the same as the SO27A, although the slimmer side-by-side configuration trims another 0.2kg (0.5lb) off the overall weight. Guns available in the .410 calibre are currently going through something of a renaissance. The small calibre is ideal for use in light hunting roles, such as vermin control. Falco not only make .410 guns with a conventional shotgun layout, but also a series with true pistol grips (no shoulder stocks) with either external hammers or a hammerless arrangement.

Light and handy to use, the Falco series of shotguns are ideally suited to convenient hunting. Note the double triggers and sling swivels fitted to the stock and fore-end.

Fausti Style ST

$–$$

Building on Italy's traditions of fine gunmaking, Stefano Fausti established his company in 1948 in Marcheno (Brescia), Italy. Still in Fausti family hands, the Fausti Stefano Arms Factory is known for high-quality, often reasonably priced, shotguns.

SPECIFICATIONS: Fausti Style ST

GAUGE/CALIBRE: 12, 16, 20, 24, 28, 32, .410

BARREL LENGTH: 60cm (24in), 63cm (25in), 65cm (25.5in), 68cm (27in), 71cm (28in), 77cm (30in)

WEIGHT: 3.4kg (7.5lb)

EJECTOR TYPE: ejectors or extractors

CHOKES: fixed or multichokes

FEATURES: multiple options on triggers, barrels, chambers

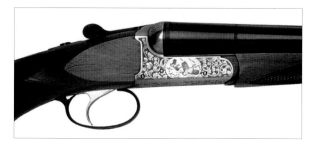

Fausti is known particularly for the excellence of its engraving, and the steel receiver has a deluxe engraving option for those wanting more visual impact.

Fausti has kept its production of shotguns to limited numbers, although the latest Cad-Cam technologies are used in the designs. The company also took over manufacture and distribution of Emilio Rizzini brand weapons in 1999, further widening its credentials as a quality gunmaker.

Fausti's range is a broad one within the confines of over-and-under and side-by-side shotguns. Its side-by-side models include fine-hammer gun models such as the Classic and Noblesse and the superb Senator sidelock, but for entry-level shooters the Style ST boxlock is a good foundation to a working collection.

Multiple gauges

The Style ST is available in an unusually wide selection of gauges – 12, 16, 20, 24, 28, 32 or .410 –

hence meeting almost any field-shooting demand except those wanting the heaviest wildfowling gauges. Barrel and chamber lengths come in similar wide varieties, the latter being 70mm (2.75in), 76mm (3in) and even a potent 89mm (3.5in). Recoil from the 89mm (3.5in) shells must be vigorous, although the Style ST has a respectable weight for a side-by-side, tipping the scales at around 3.4kg (7.5lb). This, along with the gun's good balance, will put the recoil within controllable limits. Locking is performed by a solid barrel-block locking system.

Fausti guns tend to offer a great number of options at purchase, and the Style ST is no exception. Chokes are either fixed (typical options here are Improved Cylinder and Modified, Modified and Full, Improved Modified and Full, or Full and Full) or multichokes. Single or double triggers are also available.

A splinter fore-end gives the Style ST a light and slender contour. Although this gun has a single trigger, double trigger versions are available for those wanting instant barrel selection.

Krieghoff K-80

$$$$–$$$$$

The K-80 is one of Krieghoff's most prestigious series of competition guns. With a new gun slotting into the c.$9–15,000 range (depending on choice), a K-80 is not affordable to many, but it guarantees state-of-the-art shooting performance.

SPECIFICATIONS: **Krieghoff K-80 Super Sport**

GAUGE/CALIBRE: 12

BARREL LENGTH: 71cm (28in), 76cm (30in), 81cm (32in), 86cm (34in)

WEIGHT: 3.9kg (8.75lb)

EJECTOR TYPE: automatic ejectors

CHOKES: interchangeable

FEATURES: adjustable trigger pull; easily changeable stocks; patented action

The balance of a Krieghoff K-80 is phenomenal despite its weight, making it a joy to control.

Krieghoff's reputation is built upon the excellence and robustness of its gun actions, and the high quality of aesthetic appearance. All K-80s are built around the same action, the K-80's top latch locking the barrels. All internal parts of the K-80 are hand finished to produce one of the most durable actions around. Sophistication abounds throughout the rest of the gun. The trigger is length-adjustable, and the barrel-selector switch is set just in front of the trigger. For high-level competition shooters, the manual safety switch can be locked into the 'Off' position to prevent lost clays because the safety has been accidentally knocked on.

Barrel types

The barrels essentially define the model of the K-80, current models being the Trap, Trap Special, Skeet, Sporting and Super Sporting. Multichokes are standard, with the new Super Sporting model receiving titanium chokes to keep down the weight. This is important, as the K-80s are weighty guns – the Sporting model weighs in at 4kg (9lb). Such weight precludes some shooters from comfortably using the K-80, although the gun is so well balanced that the weight does not feel awkward. A selection of ribs is available, each set for the particular clay discipline, and on the Trap Special model the high-post tapered rib is fully adjustable to alter the point of impact.

Krieghoff stocks are made from the finest-quality European walnut. They can be easily changed or removed for cleaning using a supplied stock wrench, and this means that the shooter can have several K-80 guns built around the same action by having different stock and barrel configurations. Stocks with adjustable combs are also available.

The finish to Krieghoff actions ranges from very plain styling through to exquisite engraving.

Krieghoff KX-5

$$$$

Single-barrelled shotguns take up a small percentage of trap gun sales internationally. Krieghoff's KX-5 belongs in the top echelons of this bracket, offering Krieghoff's exceptional levels of engineering in a single-barrel package.

SPECIFICATIONS: **Krieghoff KX-5**

GAUGE/CALIBRE: 12

BARREL LENGTH: 76cm (30in), 81cm (32in)

WEIGHT: 3.9kg (8.75lb)

EJECTOR TYPE: automatic ejectors

CHOKES: multichokes

FEATURES: adjustable rib; adjustable trigger pull

Krieghoff actions are incredibly smooth on opening and closing, with the most robust of locks before firing. Note here the rear end of the adjustable rib.

The KX-5 builds upon the KS-5 Special Trap gun, adding more technological refinements. With a 76cm (30in) or 81cm (32in) barrel (trap shooters prefer longer barrel lengths to improve reach and shot-pattern density at range), the KX-5 also has a fully adjustable rib.

Straight from the factory the rib is set to produce a 65 per cent/35 per cent pattern (meaning 65 per cent of the pattern is thrown above the point of aim). However, a dial control at the muzzle allows the shooter to make dramatic alterations to this pattern, up to 90 per cent high or down to a flat 50 per cent/50 per cent.

The barrel has a high, tapered rib with spacious ventilation to prevent heat distortion from the barrel spoiling the shooter's visual acquisition of the target.

Custom fit

Krieghoff Trap guns come fitted with a Monte Carlo stock (that is, a raised cheek-piece section) with an adjustable comb for a precise custom fit. To further personalize the weapon for the user, the trigger is adjustable for length of pull. The fore-end has a push-button lock to attach it to the barrels, this, according to Krieghoff, 'providing a better and stronger latch to the barrel'.

Although it is a single-barrel gun, the KX-5 comes with multichokes in three constrictions – Modified, Improved Modified and Full – although the gun can take any of Krieghoff's full range of chokes, which run from Cylinder to Super Full.

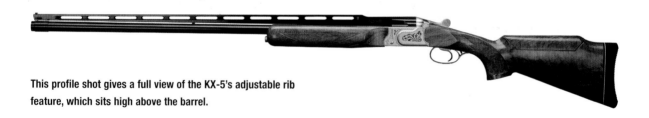

This profile shot gives a full view of the KX-5's adjustable rib feature, which sits high above the barrel.

Lanber Deluxe Sporter

$

Lanber entered the clay-shooting market with its Sporter models in the 1980s. Since then Lanber over-and-unders have become competitively placed for people wanting their first serious sporting shotgun.

SPECIFICATIONS: **Lanber Deluxe Sporter**

GAUGE/CALIBRE: 12	
BARREL LENGTH: 71cm (28in), 76cm (30in)	
WEIGHT: 3.5kg (7.7lb)	
EJECTOR TYPE: automatic ejectors	
CHOKES: interchangeable	
FEATURES: reliable action; superb value for money	

In many ways the Lanber range of sporting shotguns is an entirely conventional series of boxlock weapons. The action of the guns has the hammers powered by two coil springs, with hammer-restraint provided by sears that are suspended from the top of the action body. The barrels are locked for firing by a full-width locking bolt that engages a slot beneath the bottom barrel. When the gun is broken, the triggers are re-cocked and the ejectors are opened by rods running through the bottom of the action, these being driven by a cam in the fore-end.

Deluxe model

Internally, the Deluxe Sporter is much the same as the previous models although its UK importer, GMK, asserts that the 'action, now highly polished by means of Lanber's pulse-plasma-nitriding technology, gives a superlative level of strength and protection to the steel'. Externally, the Deluxe Sporter follows fairly standard configurations for a sporting shotgun.

It has 71cm (28in) or 76cm (30in) barrels, the bores being chrome-lined for corrosion protection, with 76mm (3in) magnum chambers and a set of screw-in multichokes. The multichokes are flush-fitting, but non-proprietary extended chokes are available for Lanber guns.

Quality stock

Woodwork quality has been improved, and the laser-cut checkering provides a good grip at the neck of the stock. The Schnabel fore-end (a Schnabel fore-end flares out at the front edge) is an improved design and sits comfortably in the front hand.

Overall the Lanber is a reliable and competent competition gun. Most importantly, its price puts a lot of gun on the market for around $1000 or less, competing with many similarly priced brands from the likes of Beretta and Bettinsoli. In fact, the sub-$1000 price bracket is becoming one of the most hard-fought sectors of the shotgun market. Companies such as Zoli, FAIR, Rizzini and Baikal/Remington all have good models in the budget category, and the competition leads to more features for less spend.

The Lanber Sporter is a good buy for those wanting their first shotgun for use in hunting or against clays.

Laurona Classic Trap

$$

The Classic Trap is a fine shotgun from the Spanish Laurona concern. Other Classic models from Laurona include the Classic Sporting and Classic Becada, for clay and field use respectively.

SPECIFICATIONS: **Laurona Classic Trap**

GAUGE/CALIBRE:	12
BARREL LENGTH:	74cm (29in), 76cm (30in)
WEIGHT:	3.45kg (7.6lb)
EJECTOR TYPE:	automatic ejectors
CHOKES:	fixed or interchangeable
FEATURES:	interchangeable billets

Laurona was established in 1941, and experienced slow but steady growth over the first three decades of its existence. In 1964 it produced its first over-and-under extractor gun, and at the beginning of the next decade it relocated to its modern-day factory in Eibar. Since then Laurona has specialized in shotguns for the clay and field markets, not only producing conventional shotguns but also over-and-under rifles and combination guns.

Classic design

The Classic Trap and the Classic Sporting are extremely strong, well-balanced shotguns. Laurona use very strong grades of steel in their shotguns, and the locking mechanisms use a rigid under-bolt system. The Classic Trap comes in 74cm (29in) or 76cm (30in) barrel lengths and there is the option of having either fixed or multichokes. (The Laurona multichokes are suitable for use with either lead or steel shot. This is an important consideration, as more

and more shooting grounds have to comply with lead-shot prohibitions.) Atop the barrel is a ventilated rib that narrows from 11mm (0.4in) to 7mm (0.27in). While Laurona used to make guns with a distinctive double-trigger system, in which the triggers could be pulled individually or either of the triggers could be used to fire both barrels in turn, today it makes the more popular single triggers, and these are adjustable.

The beavertail fore-end wraps the lower barrel, and provides a good wide base for a trap-shooting front grip, while the stock is a sharply curved pistol grip. The billets on the receiver are interchangeable, with bare steel or grey metal being options.

The Classic Trap has a strong under-bolt locking system and automatic ejectors. The action decoration here shows what the gun was designed for.

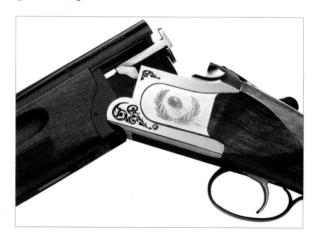

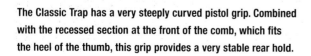

The Classic Trap has a very steeply curved pistol grip. Combined with the recessed section at the front of the comb, which fits the heel of the thumb, this grip provides a very stable rear hold.

MacNab Highlander

$$–$$$$

John MacNab recently brought out two new models: the Lowlander and the Highlander. The former gives the shooter a first serious competition gun at budget price; the latter takes the quality to the next level.

SPECIFICATIONS: **MacNab Highlander**

GAUGE/CALIBRE: 12
BARREL LENGTH: 74cm (29in)
WEIGHT: 3.4kg (7.5lb)
EJECTOR TYPE: automatic ejectors
CHOKES: fixed with multichoke option
FEATURES: lightweight version available

The MacNab Lowlander has received much critical acclaim in the shooting press. Richard Rawlinson, writer for the British *Clay Shooting* magazine, acknowledged that 'here was a budget gun … that felt like a more expensive model', (August 2005), and felt that the Lowlander tended to avoid the trap of trying to be both a game gun and a clay gun.

So what does the Highlander give that the Lowlander doesn't? For a start, the Highlander drops into much different price categories, moving from just over $1000 up to nearly $6000 depending on the model. (It is designed and made by Giorgio Guerini in Val Trompia, Italy, and many of MacNab's guns have Italian design input.) Predictably, therefore, the quality of the finish in the Highlander is far superior to that of the Lowlander, with the grain of the walnut stock and fore-end having a luxurious appearance. The fore-end also differs in shape from the Lowlander, having a Schnabel configuration rather than the Lowlander's beavertail fore-end.

Balance

The Highlander is primarily a game gun. Its weight comes in at 3.4kg (7.5lb), a respectable enough weight for carrying around on a day's shooting. MacNab also produce the Highlander Light, a weight-reduced shotgun (using lightweight alloys) that takes the weight down to a remarkable 2.5kg (5.5lb), although many shooters would find such a floaty gun difficult to control on long birds requiring a smooth, fluid swing.

As standard, the chokes on the Highlander are fixed, set at Improved Cylinder and Modified. For those wanting a little more control over their chokes, a multichoke option is available.

MacNab utilizes some of the best-known Italian gunsmiths in the crafting of its shotguns.

MacNab Side-by-Sides

$$$$$

MacNab offers a range of high-quality side-by-sides produced by some of Europe's most prestigious gun houses. Current models include the Woodcock, Garbi, Teal and the Arrieta.

SPECIFICATIONS: **MacNab Arrieta**

GAUGE/CALIBRE: 12, 20, 28, .410	
BARREL LENGTH: 74cm (29in)	
WEIGHT: up to 2.95kg (6.5lb)	
EJECTOR TYPE: automatic ejectors	
CHOKES: fixed	
FEATURES: sidelock mechanism	

A recent addition to the MacNab fold, and a gun representative of its side-by-sides, is the Woodcock. Ugartechea in Spain makes it but, as with other MacNab shotguns produced outside the UK, the specifications are set by MacNab. The Woodcock is a classic side-by-side field gun. It is a sidelock design, although some reviewers feel that it is not a pure sidelock because it uses coil springs in its mechanism instead of the traditional V-springs.

Yet the gun is undoubtedly made to the highest standards, with double-bolt locking and the chopper-lump barrels making for a solid mechanism and the sidelock plates receiving excellent decorative engraving. The splinter-type fore-end is push-button released. Barrel lengths are 74cm (29in) or 76cm (30in), and the weight is kept to around 2.8kg (6.3lb). Its appearance and robust construction make it a good field weapon in the sub-$3000 bracket. It is available in both 12- and 20-gauge versions.

Arrieta

The Arrieta is one of MacNab's most prestigious side-by-sides. Arrieta is a Spanish gunmaker known for over 80 years for producing high-grade sidelock side-by-sides, and with whom MacNab has had a working association for over 20 years. The Arrieta shotgun has a Holland & Holland type sidelock

mechanism and an exceptional quality of engraving that runs from the sideplates to beneath the action and around the trigger guard. Like the Woodcock, the Arrieta has chopper-lump barrels (the strongest type of fixing for a side-by-side) and fixed chokes, but comes in a greater range of calibres – 12, 20, 28 and .410. Barrel length is 74cm (29in).

Arrietas come with a hefty price tag on account of the hand-finishing processes the guns receive, but the guns are as much collector's pieces as they are fine working firearms.

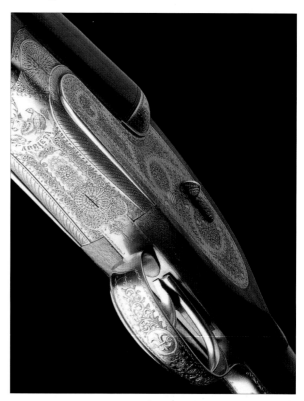

With their lavish engraving, MacNab Arrieta shotguns sell to only the most discerning customers, with the current client list including the Spanish Royal Family.

Marlin LC Range

$$

The side-by-side shotguns made by the Hunter Arms Company, Fulton, New York, were much respected during the 1940s. Now Marlin has brought back Hunter's venerated L.C. Smith shotgun.

SPECIFICATIONS: Marlin LC20-DB
GAUGE/CALIBRE: 20
BARREL LENGTH: 66cm (26in)
WEIGHT: 2.7kg (6lb)
EJECTOR TYPE: automatic ejectors
CHOKES: interchangeable
FEATURES: sideplates

Marlin bought the Hunter Arms Company in 1945, and several years later discontinued the L.C. Smith line. Its re-creation of the Smith shotgun is not a pure reproduction, but it has created a stir amongst those hunters wanting an American classic for their field shooting. Side-by-side shotguns have an enduring appeal even amongst those who have previously been confirmed over-and-under shooters. The L.C. Smith shotguns are aimed at those who want to bring a certain nostalgia into their gun collection.

Marlin's L.C. Smith range offers four guns. Two of them are 12 gauges (LC12-DB and LC12-OU) and two are 20 gauges (LC20-DB and LC20-OU). As the designations suggest, each gauge is available in side-by-side or over-and-under configurations, although the company acknowledges that Smith never produced any over-and-under guns. The side-by-side models are not true sidelocks like the Smith guns, but are conventional boxlocks fitted with sideplates.

Features

All of the guns, except the LC20-OU, come with 71cm (28in) barrels, the mentioned gun having 66cm (26in) barrels. Three choke tubes are supplied – Improved Cylinder, Modified and Full – and the guns are chambered for 76mm (3in) cartridges. Automatic selective ejectors are fitted.

On the side-by-side models the rib is solid, whereas the over-and-under models have ventilated top and mid ribs. The woodwork is walnut of a fine quality, and all the guns in the series have beavertail fore-ends. A modern recoil pad is fitted to the stock for comfort. The stock has a pronounced drop at comb, so shooters are advised to try one for fit before purchasing.

Weight configurations

The different configurations of the LC guns make for different weights. Of the side-by-side guns, the LC12-DB weighs 2.8kg (6.25lb) while the LC20-DB is 2.7kg (6lb). In over-and-under format the weight jumps pronouncedly: the LC12-OU is 3.3kg (7.25lb) and the LC20-OU is 3kg (6.6lb). Apart from some occasional reservations about how the gun fits, the press concerning the new L.C. Smith range has been generally favourable, and they are respectable game guns for a good price.

The L.C. Smith range of shotguns are all light and durable field guns, with a classic styling reminiscent of the American 1940s.

Marocchi Model 99

$$$–$$$$

Marocchi's Model 99 is a series for dedicated competition shooters, and has some of the company's flagship models. While much is familiar about the guns, Marocchi is keen to emphasize the technology behind their creations.

SPECIFICATIONS: **Marocchi Model 99 Sporter**

GAUGE/CALIBRE: 12

BARREL LENGTH: 71cm (28in), 76cm (30in), 81cm (32in)

WEIGHT: 3.5kg (7.7lb)

EJECTOR TYPE: automatic ejectors

CHOKES: Inchoke interchangeable

FEATURES: Schnabel fore-end; Boss action

The Model 99 has six versions, all united by a 12-gauge calibre, 70mm (2.75in) chambers and the stock configuration. They also use the same internal mechanism, which revolves around the Boss-type locking system – a bifurcated bolt moving through the standing breech engages with bites in the monobloc beneath the bottom barrel.

Because the hammers are driven by powerful coil springs, the trigger mechanism has been designed for very fast lock times. Length of pull on the trigger is fully adjustable, and the sear and hammer engagement can also be adjusted by a gunsmith. On firing, the gun's hammers rebound and withdraw the firing pins as a safety feature; the pins cannot accidentally strike the cap of a cartridge when a freshly loaded gun is shut.

Those guns fitted with multichokes use Marocchi's own Inchoke system. The chokes are made from the same material as the barrels themselves and can handle steel shot.

Versions

The current Model 99 range consists of the Sporter, Trap, Double Trap – Skeet, Electrocible-Box Bird, High Grades (II and III) and Custom Grades. The Sporter comes in the three typical sporting barrel lengths – 71cm (28in), 76cm (30in) and 81cm (32in) – and has multichokes. Like the lighter Electrocible, it also has a Schnabel fore-end, while the other guns have beavertail front woodwork.

The woodwork on all the models is oil-finished walnut, and they also all share 10mm (0.4in) ventilated top ribs. The Trap and Skeet guns come with fixed chokes set appropriate to the discipline, while the Double Trap can have either fixed or multichokes. The High Grades and Custom Grades offer greater standards of decoration.

The Marocchi Model 99 utilizes the redoubtable Boss locking system, one of the most trusted locking systems on the shotgun market.

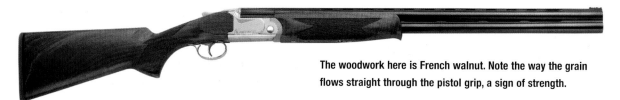

The woodwork here is French walnut. Note the way the grain flows straight through the pistol grip, a sign of strength.

Merkel Side-by-Sides

$$$–$$$$

The master gunmakers of Merkel based in Suhl, Germany, produce a broad range of breech-loading hunting weapons, from light game guns through to powerful 'safari' weapons.

SPECIFICATIONS: Merkel 280/360EL

GAUGE/CALIBRE: 20, .410	
BARREL LENGTH: 71cm (28in)	
WEIGHT: 2.5kg (5.5lb)	
EJECTOR TYPE: automatic ejectors	
CHOKES: fixed	
FEATURES: interchangeable barrel sets	

Merkel was founded in 1868, although the roots of the company go back into the sixteenth century. Today, Merkel is known worldwide for superior firearms, and their shotguns and rifles are on the wish lists of many discerning shots, particularly their side-by-side weapons.

Merkel 40E

A classic Merkel side-by-side is the 40E, available in 12-, 16- and 20-bore versions. This boxlock has a rugged locking action based on a Greener-style crossbolt and double bottom bite and Anson & Deeley lockwork (the lockwork also features cocking indicators). The standard gun comes with a double trigger (single trigger is an option).

Quality sidelocks

The Merkel side-by-side range rises up to guns like the 61E, which has Merkel sidelocks and is in 28 or .410 gauges. The barrel length is 71cm (28in), contributing to an overall length of 113cm (44.5in), and weight is around 2.5kg (5.5lb). The 280/360EL pictured here comes supplied with two barrel sets, in 28 gauge and .410 gauge. It has 71cm (28in) barrels operated by a double-trigger system. Chambers for the 28-gauge barrel are set at 70mm (2.75in), while the .410-gauge barrels have 76mm (3in) chambers. Weight for both of the guns is around the same, 2.5kg (5.5lb). Safety function on the gun is automatic, the safety being a conventional thumb-operated switch mounted just behind the top lever.

Standard Merkel engravings on the sidelocks are of superb quality, but the custom-grade engravings make the guns objects of exceptional beauty, with relief, Bulino-style work, coloured case hardenings and inlays transforming the metalwork. Combination guns are also one of Merkel's specialities, mixing rifled barrels with smoothbore barrels. However, the ability to select shotgun barrel sets is particularly useful, the same gun being used for light vermin through to upland bird shooting.

Right: This barrel set from the Merkel 280/360EL clearly shows the barrel hinge and the large locking lug just behind the fore-end.

The heavily decorated sideplates of the 280/360EL, plus its fine woodwork, make it a particularly attractive side-by-side.

Merkel 2001EL Sporter

$$$

Merkel produced its first over-and-under model at the end of the nineteenth century. The series 2000 continues the tradition in the modern age with a range of technologically advanced boxlocks.

SPECIFICATIONS: **Merkel 2001EL Sporter**

GAUGE/CALIBRE: 12, 20, 28	
BARREL LENGTH: 71cm (28in)	
WEIGHT: approx 3.1kg (6.8lb)	
EJECTOR TYPE: automatic ejectors	
CHOKES: fixed or interchangeable	
FEATURES: multiple options of customization	

The 2000 series of guns, at time of writing, consists of nine different models, ranging from a selection of 12-gauge shotguns suitable for game or clays, through to over-and-under rifles such as the 2022D. The 2001EL is a striking boxlock with a slightly couched outline that conveys power and balance.

Gauge choice

The 2001EL is available in 12-, 20- or 28-gauge versions, appealing to a broad range of shooters who want guns ranging from wildfowling pieces through to light bird guns. For fixed-choke guns the combinations are Improved Cylinder and Modified, Improved Cylinder and Improved Modified, and Modified and Full, according to the customer order.

The Merkel 2001EL has a cold-hammer-forged steel barrel with a solid sighting rib running along top. Its weight, however, is still kept at a manageable level.

However, interchangeable chokes are an option (few manufacturers make over-and-unders without multichoke as standard or optional). The locks are of a modified Anson & Deeley type, and the Kersten crossbolt slots into an adjustable bite plate. Barrel length is 71cm (28in) for the 12-gauge weapon, and 68cm (27cm) for the 20 and 28 gauges. Steel receivers are slimmed down to the bore diameter to give the gun a slender appearance. A simple thumb switch provides safety, but the 2000 series also has intercepting sear safety to prevent the guns going off if they are knocked or jarred.

Options

All 2000 series weapons offer multiple options for the purchaser, hence giving the buyer a gun more customized to his or her particular needs. The automatic ejectors can be deactivated to become extractors, useful if the shooter wants to avoid environmental pollution from ejected rounds. A single trigger is standard, but options include a single selectable trigger, an adjustable-length single trigger and a double trigger.

The stock comes either with or without a cheek piece, and a straight-stock option is also available. Company promotional material also states that 'A painstakingly hand-crafted three-piece forearm is also available as a stylish feature for this particularly responsive and elegant shotgun.'

Miroku MK60/70

$$

Miroku guns, intimately associated with Browning after the Japanese company's major stock purchase in the 1960s and 1970s, are rugged, reliable weapons that are priced competitively.

SPECIFICATIONS: Miroku MK70 Sporting

GAUGE/CALIBRE: 12, 20, 28	
BARREL LENGTH: 71cm (28in), 76cm (30in), 81cm (32in)	
WEIGHT: 3.5kg (7.7lb)	
EJECTOR TYPE: automatic ejectors	
CHOKES: Invector interchangeable	
FEATURES: reliable Browning-type mechanism	

Miroku shotguns are reliable, effective weapons for game shooters and sportsmen.

Today Miroku produces a wide range of shotguns for Browning, and the synergy between the two is clear. However, Miroku guns tend to be somewhat cheaper, although that fact in no way casts doubt on their quality. Many a shooter has begun his pastime or career with a Miroku, only to find many years later that he still has little reason to change his gun. The second-hand market in Mirokus is also extremely buoyant, most dealers being able to offer some real bargains at the sub-$500 mark.

Sporting and game

The MK60 and MK70 are essentially the same gun. Both are available in either Game or Sporting models, the former having fixed chokes and the latter having Browning's Invector multichokes. The differences between the two series of guns revolve around subtleties of format rather than the mechanism. The action is at the heart of the Miroku guns' reliability. It is actually based upon the mechanism of the Browning B25. The tumblers are driven by coil springs, the sear engaging with the tumbler from its position on the top strap of the action. The hinge lumps are beneath the barrel and lock onto a full-width hinge pin. This gives the Miroku guns – much like many of the Browning models – deeper actions than guns such as the Berettas, which use the 'bifurcated lumps' system. Locking is accomplished by a flat bolt slotting into bites in the bottom of the monobloc. The system is simple, and consequently reliable.

All MK60 models come with 70mm (2.75in) chambers, whereas the 71cm (28in) and 76cm (30in) models of the MK70 have 76mm (3in) chambers. The MK60 and MK70 Game guns have 6.2mm (0.24in) ventilated top ribs, whereas the Sporting models take the rib width up to 10mm (0.39in).

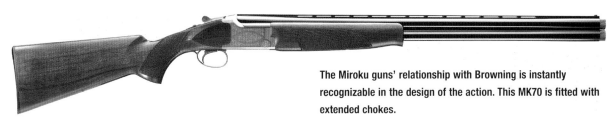

The Miroku guns' relationship with Browning is instantly recognizable in the design of the action. This MK70 is fitted with extended chokes.

Miroku Mk-10

$$

The Mk-10 is another popular series from Miroku. Available in trap, skeet or sporting versions, it is a good gun for a beginner wanting to get serious about his chosen clay discipline.

SPECIFICATIONS: **Miroku Mk-10 Trap**

GAUGE/CALIBRE: 12	
BARREL LENGTH: 76cm (30in)	
WEIGHT: 3.5kg (7.7lb)	
EJECTOR TYPE: automatic ejectors	
CHOKES: Invector-Plus interchangeable	
FEATURES: back-boring technology	

The Mk-10 Trap model has 76cm (30in) barrels and the top rib tapers down from a wide 13mm (0.51in) to 10mm (0.39in). The sighting plane it provides is therefore very clear, while the 76cm (30in) barrel length keeps the shot patterns tighter at the range typical of trap shooting, and also aids the 'pointability' of the gun when a target is making a crossing trajectory.

Miroku has also invested the gun with an adjustable trigger pull, and the Invector-Plus multichokes ensure that the shot makes a smooth transition into the choked section, thereby producing better patterns (depending, of course, on the quality of the cartridges) through less shot deformation.

The main Miroku competitor to the Mk-10 Trap is the Mk-38 Trap. This is also available in an 81cm (32in) barrel version (the lengthier barrels are particularly popular with more professional trap shots). The Mk-38s also come with a selection of rib widths and the adjustable comb model has recently been introduced to give the shooter a precision mount.

Mk-10 Sport

During the early 1990s, second-hand Mk-38s were frequently converted into sporting models through the addition of a set of non-proprietary multichokes and some modifications to the dimensions of the woodwork. Eventually, Miroku produced a dedicated Mk-38 Sport, with a Schnabel fore-end, along with modified stock dimensions. The Mk-10 Sport fleshes out Miroku's sporting range, with its Invector-Plus chokes, and the 'back-boring' technology used by Browning produces excellent shot patterning (the Mk-38 is also a back-bored gun).

There are also two grades of finish to the Mk-10 Sport – Grade 1 and Grade 2. The second-hand market for Miroku guns is good, so anyone wanting to buy a new Miroku is advised to make an initial check of local gun stores for any mint-condition weapons. As long as there are no significant signs of damage and the barrels fasten tightly to the action, the second-hand Miroku should continue to provide years of good service.

The Mk-10 provides plenty of gun for the money. The Sport model can also serve well as a field gun, although the double ventilated rib will need diligent cleaning after a wet trip.

Perazzi MX 410

$$$$$

Based in Brescia, Italy, Perazzi is one of the most respected names in the world of shotgunning, its guns serving some of the world's medal-winning competitive shooters.

SPECIFICATIONS: **Perazzi MX 410 Basic Grade**

GAUGE/CALIBRE: .410

BARREL LENGTH: 66cm (26in), 68cm (27in), 71cm (28in), 74cm (29in)

WEIGHT: N/A

EJECTOR TYPE: automatic ejectors

CHOKES: fixed or interchangeable

FEATURES: customized finish and stock dimensions

Perazzi has retained a bespoke emphasis in its production, customizing guns to fit its clients and producing a limited number of weapons – at the time of writing, only 12 guns a day. Those shooters fortunate enough to buy from the Perazzi factory can select their own stock blank, from which their gun stock will be cut, using the shooter's body measurements.

Small-gauge guns

The Perazzi reputation has been consolidated by a string of major victories for Perazzi shooters on the world stage. In the 2000 Sydney Olympics, for example, Perazzi guns were used to win three gold medals, one silver medal and five bronze medals.

Nevertheless, Perazzi also invests in producing a range of excellent field guns, including the small-gauge MX 410 Game models.

The basic MX 410 Standard Grade model is a .410-calibre over-and-under shotgun available in 66cm (26in), 68cm (27in), 71cm (28in) or 74cm (29in) barrel lengths. Chokes are either fixed or multichoke, depending on the requirements. The trigger group consists of a single, selective trigger and the stock has an 'English game' fore-end. While the Standard Grade model is attractive in itself, with a deep grain in the select Asian walnut and high-quality engraving, other models push the external appearance even further. The MX 410 SCO Grade with Sideplates gives – as the name suggests – the engraver's art more scope for expression by including sideplates.

Other versions have more functional changes: the MX 410 Extra Grade, for example, has a ventilated top rib in contrast to the solid rib of the Standard Grade. Whatever the grade or finish, the MX 410s are totally dependable .410 shotguns for prolonged field use.

The Perazzi MX 410 Extra Grade features lavishly decorated sideplates and a ventilated top rib.

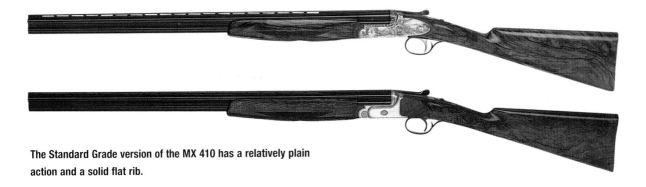

The Standard Grade version of the MX 410 has a relatively plain action and a solid flat rib.

Perazzi MX 8

$$$$$

Compared with many of Italy's more venerable gun producers, Perazzi is the new kid on the block (it was founded in 1952). However, it has built a reputation as one of the world's finest producers of competition guns.

SPECIFICATIONS: **Perazzi MX 8 Trap**

GAUGE/CALIBRE: 12

BARREL LENGTH: 75cm (29.5in), 80cm (31.5in)

WEIGHT: 3.9kg (8.5lb)

EJECTOR TYPE: automatic ejectors

CHOKES: fixed

FEATURES: customized finish and stock dimensions; detachable trigger group

Based in Botticino Mattina, Brescia, Perazzi has achieved its global prominence through the sheer pleasure that shooting a Perazzi weapon offers, and through many Olympic medal triumphs. A defining moment was at the 1996 Olympics in Atlanta, when Perazzi-armed competitors took gold, silver and bronze medals.

The MX 8 has been designed for the worlds of trap and skeet, the disciplines that have brought the gun fame, and it incorporates a high degree of user-friendliness. A distinguishing feature is its detachable

trigger mechanism. The safety switch is pushed fully forward to release a retaining pin. The trigger plate is then removed, and with it the whole firing mechanism. There should, however, be infrequent need to remove this mechanism for maintenance, as the Perazzi system is simple and reliable, and imparts crisp trigger pulls and fast lock times. However, some competitive shots like the easier switching of trigger groups. The MX 8 Special model also has a four-position adjustable trigger.

Attention to detail

An H-shaped locking bolt that engages with bites either side of the barrel, this being cammed off the top-lever spindle, locks the MX 8. Replacement H-bolts are available should the gun become worn over a long time and from heavy use. The barrels are manufactured to extraordinarily high standards, with chrome-lined chambers and chokes and a flawless blacking. Barrel lengths are 75cm (29.5in) with the chokes set at Improved Modified and Extra Full, or 80cm (31.5in) with Full and Extra Full. The skeet version has a 71cm (28in) or 75cm (29.5in) barrel, the latter having multichokes instead of fixed chokes.

Many different grades and configurations of woodwork are available with the MX 8, as with all Perazzi guns, resulting in wide variations in final price. Any MX 8, however, is a durable and sage investment for heavy shooters.

A trap shooter puts her head down hard against the stock of an MX 8. Trap shotguns are designed to throw patterns high so the shooter can keep the target above the barrel at all times.

Perazzi MX 2000

$$$$

The MX 2000 is aimed at many different clay disciplines, with representatives for trap, double trap, skeet and sporting clays. All guns in the series are top-quality competition weapons.

SPECIFICATIONS:

Perazzi MX 2000 Olympic/Double Trap

GAUGE/CALIBRE: 12

BARREL LENGTH: 75cm (29.5in), 80cm (31.5in)

WEIGHT: N/A

EJECTOR TYPE: automatic ejectors

CHOKES: fixed or interchangeable

FEATURES: adjustable stock; adjustable rib; detachable trigger group

Indicative of Perazzi's emphasis on customization, the MX 2000 presents numerous different configurations for every major clay discipline. For trap shooters alone, the choices are impressive. Single-/double-barrel combo sets are available for those wanting to use a single gun for both trap and double-trap events.

The single-barrel option is for an 81cm (32in) or 86cm (34in) barrel, while the double-barrelled set has 75cm (29.5in) or 80cm (31.5in) lengths. In terms of chokes, both sets can be either fixed or multichoke, according to preference.

Although a shooter might automatically lean towards the idea of a multichoke weapon, he often finds that, once fitted, the chokes are rarely changed, so a fixed-choke gun can reduce the time spent on cleaning and maintenance. The barrel sets are available with either fixed or adjustable ribs. The adjustable-rib system features four notches for different stages of rib elevation, this giving the shooter a useful way of adjusting his point of impact depending on his shooting style or mounting technique. Adjustable stocks are also standard – the comb can be altered for both drop and cast for a precision fit.

Skeet and sporting

While Perazzi has forged a major presence on the trap circuit, its MX 2000 series also has fine skeet and sporting models. The skeet model comes in four different barrel lengths ranging from 67cm (26.5in) up to 75cm (29.5in).

The shorter barrel lengths are matched by more open fixed-choke options – the standard fixed configuration is Cylinder and Cylinder – although multichokes are another option. Reliability is prodigious, with some shooting magazines talking of a professional firing over one million rounds without any significant malfunction. The sporting model comes in four other barrel lengths common to the discipline and only has a multichoke configuration, so the shooter can select chokes according to stand presentation.

Below is an MX 2000 S 12 gauge. The MX 2000 models are some of the most technologically advanced on the market, particularly when it comes to rib options for trap shooters.

Perazzi MX 2005

$$$$

Perazzi's MX 2005 guns are the latest incarnation of a prestigious line of Perazzi weapons designed for the serious trap shooter, and they are strong competition for guns such as the Krieghoff K-80.

SPECIFICATIONS: Perazzi MX 2005
GAUGE/CALIBRE: 12
BARREL LENGTH: 75cm (29.5in), 77cm (30.4in), 80cm (31.5in)
WEIGHT: 4.2kg (9.25lb)
EJECTOR TYPE: automatic ejectors
CHOKES: fixed top barrel, interchangeable bottom barrel
FEATURES: adjustable stock; adjustable rib; detachable trigger group

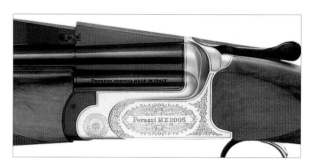

The MX 2005 features a superb standard of engraving on the side of the stylishly crafted nickel-plated action.

Some features of the MX 2005 are very familiar to existing Perazzi trap-gun users. The MX 2005, for instance, has the MX 8's detachable trigger group. This is equipped with V-springs to power the hammers – although Perazzi has used coil springs in many of its trigger systems, with few complaints, many of the most dedicated trap shooters have a preference for the crisp, fast pulls imparted by V-springs.

Trigger-pull weights on an on-test out-of-the-box MX 2005 are around 2.2kg (3lb) for the bottom barrel and 2.3kg (5lb) for the top barrel. The top barrel is a fixed choke, bored out to Maximum Full, while the bottom barrel is multichoke, giving the shooter more control over the pattern of the first shot.

Ribs and bores

The adjustable-rib system is used on the MX 2005. First impressions of the rib are striking – it stands some 3cm (1.2in) above the barrel. By setting the rib high, the shooter has a very unobstructed view of the clay rising fast out of the trap. Each end of the rib sits in a notched holder, and the rib pivots in the middle. The lower the notch setting at the back (and the higher at the front), the flatter the pattern thrown, and vice versa. Add in the fact that the stock comb is also fully adjustable, and some experimentation is obviously required to bring the gun to the correct personal configuration.

Despite the sci-fi appearance of the MX 2005's rib setup, the rest of the gun has traditional, and highly attractive, woodwork, with a deep beavertail fore-end and a highly engraved nickel-plated action.

The rib profile on the Perazzi MX 2005 is almost alarming at first glance, though less so when you look at the level of the adjustable comb on the stock.

Renato Gamba Ambassador $$$$$

Any book on sporting guns would be incomplete without at least one or two of the world's superlative models, occupying the highest price brackets. One such model is the Renato Gamba Ambassador Sidelock.

SPECIFICATIONS: **Renato Gamba Ambassador**

GAUGE/CALIBRE: 12

BARREL LENGTH: 66cm (26in), 71cm (28in)

WEIGHT: depends on stock dimensions

EJECTOR TYPE: automatic ejectors

CHOKES: fixed

FEATURES: demi-bloc construction

A close-up view of the top lever on the Ambassador sidelock, with the ejectors visible top left.

It is arguable that if you can spend up to $10,000 on a shotgun, then any weapon priced beyond that will give you nothing extra in terms of functionality and performance. Nevertheless, the lure of shotgun excellence is strong, and there remain plenty of investors in the market for guns priced upwards of $100,000 – and even beyond. Although such purchases are rarely fired, many are bought as collector's pieces to hold and improve their value over many years. What you get is exquisite appearance, rock solid and often hand-finished engineering, and pure joy to shoot.

Pure excellence

A review on the Internet of the Ambassador sidelock discovered the sale of one example, built in 1979 and formerly owned by Prince Faisal M. Al Saud, with a price tag of over $56,000, although other second-hand models are available closer to the region of $15,000. The Ambassador itself is a 66cm (26in) or 71cm (28in) side-by-side gun. It has demi-bloc barrels, meaning that the lumps are forged integrally with the barrel they join, the two barrel sets then being set together.

Demi-bloc barrels have a very favourable strength-to-weight ratio, and they also allow close setting of the barrels at the breech end so that it is easier to regulate the point of aim for the pair of barrels. A three-bite double Purdey locking system is used, single or double triggers can be ordered, and the woodwork is of the finest quality. The gun is made with a personalized fit, and it is doubtless something the shooter will treasure for many years.

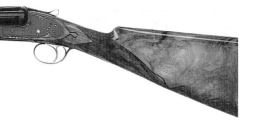

The quality of the woodwork here is as good as it gets in terms of shotgun manufacture, with a deep lustrous grain and a flawless strength.

Renato Gamba Daytona

$$$$–$$$$$

Renato Gamba does not enjoy the same high profile as Beretta or Perazzi, but its guns are of undoubted quality. As a premier-grade sporting clays gun, the Daytona is a fine choice.

SPECIFICATIONS: Renato Gamba Daytona Sporter

GAUGE/CALIBRE: 12	
BARREL LENGTH: 71cm (28in), 76cm (30in), 81cm (32in)	
WEIGHT: 3.8kg (8.5lb)	
EJECTOR TYPE: automatic ejectors	
CHOKES: fixed or interchangeable	
FEATURES: adjustable trigger; detachable trigger group	

At the core of the Daytona action are strong construction techniques, providing the dependability essential for a competition gun destined for hard use. A tri-alloy steel forging forms the action body, which has a slim profile and a black metal exterior to create a striking visual contrast with the woodwork. Two oversize locking bolts achieve locking, giving a smooth and rigid closure.

Like many Perazzi weapons, the Daytona's trigger group is removable. Hammers are powered by coil springs and lock times are very fast – the hammers are designed for a perfect 90-degree strike on the firing pins. The firing pins also shift back slightly after firing. This prevents the head of a firing pin from becoming damaged by dragging against a cartridge primer when the gun is opened.

Trigger settings

If so ordered, the Daytona can be fitted with an adjustable trigger so that the length of pull can be altered to fit the hand (the adjustable trigger has up to 2.5cm/1in of lateral movement). Trigger pull is fast, responsive and has no creep.

The Daytona's barrels are lined with chrome for corrosion resistance, and come with either Rhino multichokes or fixed chokes. The chambers are set for 70mm (2.75in) cartridges. In its Sporter configuration, a Daytona with 81cm (32in) barrels weighs around 3.8kg (8.5lb), but the gun comes in several other different configurations, among them models for trap and skeet. For those wanting an even more prestigious weapon, the Daytona range includes the SL sideplate model and the SLHH sidelock model, for a significant increase in price and aesthetic appearance.

The Renato Gamba Daytona is available in a plain black action or in several silver actions, the latter being able to take more engraving and delicate styling.

Rizzini Premier Sporting $$$

Rizzini is another shotgun manufacturer based in the Brescia region of Italy. It concentrates purely on over-and-under shotguns, and the Premier Sporting is configured for the varied presentations of a sporting layout.

SPECIFICATIONS: **Rizzini Premier Sporting**

GAUGE/CALIBRE: 12, 20

BARREL LENGTH: 71cm (28in), 75cm (29.5in), 78cm (31in), 81cm (32in)

WEIGHT: 3.4kg (7.5lb)

EJECTOR TYPE: automatic ejectors

CHOKES: fixed or interchangeable

FEATURES: selective trigger

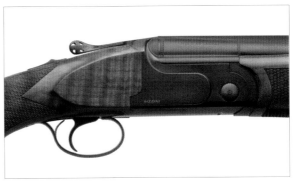

The smooth black styling on the Rizzini Premier Sporting is the most immediately striking feature of the gun, and little details like the ventilated top lever also grab the attention.

The Premier Skeet and the Premier Trap accompany the Premier Sporting. All three come in either 12- or 20-gauge versions, and the key differences lie in the barrel and chamber dimensions. The Premier Skeet has, predictably, the shortest barrels of the range, being 68 and 71cm (27 and 28in). Premier Trap models come in either 75cm (29.5in) or 78cm (31in), and also have slightly different stock dimensions to the Skeet and Sporting guns.

Barrel lengths

Finally, the Premier Sporting has the greatest variety in barrel lengths: 71, 75, 78 and 81cm (28, 29.5, 31 and 32in). Choosing the correct barrel length for the shooter depends on several factors, including confidence (longer barrels give tighter patterns of shot at closer ranges, requiring greater accuracy), size and the types of shooting ground commonly tackled.

Common features

Apart from the barrel differences, the Premier range shares most of its features between the models. Chokes are either fixed or interchangeable (surprisingly, fixed is listed as an option on the Sporting model), there are automatic ejectors, and the boxlock action is completely blued, although a chromed action is also available. Bores are lined with chrome, and both ribs are ventilated. The top rib of all the guns is a wide 10mm (0.39in), and it does not taper along its length. All of the guns have single triggers, but the Sporting model's trigger is selective. The checkering on the woodwork is done by hand, and the finish on the Rizzini weapons is of a very high quality.

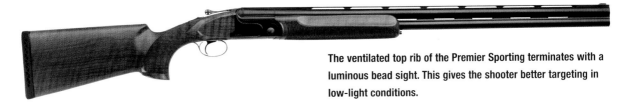

The ventilated top rib of the Premier Sporting terminates with a luminous bead sight. This gives the shooter better targeting in low-light conditions.

Ruger Gold Label

$$

The Gold Label is a classic-style side-by-side shotgun from Sturm, Ruger & Co. For those wanting a light, effective game gun, it is a good option around the $2000 mark.

SPECIFICATIONS: **Ruger Gold Label**

GAUGE/CALIBRE: 12	
BARREL LENGTH: 71cm (28in)	
WEIGHT: 3kg (6.6lb)	
EJECTOR TYPE: automatic ejectors	
CHOKES: interchangeable	
FEATURES: option of straight or pistol-grip stock	

Weight reduction is the main focus of the Gold Label. The barrels are made from lightweight metal and the extremely shallow receiver is constructed of stainless steel – resulting in a gun that only weighs 3kg (6.6lb). The interchangeable chokes also have very thin walls, and the gun comes with a five-choke set (these are ranged from Skeet to Full), so the shooter can set the pattern according to their particular style of shooting or hunting. The chokes are also fine for shooting with steel shot, so can be used in environmentally sensitive areas (typically wetlands) or countries (throughout most of the European Union, for example, lead shot is banned).

Lightweight power

Although a very light gun, the Gold Label is chambered for 76mm (3in) magnum cartridges – recoil must be quite firm when firing heavy shot loads. Only a 71cm (28in) barrel length is available, and this has a full-length rib with a simple bead sight

at the muzzle end. The woodwork is American walnut, and the stock is available either with a classic straight neck or with a pistol-grip configuration. The fore-end is of the splinter type, and the weight of the gun balances at the junction of fore-end and receiver. An auto-safety reduces the risk of an accident in the field, and the safety switch is combined with the barrel selector.

Shooting reviews of the Gold Label have been very favourable, noting the gun's natural 'pointability' and its ease of transportation.

Above: A close-up view of the Gold Label's shallow stainless-steel receiver. The break action of the gun also features spring-assisted opening.

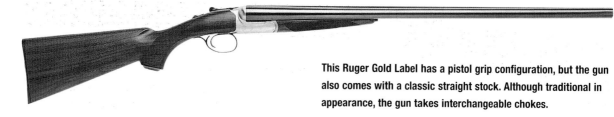

This Ruger Gold Label has a pistol grip configuration, but the gun also comes with a classic straight stock. Although traditional in appearance, the gun takes interchangeable chokes.

Ruger Red Label

$$

Ruger Red Labels are veteran American shotguns, having been introduced by the Ruger Company back in 1978. With prices around the $1600 mark, they are extremely popular as first or second guns.

SPECIFICATIONS: Ruger Red Label
GAUGE/CALIBRE: 12, 20, 28
BARREL LENGTH: 66cm (26in), 71cm (28in), 76cm (30in)
WEIGHT: 3.6kg (8lb)
EJECTOR TYPE: automatic ejectors
CHOKES: interchangeable
FEATURES: option of straight or pistol-grip stock

The 12- and 20-gauge Red Label have 76mm (3in) chambers, while the 28-gauge gun has 70mm (2.75in) chambers.

Today the Red Label shotguns are split into three basic categories: Red Label, Engraved Red Label and Satin Grey All-Weather® Red Label, with subtle model differences within these categories. The company website, however, defines all models as particularly suitable for 'sporting clays, pheasants and waterfowl', and the gun does seem to fulfil its all-round brief.

Gauge

Three gauges are available in this series: 12, 20 and 28. The subdivisions within the basic Red Label category centre not only around the calibre, but also around whether a straight or pistol-grip stock is selected. Barrel lengths for Red Label shotguns are 66cm (26in), 71cm (28in) or 76cm (30in), with ventilated ribs and a simple front bead sight. Weights for a 71cm (28in) barrel Red Label gun are around the 3.6kg (8lb) mark.

The engraved Red Label, as the name suggests, comes with a higher standard of scrollwork on the receiver, which also features a 24-carat gold game representation. This extra luxury raises the price over the standard Red Label by around $200. The Satin Grey All-Weather® Red Label, however, is modelled very differently. Designed for highly corrosive environments – particularly wetlands and coastal shooting – this gun has stainless-steel metallic parts and a black synthetic polymer stock and fore-end that resist the wet. The All-Weather® Red Label comes in 12 gauge only, and also has a camouflage version with all parts rendered in a photo-realistic grade of woodland camouflage. Red Labels are proven guns, which have been tried and tested in all manner of shooting conditions over the past 30 years and more.

The standard Red Label comes with an American walnut stock – as seen here – although black synthetic versions are available for field shooters who want a bit more stealth.

Salvinelli Sporting Guns

$$–$$$

Salvinelli have recently produced a range of sporting shotguns that offer the shooter affordable, good-quality guns for any sporting clay discipline.

SPECIFICATIONS: **Salvinelli Sporting EXL**

GAUGE/CALIBRE: 12	
BARREL LENGTH: 70cm (27.5in), 72cm (28in), 76cm (30in)	
WEIGHT: 3.5kg (7.7lb)	
EJECTOR TYPE: automatic ejectors	
CHOKES: Investarm interchangeable	
FEATURES: personalized stock dimensions; elongated forcing cones	

The Salvinelli brothers, who began making fine-quality sporting guns back in the 1950s, also founded Investarm SpA in 1975. While the Investarm brand has been known for many of its budget models, Salvinelli makes some of the finest shotguns and rifles on the market. Its premium boxlock and sidelock shotguns and double rifles feature superb standards of engraving and manufacture, and include collector's pieces such as the Rombo four-barrelled gun.

Form and function

Salvinelli's Sporting range comes in seven different models – L1, L2, XL1, XL2, EXL, EXO and EXL

Sideplates. Depending on the model, 70cm (27.5in) to 76cm (30in) barrels are available for these competition guns. As you would expect on a sporting shotgun, multichokes are standard, these being very thin-walled fittings made by Salvinelli itself. A combination of these chokes and long forcing cones (the latter reducing risk of pellet deformation) produces excellent patterns.

Cosmetically the Sporting guns are finished to a high standard. Options are available for stock-quality upgrades, and the computerized stock-making technologies in the Salvinelli factory mean that stocks can be personalized to the buyer's physique. The EXL Sideplates features a sideplate design. The total weight of a 76cm (30in) Sporting is around 3.5kg (7.7lb).

Reviews of the Sporting series often point to a debt to the internal mechanics of Boss and Perazzi, and Salvinelli have indeed created a very solid and reliable action. The Sporting series guns have bifurcated lumps fitting the barrels to the receiver (a traditional form of barrel/receiver locking that gives guns a slimmer profile) and locking is via a bolt from the breech face engaging with lugs either side of the bottom barrel.

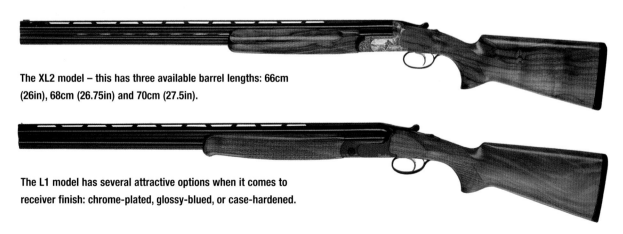

The XL2 model – this has three available barrel lengths: 66cm (26in), 68cm (26.75in) and 70cm (27.5in).

The L1 model has several attractive options when it comes to receiver finish: chrome-plated, glossy-blued, or case-hardened.

Weatherby Athena Grade V Classic $$$

Weatherby have been specializing in the production of sporting rifles and shotguns since 1945, and they also produce many types of ammunition. The Athena Grade V Classic is one of Weatherby's top-of-the-line field guns.

SPECIFICATIONS: Weatherby Athena Grade V Classic
GAUGE/CALIBRE: 12, 20
BARREL LENGTH: 66cm (26in), 71cm (28in)
WEIGHT: (12 gauge) 3.3kg (7.25lb)
EJECTOR TYPE: automatic ejectors
CHOKES: interchangeable
FEATURES: selective trigger; patented sear block safety; back-boring

The Grade V is an extremely attractive field gun, with lines that seem to combine both traditionalism and modernity. The first aspect to grab the attention is the silver/grey nitride sideplate receiver decorated with rose and scroll engraving. The American Claro walnut stock and fore-end are also richly oiled to bring out the strong grain. The hand of the stock (the part that forms the pistol grip, where the trigger-hand sits) is slender and flows backwards at a shallower angle than many modern guns, which often have quite angular pistol grips. There are finely cut checkering sections on both sides of the pistol grip and running along the underparts of the fore-end. The heel of the thumb sits neatly in a recess cut into the front of the comb. The overall impression is of a well-balanced field gun with a high grade of aesthetic appeal thrown into the mix.

Format

The Athena Grade V Classic is a boxlock (it has sideplates, not sidelocks) and can be bought in either 12 or 20 gauge. Both gauges are available in either 66cm (26in) or 71cm (28in), the lack of a 76cm (30in) model indicating that the series is squarely intended for field rather than clay shooting (although the Athena will perform perfectly well in clay shooting). The overall length of the 66cm (26in) gun is 109cm (43in) with the 71cm (28in) gun being 5cm (2in) longer. Weatherby shotguns are supplied with a set of Integral Multichoke (IMC) interchangeable chokes. These are steel-shot capable (something not all interchangeable chokes can handle) and have 10 different levels of constriction, ranging from Cylinder to Extra Full.

Trigger safety

The Athena's trigger is selective and is also gold-plated for protection against corrosion. For additional safety, Weatherby's over-and-unders have a patented sear block safety design: should the gun be closed with the trigger depressed and the safety off, the gun will not fire. This is a useful safety feature for episodes of rapid-firing, such as those that occur in wildfowling or pigeon shooting, when a shooter's normally controlled approach to safety might be rushed in the heat of the moment.

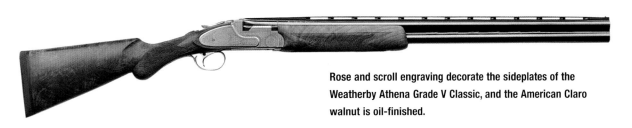

Rose and scroll engraving decorate the sideplates of the Weatherby Athena Grade V Classic, and the American Claro walnut is oil-finished.

Weatherby SBS Athena D'Italia Deluxe

$$$$

The Italian-made Athena D'Italia range entered the Weatherby line-up in 2005, and offers high-grade side-by-side shotguns with modern engineering and beautiful standards of finish.

SPECIFICATIONS: **Weatherby SBS Athena D'Italia Deluxe**

GAUGE/CALIBRE: 12, 20

BARREL LENGTH: 66cm (26in), 71cm (28in)

WEIGHT: (12 gauge) up to 3.3kg (7.25lb)

EJECTOR TYPE: automatic ejectors

CHOKES: interchangeable

FEATURES: back-boring; lengthened forcing cones; high standard of finish

The 'basic' SBS Athena Classic is a 12- or 20-gauge shotgun with an ornate sideplate design. Its Anson & Deeley action is combined with Purdey double locking for the most solid of barrel closures. As with most modern shotguns, the barrels themselves are lined with chrome to resist corrosion.

Barrel type

They are also the recipients of back-boring, which the shooting world generally feels produces better shot patterns. Similarly, the D'Italia has lengthened forcing cones (the forcing cones are the constricting transitional stages between the chambers and the bores). By lengthening the cones, the movement of the shot into the bores is less violent, and so the risk

The Athena D'Italia guns have the classic straight stock style, which gives them a beautiful, slender continuity from the muzzles to the butt plate.

of shot deformation is lessened. (Deformed shot slow down more quickly in the air and make erratic flight paths, resulting in holes in the shot pattern.)

Deluxe model

The next step up from the Athena D'Italia is the D'Italia PG, which has the same action as the D'Italia but features a rounded pistol and semi-beavertail fore-end. It is also available in 28 gauge. The checkering is laser-cut for accuracy, and features 20 lines per inch (LPI). Top of the range, however, is the D'Italia Deluxe. Superlative standards of engraving and hand-rubbed wood finishing push the Deluxe up just short of the $8000 mark. Stylistic features include the option of a trigger personalized with the shooter's initials, sculptured frameheads and an exquisitely crafted game scene signed by the artist. The checkering quality rises to 24 LPI, and is hand- cut.

Such fine guns always raise the question as to whether you would want to take them out into the field in the first place. However, the D'Italia Deluxe is as strong on function as form, and for pursuits such as pheasant shooting it must be a pleasure to use.

Winchester Select Energy Trap

$$

Over recent years the likes of Browning and Perazzi have produced a new breed of visually striking high-performance trap guns. The Select Energy Trap is Winchester's contribution to this market.

SPECIFICATIONS: **Winchester Select Energy Trap**

GAUGE/CALIBRE: 12

BARREL LENGTH: 76cm (30in), 81cm (32in)

WEIGHT: (76cm/30in barrels) 3.4kg (7.5lb)

EJECTOR TYPE: automatic ejectors

CHOKES: interchangeable

FEATURES: distinctive grip and fore-end checkering; adjustable comb

First impressions of the Select Energy Trap confirm a very modernistic approach to the gun, particularly in the design of its woodwork. The checkering along both the pistol grip and fore-end is placed in lozenge-shaped sections rather than a continuous patch. This design has no significant advantage over more traditional types of checkering, and it is up to the buyer to decide whether he or she likes the gun's appearance. The receiver is very lightly decorated with the name of the gun, and the weapon has a minimalist feel to it overall. That said, the stock is fitted with an advanced adjustable-comb system, which can alter the stock for drop, cast and tilt.

Performance

Being specifically a trap gun, the Select Energy Trap has 76cm (30in) or 81cm (32in) barrels. Some may feel that an 81cm (32in) barrel is preferable for classic down-the-line shooting, but the length of the 76cm (30in) barrels is extended slightly by Winchester's excellent Signature Invector-Plus multichokes, which

come with the gun. (The chokes have colour-coded bands running around the front edge, with difference colours signifying different chokes.) Both the top and mid ribs are ventilated; at the muzzle end is an elongated Truglo® fibre-optic sight, and there is a corresponding bead sight halfway along the top rib.

While the shooting press has had some marked reservations about the Select Energy Trap's appearance, it has been much more enthusiastic about its shooting ability. A gun test in the British *Sporting Shooter* magazine (July 2006) noted that recoil was 'extraordinarily light' and that the gun produced 'some of the best patterns we have seen in any gun'. Patterning is a concern for any clay shooter, but even more so for the competitive trap shooter, so the Select Energy Trap may well make a significant impact on the market.

The back-bored barrels that are a key feature of the Select series produce good dense patterns that can turn a clay into dust with the right choke combination.

Winchester Select White Field

$$

The Select White Field contains much the same technology as is invested in the Select Energy Trap. However, it is configured as a field gun, with shorter barrels, a solid stock and lighter weight.

SPECIFICATIONS: **Winchester Select White Field**

GAUGE/CALIBRE: 12	
BARREL LENGTH: 66cm (26in), 71cm (28in)	
WEIGHT: 3.2kg (7lb)	
EJECTOR TYPE: automatic ejectors	
CHOKES: interchangeable	
FEATURES: back-boring; 76mm (3in) chambers	

The Select family of Winchester guns is a broad one – at the time of writing 11 different models were listed under the Select name. These include the Select Energy Sporting, and the same model but with an adjustable comb.

The Winchester Select Platinum is a premium-grade competition model, with a Schnabel fore-end,

a slimmer grip area and fine engraving. Other models include the Select Traditional Elegance, the Select Model 101 and the Select Extreme Elegance. Several common ingredients unite all the Select models. The receivers have quite a low profile, and have two side-locking lugs with a third lug set beneath the receiver for added solidity. The length of the trigger pull is adjustable. The barrels are back-bored to improve shot patterning – something we have seen in the review of the Select Energy Trap above.

Field gun

The Select White Field has a far more traditional appearance than many other guns in the Select range. Gone is the oval-section checkering, replaced by single panels either side of the pistol grip and the fore-end. (The Select White Field Extreme model keeps the ovals, however.) Barrel lengths are typical of those for field shooting – 66cm (26in) and 71cm (28in) – and the Invector-Plus chokes are flush-fitting, not extended like those of the Trap models. (New White Field shotguns are supplied with Full, Modified and Improved Cylinder chokes.)

The Select White Field has 76mm (3in) chambers, to give it more hunting versatility. The weight of the 66cm (26in) model is a manageable 3.2kg (7lb), so it should be a comfortable gun for a day's shoot.

The Select White Field, as its name implies, is designed principally for field use, particularly bird shooting.

Zabala Beri-Lux

$

Zabala's Beri-Lux is a .410 side-by-side shotgun built with a sub-$1000 price tag in mind. It offers great performance for light hunting duties.

SPECIFICATIONS: **Zabala Beri-Lux**

GAUGE/CALIBRE: .410	
BARREL LENGTH: 71cm (28in)	
WEIGHT: 3kg (6.6lb)	
EJECTOR TYPE: ejectors	
CHOKES: interchangeable	
FEATURES: single selective trigger	

The Spanish gunmaker Zabala makes a versatile range of both side-by-side and over-and-under shotguns. At the 'big guns' end of the scale is the Canardier. This is a mighty 12-gauge side-by-side shotgun that has 89mm (3.5in) chambers. The Canardier has two triggers in its setup, but the rear trigger actually fires both barrels simultaneously. The author has not had the chance to fire this gun, but press reports speak of a ferocious punch from the both-barrel firing even when using light game loads in 70mm (2.75in) cartridges.

Lightweight

The Beri-Lux resides at the opposite pole to the formidable Canardier, being a simple .410 side-by-side. Its negligible recoil make it the ideal gun for a young shooter, or for those who want a highly portable firearm for use controlling small vermin.

For its value price (it retails for less than £600 in the United Kingdom), the Beri-Lux packs in a good build quality alongside a suprising number of features. It has ejectors, something not typical of small-bore guns. It also has a single selective trigger, and the overall mechanism – based on the tried-and-tested Anson & Deeley system – is rugged and reliable.

Layout

In terms of overall layout, the Beri-Lux has 71cm (28in) barrels of a monobloc construction and with a slender solid top rib running up to a simple brass bead sight at the muzzle end. Press reviews have generally picked up on the good quality of the barrels when considering the price of the gun. The chambers of the gun – again surprisingly – are 76mm (3in), giving the Beri-Lux that little extra power and range to take on a good-sized rabbit or even an overflying pigeon.

The woodwork is also of a respectable quality, the fore-end being of a splinter/beavertail combination that sits easily in the front hand. There is pressed checkering featuring a simple fleur de lys pattern.

The Zabala Beri-Lux is an excellent small-gauge shotgun. In addition to many other features, the gun is also a multichoke, and comes supplied with three different choke tubes.

Zabala Century Classic

$

The Zabala Century Classic is another popular over-and-under model from the Spanish gunmaker. Like the Beri-Lux, it is also a budget gun providing great value for money.

SPECIFICATIONS: **Zabala Century Classic**

GAUGE/CALIBRE: 12, 20	
BARREL LENGTH: 71cm (28in)	
WEIGHT: 3.6kg (8lb)	
EJECTOR TYPE: automatic ejectors	
CHOKES: interchangeable	
FEATURES: single selective trigger	

Zabala Hermanos has, during its lifetime, produced over one million guns. Alongside its very traditional styles of side-by-sides, it has not been afraid to innovate. It now produces a very respectable range of over-and-under sporting guns, such as the XL-90 Interchoke and the Suprema. The Century Classic also falls into this category, and with a retail price of less than $1000 (it retails for around £500 in the United Kingdom).

Heavy chambers

As with the Zabala Beri-Lux reviewed previously, the Century Classic delivers plenty of gun for the money. Its key feature is the 89mm (3.5in) chambers. This size of chamber usually means that the gun is intended for wildfowlers, and for that market the gun also has to be tough. This requirement the Century Classic satisfies admirably. The gun is locked prior to firing by a heavy barrel bite located beneath the monbloc. The chambers and the bores are chromium-lined to give them excellent resistance to rust, dirt and corrosive propellant deposits. The trigger system is extremely simple and hence reliable, the hammers behind powered by straight coil springs.

Power option

When the Beri-Lux was discussed, we also noted Zabala's mighty Canardier, with its simultaneous both-barrel fire option. The standard version of the Century Classic has a simple combined safety/selector switch on the neck of the stock. (Note that the safety is of the manual, rather than the automatic type, a fact that causes safety concerns with some).

However, another version has the ability to opt for the Canardier's double-barrel fire, simply by pushing the selector switch over to the left. As with the Canardier, there is a big question mark over when a shooter would want to use such a feature.

Certainly, two 89mm (3.5in) shells detonating simultaneously would have an enormous impact on the shooter's shoulder and could well destroy the target entirely.

Notwithstanding this option, the Century Classic is a solid, well-thought-out gun.

The Century Classic is another robust gun from Zabala. It comes with stainless steel multichokes and a rubber recoil pad as standard fitting.

Zoli Kronos

$$

The Zoli Kronos is a competition-standard over-and-under from the Italian Zoli company. Available in either sporting or trap versions, it represents a major technological investment for the firm.

SPECIFICATIONS: **Zoli Kronos Sporting**

GAUGE/CALIBRE: 12

BARREL LENGTH: 71cm (28in), 75cm (29.5in), 81cm (32in)

WEIGHT: 3.5kg (7.7lb)

EJECTOR TYPE: automatic ejectors

CHOKES: fixed or interchangeable

FEATURES: removable trigger unit; quick-release stock

The Kronos squares up to direct competition such as the Beretta 682 Gold E and the Blaser F3 with confidence. It is 12 gauge only, and the Trap models have 75cm (29.5in) or 81cm (32in) barrels while the Sporting models are the same with the addition of a 71cm (28in) barrel version. All models come with multichokes, although fixed-choke Trap models are another option.

Magnum chambers

Although 70mm (2.75in) shells are the standard for most clay-target disciplines, the Kronos is fitted with 76mm (3in) chambers. Bifurcated lumps either side of the monobloc make for a very positive and strong locking action. The Kronos' trigger group is also detachable once it is loosened with the provided Allen key, revealing hammers powered by coil springs.

To demonstrate its seriousness as a competition gun, the Kronos' stock can also be instantly removed using a key slipped through a hole in the recoil pad.

This means that a shooter can select the stock type depending on the shooting event. An adjustable-comb stock is available, and all stocks come fitted with a rubber pad to cushion against recoil

The bores on the Kronos are taken out to 18.5mm (0.72in), which is fractionally bigger than the standard bore diameter on most 12 gauges. This 'over-boring' gives the guns better patterns, and also reduces felt recoil. Competition shooters will appreciate Zoli's inclusion of spare coil springs and strikers. This means that should the gun have a simple breakdown, the removable trigger unit will give easy access to the problem, which should hopefully be repairable with the spares supplied.

A shooter takes aim with the Zoli Kronos. The beavertail fore-end provides a stable front to the gun. Note the high-visibility luminous sight.

CHAPTER 2

SEMI-AUTOMATIC & PUMP SHOTGUNS

A semi-automatic shotgun is quite a different purchase from a double-barrelled gun. Although the ballistic capabilities of the two types of firearm remain the same – remember that the cartridge, not the gun, is the chief determinant of performance – the practical usage alters.

Semi-auto shotguns, while not having the aura of sophistication surrounding the double-barrel guns, are the true workhorses of hunters worldwide. Their extended magazine capacity makes them ideal for wildfowlers and their semi-auto mechanisms mean they can soak up the recoil of the heaviest loads.

The most obvious difference is that a semi-automatic has a single barrel rather than two barrels. Only one choke pattern, therefore, is in operation, hence the majority (but by no means all) of clay shooters prefer the two-choke option of a double-barrelled gun. Furthermore, some clay grounds can be slightly more wary of semi-automatics because they are magazine-fed rather than breech-loaded, hence they cannot be 'seen to be safe' as is the case with a broken-open shotgun. Furthermore, some argue that semi-automatics are much less reliable than break-barrel guns because of their more mechanically complex semi-automatic systems.

Many of these arguments, on closer inspection, lose their validity. In terms of choke, the semi-automatic shooter with Modified will probably shoot a sporting layout just as well as with a Modified/Improved Modified over-and-under. Good safety discipline – particularly muzzle awareness and opening the bolt when not shooting – reassures most fellow shooters.

A hunter advances on his prey armed with a Browning Gold Hunter pump shotgun. The basic Browning Gold model is 12- or 20-gauge.

example, limits a semi-automatic's capacity to two shells in the magazine and one in the chamber.) Many bird shooters prefer the greater capacity of a semi-automatic over a double gun, particularly for sports such as pigeon shooting or wildfowling, in which multiple shots often have to be taken in quick succession before an entire flock gets out of range. Semi-automatics also have particularly light recoil – the gas, inertia, or recoil mechanism soaks up much of the kick. Not only does this mean that semi-automatics are good for small-framed people or those suffering with shoulder complaints, but also that these guns are ideal for taking very heavy hunting loads, such as those found in 89mm (3.5in) shells. (This is another reason why wildfowlers often prefer the semi-automatic, the big magnum cartridges being used against large or high-flying geese.)

Regarding reliability, I have seen just as many misfires and breakdowns with double guns as I have with semi-automatics. However, it is a fact that semi-automatics require much more careful cleaning and handling, because dirt or fouling in a semi-automatic mechanism can easily cause a misfeed. Drop one in the mud, and it may well require full stripping.

Semi-automatic sport

There are many areas where a good semi-automatic is a perfect choice. Depending on the gauge, a semi-automatic's magazine will typically hold three to six cartridges. (Note that the magazine capacity can be limited depending on the country. The UK, for

A major percentage of semi-automatic shotguns are operated using gas. In this system, some of the gas created by the propellant powder when burnt is siphoned downwards through a port in the barrel into a cylinder set beneath the barrel. The gas drives

The barrel of a modern gas-operated semi-auto. Gas-operated guns may be mechanically complex, but they are very smooth to shoot, and reliable as long as they are cleaned properly.

a piston backwards, and this rearward force, through a series of connected mechanisms, unlocks the bolt and forces it backwards.

During this stage of movement the spent cartridge is extracted and ejected. Finally, the recoil spring forces the bolt to return forward, picking up a new cartridge and driving it forward into the chamber for the next shot.

The other methods of semi-automatic operation are recoil and inertia. In both methods the gun uses the force of recoil alone to operate the weapon, the recoil action using the force of the barrel and bolt assembly being driven backwards, the latter using the energy stored in an inertia spring as the moveable

parts of the gun go backwards. All are sound operating systems if maintained well, with recoil and inertia having the advantage that no gases are vented into a piston system, but are all kept within the barrel.

Pump guns

Of course, there is an alternative to a semi-automatic shotgun – the pump-action shotgun. Pump-action guns have their place at the tough end of shooting. They are extremely reliable regardless of the conditions, having greater mechanical simplicity than a semi-automatic system. Furthermore, modern pump-action mechanisms are extremely fast, and even utilize the force of recoil to assist the hand movement of the slide. As such, there is little if any difference between the reload speed of a semi-automatic and that of a pump-action gun in competent hands.

A hunter crouches in the grasses with his Remington shotgun, waiting for a flight of birds. Many semi-auto shotguns are available in photo-realistic camouflage to aid concealment.

ARMSCOR M30 DI

$

The Arms Corporation of the Philippines, better known as ARMSCOR, has been manufacturing firearms and importing them into the United States and other countries since the 1950s.

SPECIFICATIONS: ARMSCOR M30 DI/C

GAUGE/CALIBRE: 12	
BARREL LENGTH: 66cm (26in), 71cm (28in)	
WEIGHT: up to approx 3.5kg (7.7lb)	
MECHANISM: pump action	
CHOKES: interchangeable	
FEATURES: three choke tubes supplied	

ARMSCOR produces a particularly broad range of personal weaponry, from combat handguns through to semi-automatic .22 calibre M16 and AK47 assault-rifle imitations. They also manufacture semi-automatic shotguns under the M30 designation. M30 shotguns differ greatly in their configuration and purpose, and here we will look at their sports and hunting models. Chief amongst these is the M30 DI/C.

All guns belonging to the M30 range are pump-action weapons, and the magazine of the DI/C has a four-cartridge capacity when using 76mm (3in) shells, rising to five cartridges for 70mm (2.75in) ammunition. (In addition, one cartridge can be held in the chamber when the magazine is full.) Barrel lengths are 66cm (26in) and 71cm (28in), and all barrels have a blued/parkerized finish.

Sporting chokes

Those shooters who take their guns into the roughest conditions often prefer pump-action weapons – a manually operated firearm is much less likely to jam through the ingress of dirt than a gas- or inertia-operated system. The M30 DI/C has interchangeable chokes to give the hunter a shot spread appropriate to the quarry he is hunting. Three choke tubes are supplied: Improved Cylinder, Modified and Full, although many M30 shotguns come with fixed chokes. Recoil reduction is limited and comes principally in the form of a ventilator rubber recoil pad fitted to the rear of the stock.

The other M30, classed as a 'Sports and Hunting' model, is the DG8, which has rifle-type sights (ramp front sight, leaf-type rear sight) and a shorter barrel, but a longer magazine capable of holding seven 70mm (2.75in) shells – one less for the 76mm (3in) rounds.

As with many pump-action guns, the M30 is a model of rugged reliability. The external features of the gun are fairly minimal so this reliability isn't compromised by sophistication The wood is an indigenous Philippine hardwood, polished to a good shine, and all the metalwork has a blued/parkerized finish to protect it against the elements. One notable feature is that the checkering is done by hand.

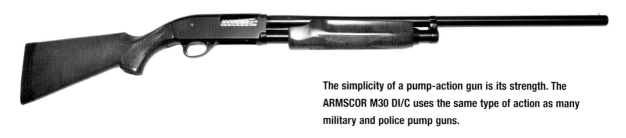

The simplicity of a pump-action gun is its strength. The ARMSCOR M30 DI/C uses the same type of action as many military and police pump guns.

ARMSCOR M30R6

$

ARMSCOR's M30 range includes a selection of guns listed as 'For Law Enforcement and Security'. Although not strictly sporting weapons, some people buy them for combat shooting sports.

SPECIFICATIONS: ARMSCOR M30R6

GAUGE/CALIBRE: 12

BARREL LENGTH: 47cm (18.5in)

WEIGHT: up to approx 3.5kg (7.7lb)

MECHANISM: pump action

CHOKES: fixed

FEATURES: polymer stock and fore-end

The ARMSCOR 'Law Enforcement and Security' guns are, as their category suggests, first-rate home-defence firearms (if the limits of national law permit the ownership of such weapons for this purpose). Their reliability and speed of loading makes them appreciated also by practical shooting enthusiasts.

Combat models

The other security models in the M30 move away from conventional shotgun layout. The M30BG, for example, has no stock. Instead, it has a pure pistol grip to give the weapon a very short overall length, which, in turn, makes it very easy to conceal or wield within a confined building interior. However, it retains the 5+1 magazine capacity (with 70mm/2.75in shells) of the longer M30R6. The M30FS has a similar polymer pistol grip and fore-end, but also has a collapsible metal stock that can be extended and locked for when the user wants to shoulder the weapon. For those who need even more capacity from their pump-action gun, there is the M30SAS. Loaded with the 76mm (2.75in) cartridges, this has a capacity of 7+1, dropping to 6+1 for the 89mm (3in) shells. It differs from the R8 in its black heat-shielded barrel.

Sports for which ARMSCOR's security products might be suitable include Practical Shooting disciplines, in which the participant shoots a range of quick-fire targets at varying ranges and with various firearms, typically a pistol, rifle and shotgun.

At the time of writing, the ARMSCOR website lists five different types of M30 security shotgun: the M30BG, M30R6, M30R8, M30SAS and M30FS. There are some interesting types within this range, although all the models centre around a simple pump-action mechanism. The M30R6 is the most conventional-looking pump-action shotgun. It has a 47cm (18.5in) barrel and a cartridge capacity of 4+1 for 76mm (3in) shells and 5+1 for 70mm (2.75in) rounds.

Rather than the Philippine wood used for the stock and fore-end of the M30 sporting models, the M30R6 uses a polymer material for great strength. The R8 is very much the same gun, except that it has a 50cm (20in) barrel and a subsequently longer magazine tube that, with 70mm (2.75in) shells, has a seven-cartridge capacity.

Baikal MP 153/Remington SPR 453

$

The Baikal MP 153, imported and rebranded by Remington in the United States as the SPR 453, is one of the best-value semi-automatic shotguns on the market, with a sub-$500 price tag ideal for the first-time buyer.

SPECIFICATIONS: Remington SPR 453

GAUGE/CALIBRE: 12	
BARREL LENGTH: 61cm (24in), 66cm (26in), 71cm (28in)	
WEIGHT: up to 3.75kg (8.25lb)	
MECHANISM: gas operated	
CHOKES: interchangeable	
FEATURES: 89mm (3.5in) chambers; tuneable gas system	

Considering its low price, the SPR 453 comes with a surprisingly upmarket range of features. Many budget guns only have fixed chokes, but the 453 comes with a four interchangeable choke tubes, the set comprising Improved Cylinder, Modified, Full and Super-full Turkey. Furthermore, all of the choke tubes are approved for use with steel shot. The gun's three barrel lengths are 61cm (24in), 66cm (26in) and 71cm (28in), and both the barrel and the receiver have a matte black finish to prevent glints of the metal warning the target. (Remington have also released the 453 in Mossy Oak® New Break-Up® camouflage.)

Heavy duty

Adding to the SPR 453's appeal, the gun can handle 70mm (2.75in), 76mm (3in), and 89mm (3.5in) cartridges, making it suitable for hunting purposes from quail and light game up to heavy-duty wildfowling.

The bolt face features dual extractors to ensure reliable ejection of the cartridges. As a further level of sophistication, the gas system is tuneable, which, in Remington's words, 'delivers smooth cycling and softens felt recoil'.

Tough stock

The 453's synthetic stock and fore-end are extremely tough and completely weather-resistant and the magazine tube can hold up to four cartridges, with an additional cartridge in the chamber. Baikal guns are known for their exceptionally robust nature, although the 453 is not excessively heavy. The heaviest 71cm (28in) barrel model tips the scales at 3.75kg (8.25lb), and its total overall length is 126cm (49.5in).

Remington's association with Baikal has brought a whole new range of budget-quality guns into the United States. It is a range that could challenge the market share of many far more expensive models.

Like its double-barrelled counterpart, the MP 153/SPR 453 is built for total reliability.

Benelli Nova Pump

$

Benelli is well known for its semi-automatic shotguns, but it also has a fine pump-action shotgun in its Nova Pump model, which, typical of the company, exhibits cutting-edge technology.

SPECIFICATIONS: **Benelli Nova Pump**

GAUGE/CALIBRE:	12, 20
BARREL LENGTH:	61cm (24in), 66cm (26in), 71cm (28in)
WEIGHT:	up to 3.68kg (8.1lb)
MECHANISM:	pump action
CHOKES:	interchangeable
FEATURES:	rotating bolt; recoil reducer as option; dual action bars

The Nova Pump is a 12- or 20-gauge shotgun with options of 61cm (24in), 66cm (26in) or 71cm (28in) barrels. In its 20-gauge incarnation the Nova Pump accepts up to 76mm (3in) cartridges, while most of the 12-gauge guns climb up to 89mm (3.5in) chambers, with the exception of some of the rifled slug models. First impressions of the Nova Pump show a gun in which the polymer stock blends seamlessly into the receiver to form a structure of considerable strength and resilience. The pistol grip and fore-end are cut with deep grooves to provide excellent grip, even in wet conditions. The stock is also hollow in structure, with the option to accept a Benelli recoil-reduction system.

Internal parts

The Nova Pump's operating system is built with the same eye for strength as the external features. It uses a Montefeltro rotating bolt for solid locking while dual action bars make the reloading mechanism extremely durable. The standard 12-gauge Nova Pump's magazine capacity is four shells (plus one in the chamber). All the guns except those with rifled barrels are multichoke, coming with the standard Benelli selection of Improved Cylinder, Modified and Full. A useful feature on the Nova Pump is a shell-stop switch beneath the fore-end, which allows the user to eject a cartridge from the chamber without the magazine feeding in another cartridge.

Several varieties of the Nova Pump are available. These include the Field & Slug Combo, which includes a cantilever, rifled barrel; the Tactical model, which has sight options that include click-adjustable ghost-ring sights; and the H20 Pump, which has a stainless-steel and nickel-plating construction.

The Nova Pump utilizes synthetic materials heavily in its construction, and comes in short-stock or long-stock configurations.

Here the Nova Pump is rendered in Advantage Timber HD® camouflage, making it a superb gun for use from a wildfowling hide.

Benelli Super Black Eagle II

$$

Benelli makes some of the world's best-selling semi-automatic shotguns. The Super Black Eagle II offers some of the company's latest technological innovations, and is a well-rounded field weapon.

SPECIFICATIONS: **Benelli Super Black Eagle II**

GAUGE/CALIBRE: 12

BARREL LENGTH: 61cm (24in), 66cm (26in), 71cm (28in)

WEIGHT: (71cm/28in barrel) 3.3kg (7.3lb)

MECHANISM: inertia operated

CHOKES: interchangeable

FEATURES: ComfortTech™ recoil-reduction system

The Super Black Eagle II delivers a string of hi-tech features, down to the smallest details of the gun. It is designed for the dedicated field shooter or wildfowler – even the trigger guard is given 30 per cent more room to accommodate gloved fingers, while the AirTouch™ checkering pattern provides a particularly adhesive grip surface in wet conditions. To cope with any shooting situation, the Super Black Eagle II can take 70mm (2.75in), 76mm (3in) and even 89mm (3.5in) shells. However, the company has also invested in an advanced recoil system to cope with the shock of firing the heaviest loads. The

ComfortTech™ system, according to the company publicity, 'reduces recoil up to 48% over the competition, without adding any moving parts or weight'. Furthermore, Benelli also states that the controlled recoil reduces muzzle climb by 15 per cent, allowing 'the shooter to get back on target up to 69% faster than the competition'. The stock is fitted with a gel-filled recoil pad to further cushion the shooter's shoulder.

Advanced parts

The Black Eagle's sophistication extends through all parts of the gun. A shooter can go straight from using the 70mm (2.75in) shells up to 89mm (3.5in) magnum loads without making any adjustments, the Benelli Inertia Driven™ bolt mechanism being able to handle the surge of power. Also, the Black Eagle's barrels are cryogenically frozen to −184°C (−300°F), this relieving the 'stresses left over from hammer forging', producing a smoother barrel and therefore better patterns and more resistance to fouling.

The Super Black Eagle II comes in many different configurations, including wood or synthetic stocks, ComfortTech™ system cheek pads and a left-handed version.

This Super Black Eagle II clearly shows the ComfortTech™ stock system, with the recoil-absorbing inserts.

The satin walnut version of the Super Black Eagle II just has a simple recoil pad to control the gun's kick.

Benelli SuperSport

$$

The Benelli Supersport has much in common with the Super Black Eagle II. Yet while the Black Eagle is designed for field shooting, the Supersport pits its technology against clays.

SPECIFICATIONS: **Benelli SuperSport**

GAUGE/CALIBRE: 12

BARREL LENGTH: 71cm (28in), 76cm (30in)

WEIGHT: (76cm/30in barrel) 3.3kg (7.3lb)

MECHANISM: inertia operated

CHOKES: interchangeable

FEATURES: ComfortTech™ recoil-reduction system

L ike the Black Eagle, the SuperSport is an inertia-cycled gun. On firing, the gun recoils and the floating bolt compresses an inertia spring. This inertia spring then drives the bolt backwards to eject the spent cartridge and re-cock the mechanism, before the bolt is pushed forward to the locked position by a recoil spring. The advantage of this system is its durability, reliability and its scope for coping with the most potent of cartridges.

Yet as well as handling the magnum cartridges, the gun will also cycle perfectly well on light 24g (just under 1oz) competition loads.

Clay-gun comfort

Chevron-shaped cut-outs in the stock are a visual signature of the ComfortTech™ recoil-reduction system. As we have already seen with the Black Eagle, this system, which operates through a controlled flexing of the stock, reduces both felt recoil and muzzle flip to give better second-target acquisition.

Like the Super Black Eagle II shotguns, the SuperSport is fitted with the ComforTech™ recoil-reduction system. Note also the cheek pad here to guard against bruised cheeks while also giving the shooter's head a much more secure fit against the stock. The gun here has a carbon-fibre-finished stock and fore-end, and has a ported barrel.

This is particularly important for clay shooters, when the second of a fast simultaneous pair can be lost if the shooter has to ride out an excessive recoil before dropping back onto the second bird. As a further limit on muzzle flip and recoil, the SuperSport has a ported barrel, which vents gas out from the sides of the muzzle.

CrioChoke tubes

Because of its declared purpose as a clay-shooting gun, the SuperSport is provided with extended CrioChoke™ interchangeable choke tubes. Benelli claims that 'When it comes to smoking targets, the SuperSport's Crio™ barrel and CrioChokes™ produce patterns 13.2% more dense than other brands'. Reviews in shooting magazines seem to bear out the claims, with one reviewer stating that with Improved Cylinder a '20-yard rabbit was turned to dust' (*Clay Shooting*, October 2005). Some sporting shooters might, therefore, feel shy about using the tighter chokes. In summary, the Benelli occupies the summit of semi-automatic technology, and will happily take on the most demanding clay grounds.

Beretta AL391 Teknys

$$

The Teknys is one of Beretta's most advanced sporting guns. A gas-operated semi-automatic gun, it is an advanced firearm suited to both sporting clays and field shooting, and a weapon known for its reliability.

SPECIFICATIONS: **Beretta AL391 Teknys**

GAUGE/CALIBRE: 12, 20

BARREL LENGTH: (12 gauge) 61cm (24in), 66cm (26in), 71cm (28in), 76cm (30in)

WEIGHT: 3kg (6.6lb)

MECHANISM: gas operated

CHOKES: Optimachoke® Plus interchangeable

SPECIAL FEATURES: Gel-Tek recoil pad; over-bored barrels; X-tra Wood finish

The gas-operated mechanism installed in the Teknys is a sophisticated but still dependable system. Its variable-gas system utilizes just enough of the propellant gas to cycle the action, and the remaining gas is expelled via ports in the underside of the fore-end.

The mechanism can handle a wide range of loads, and the gun is chambered for up to 76mm (3in) magnum cartridges.

Recoil reduction

Many people choose auto-loaders specifically for the soft recoil (much of the recoil on any semi-automatic is taken by the return spring). All Teknys guns are fitted with a Gel-Tek recoil pad, a soft pad that squashes under impact and so reduces the amount of shock transferred to the shooter's shoulder and also deadens recoil vibrations. (The pads can be changed easily.) At the shooter's request, however, a further spring-mass recoil-reduction system can be added into the stock.

Semi-automatics can be prey to corrosion in a way that breech-loaders are not: the piston and related parts are subject to the corrosive firing gases and water ingressing through the ejection port can work its way throughout the mechanism. Beretta produces any metal parts that come into contact with gas in corrosion-resistant inox steel and supplement this with further protective treatments.

The wood parts are also coated with Beretta's patented X-tra Wood finish, this giving a varnish-like depth to the wood grain while also being totally waterproof.

The more subtle features of the Teknys attest to its suitability as both a clay and a field gun. The trigger guard is enlarged to take glove-clad fingers for winter shooters. A luminous Truglo front sight stands out clearly in poor light conditions. The Optima-Bore® barrels, which have lengthened forcing cones, and the extended Optimachoke® Plus choke tubes keep the shot patterns dense and even.

This picture of the AL391 Teknys shows the deep lustre provided by Beretta's X-tra Wood finish. The choke tubes here are of the extended type, hinting at the gun's comfort as a clay-shooting semi-auto.

Beretta AL391 Urika

$$

The Urika is a high-end competition-clay shotgun with features such as cold-hammer-forged barrels and a lightweight receiver, which also can be customized for game shooting or wildfowling.

SPECIFICATIONS: **Beretta AL391 Urika**

GAUGE/CALIBRE: 12, 20

BARREL LENGTH: 56cm (22in), 61cm (24in), 66cm (26in), 71cm (28in), 76cm (30in)

WEIGHT: up to 3.3kg (7.28lb)

MECHANISM: gas operated

CHOKES: Optimachoke® Plus interchangeable

FEATURES: Gel-Tek recoil pad; over-bored barrels; X-tra Wood finish

The Urika has an unusually broad range of barrel lengths for a semi-auto, from 56cm (22in) to 76cm (30in).

The AL391 Urika and the AL391 Teknys share a great deal in common. Both are gas-operated weapons, using the same self-regulating gas system that vents excess gas from the front of the fore-end. (The gas vent directs gases down and away from the shooter's hand.) A recoil reducer in the rear of the receiver controls excessive recoil, and Optima-Bore® barrels are used in combination with Optimachoke® Plus choke tubes.

Lightweight materials

One key feature of the Urika is the attention paid to lightweight materials. The receiver is made from a special high-strength alloy, which, according to Beretta, 'is as strong as steel but 65% lighter'. Its proportions are also kept very slender so as not to obscure the shooter's view of the target. Trigger pulls are crisp, and the trigger plate has a self-lubricating system to optimize performance.

Reflecting their multipurpose use, Urika shotguns have a wide range of barrel lengths, going up in 5cm (2in) increments from 56cm (22in) to 76cm (30in). The weight of the gun depends on the barrel length and the gauge – the Urika is available in 12 or 20 gauge – and the weights run from around 2.7kg (5.95lb) through to 3.3kg (7.28lb). All the Urika guns have 76mm (3in) chambers, and the recoil-reducing features mean that even the lightest guns ride out the heavy loads. The cold-hammer-forged barrels are both lightweight and strong, and the bores are lined with chrome.

The Urika comes in three varieties of stock: walnut, black synthetic, or camouflaged synthetic. The last of these models has a total covering of Realtree camouflage, including all metal parts, which makes the Urika an excellent field weapon.

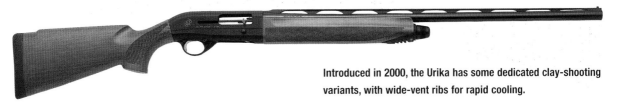

Introduced in 2000, the Urika has some dedicated clay-shooting variants, with wide-vent ribs for rapid cooling.

Beretta A391 Xtrema2

$$

The Beretta A391 Xtrema2 is purposely designed for heavyweight shooting loads. With its 89mm (3.5in) chambers, it offers a powerful addition to the gun cabinet of any wildfowler or pigeon shooter.

SPECIFICATIONS: **Beretta A391 Xtrema2**

GAUGE/CALIBRE: 12

BARREL LENGTH: 56cm (22in), 61cm (24in), 66cm (26in), 71cm (28in), 76cm (30in)

WEIGHT: up to 3.5kg (7.7lb)

MECHANISM: gas operated

CHOKES: Optimachoke® Plus interchangeable

FEATURES: Gel-Tek recoil pad; rotating-bolt locking; recoil-reduction systems

Although many field shooters are perfectly happy with 76mm (3in) chambers, the 89mm (3.5in) chambers of the Xtrema2 are not just for those with a love of power. Wildfowlers, for example, often take shots at extreme ranges and also, for legal and environmental reasons, with steel shot instead of lead shot. Steel shot slows more quickly in flight than lead shot, so having the extra charge of an 89mm (3.5in) chamber can mean that long-range patterns stay dense and forceful. (We must be cautious, however, of overstating the advantage of 89mm/3.5in over 76mm/3in cartridges.)

Beretta has built many sophisticated features into the Xtrema2 to help it cope with the heavy loads (although its self-regulating gas system also allows it to cycle easily on light 28g/1oz loads). A rotating bolt head provides locking, and the bolt and operating rods are integral for extra strength. Recoil absorbers/reducers are built into the stock and these also reduce vibrations transmitted to the shooter via bolt travel. Combined with the Gel-Tek recoil pad on the stock, the Xtrema2's recoil-control systems make for a very smooth and controllable firing experience.

Weather-resistant

Wildfowling presents some of the harshest climatic challenges for any single shotgun, and the Xtrema2 is designed to cope with the rigours. The stock and fore-end are formed from fibreglass-reinforced technopolymer, which is waterproof and resistant to scratching. All the metal parts of the gun, including the anodized-aluminium alloy receiver, have been treated with Beretta's Aqua Tek treatment, a special sealant that protects the metal from corrosive forces. Internal parts receive other forms of corrosion protection, including chrome- and nickel-plating.

To aid the shooter on the cold and gloomy foreshore, the Xtrema2's trigger is enlarged for use with gloved hands and the top rib terminates in a Truglo sight. This luminous elongated sight can be changed for sights of various different colours depending on the light conditions.

Xtrema2 Max-4 HD – the advent of photo-realistic camouflage has had a real impact for hunters. Usually, the gun's colour scheme can be matched with clothing and hide materials.

Browning BPS

$

Browning's BPS pump-action shotgun has garnered a long-standing popularity as an all-round pump gun for field shooting's most arduous challenges.

SPECIFICATIONS: **Browning BPS**

GAUGE/CALIBRE: 12, 20, 28, .410

BARREL LENGTH: from 56cm (22in) to 71cm (28in) depending on model

WEIGHT: up to 3.7kg (8.3lb)

MECHANISM: pump action

CHOKES: Invector or Invector Plus interchangeable chokes

FEATURES: bottom ejector; dual steel-action bars; fibre-optic sight on some models

As with many Browning guns, the BPS is a series rather than a single weapon. Model type depends on several factors, including chamber length, barrel length, gauge, external finish and purpose. A typical example of the BPS would be the basic Hunter model. This has two barrel lengths, 66cm (26in) and 71cm (28in), and is available in four gauges: 12, 20, 28 and .410. Chamber length depends on the gauge, with the 12, 20 and .410 taking 76mm (3in) shells while the 28-gauge model accepts only 70mm (2.75in) cartridges.

The gun is a bottom ejector with hardwearing dual steel-action bars. It comes with a plain satinwood stock and fore-end and Invector (28 or .410 gauge) or Invector Plus (12 and 20 gauge) interchangeable chokes. The retail price is around $500. Most of the BPS 12-gauge range is the beneficiary of Browning's back-bored technology, noted for producing uniform shot patterns.

Advanced finishes

Beyond the basic BPS, there are a number of models with the latest in hunting features. For the turkey shooter, there is the NWTF BPS, Mossy Oak® Break-Up®. This 12- or 20-gauge shotgun has 56cm (22in) or 61cm (24in) barrels, and the 61cm (24in) 12-gauge shotgun also has 89mm (3.5in) chambers. Features extra to the Hunter are the HiViz® TriViz™ fibre-optic sight (useful to have for low-light shooting) and the Dura-Touch® Armour Coating. The latter is a Browning stock treatment that improves the overall grip on the gun at the same time as sealing the gun against the elements. As the gun's name suggests, it is covered entirely with camouflage patterning. Other BPS models include the Upland Special, the Stalker and the Rifled Deer Hunter, the latter being a thick-barrelled version for use only with heavy slugs.

A BPS-armed hunter demonstrates the great sophistication reached by modern camouflage.

Browning Fusion Evolve II $$

Browning has a prestigious history of semi-automatics. The Fusion Evolve II has the characteristics that make Browning semi-automatics market leaders in many sectors, particularly in North America.

SPECIFICATIONS: **Browning Fusion Evolve II**

GAUGE/CALIBRE: 12	
BARREL LENGTH: 66cm (26in), 71cm (28in), 76cm (30in)	
WEIGHT: up to 3kg (6.6lb)	
MECHANISM: gas operated	
CHOKES: Invector Plus interchangeable	
FEATURES: Active Valve gas-regulation system; back-boring; Speed Loading™ system	

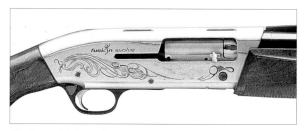

The Fusion Evolve II Gold has a high standard of receiver decoration.

The Fusion Evolve II is a gas-operated 12-gauge shotgun designed for either field shooting or clays. Three barrel lengths are available – 66cm (26in), 71cm (28in), 76cm (30in) – and like most Browning shotguns the Evolve II has the advantage of back-bored technology. By widening the bore beyond the standard measurement, less friction is experienced between the shot load and the barrel, thus reducing pellet deformation and improving velocity. The resulting patterns are very consistent, with few holes. Such is important to any shooter, but especially so to game shooters or wildfowlers who want a clean kill to the head of a goose, duck or pheasant.

Clay or pigeon shooters can appreciate the back-boring because it also results in a six per cent reduction in recoil, which is significant over a long shooting session. Back-boring is becoming widely accepted throughout the shooting industry, and not just within Browning.

Active Valve system

The Fusion Evolve II will take 76mm (3in) cartridges. As we have seen with the Beretta semi-automatic shotguns, coping with the shift from light 28g (1oz) loads through the monster 56g (2oz) loads requires a special accommodation from the gas system. Browning's Active Valve system regulates the gas used to power the piston rearwards, venting off any surplus gas through ventilation holes in the piston's sides.

Valuable to all types of shooter is Browning's Speed Loading™ express loading system. With many automatic shotguns, cartridges cannot be loaded into the magazine unless various buttons are pressed and held, such as the bolt-release button. On the Fusion Evolve II the Speed Loading™ system means that with the breech open the cartridges are simply slotted into the magazine tube single-handedly, the gun automatically chambering a cartridge when the bolt is released.

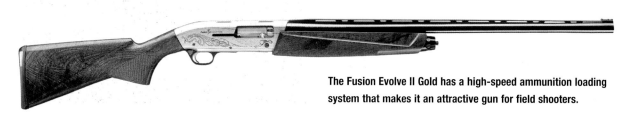

The Fusion Evolve II Gold has a high-speed ammunition loading system that makes it an attractive gun for field shooters.

Browning Gold Hunter

$–$$

Browning Gold semi-automatics come in numerous configurations and external effects, from plain wood through to complete camouflage. They are mainly intended for field shooting, and are excellent value at around the $1000 mark.

A Browning Gold Hunter rendered in the Mossy Oak® Break-Up™ camouflage.

SPECIFICATIONS: Browning Gold Hunter

GAUGE/CALIBRE: 12, 20	
BARREL LENGTH: 66cm (26in), 71cm (28in)	
WEIGHT: up to 3.5kg (7.6lb)	
MECHANISM: gas operated	
CHOKES: Invector Plus interchangeable	
FEATURES: 89mm (3.5in) chambers; Active Valve gas-regulation system	

The basic Browning Gold model is a 12- or 20-gauge shotgun. While the 20-gauge Gold is equipped with 76mm (3in) chambers, the 12 gauge can take 76mm (3in) and 89mm (3.5in) cartridges. Both guns have 66cm (26in) and 71cm (28in) barrel versions, but only the 12 gauge has a 76cm (30in). The chambers and shell sizes naturally affect how many shells can be held in the under-barrel magazine. With 70mm (2.75in) shells (12 gauge), capacity is four in the magazine and one in the chamber. The 76mm (3in) and 89mm (3.5in) cartridges reduce the number to three in the magazine and one in the chamber.

Numerous variants

The features that unite guns of the Gold shotgun range are some of Browning's most advanced. All Gold firearms have Active Valve gas regulation (useful in guns that can take such widely divergent loads). Most Gold shotguns have a magazine cut-off facility that allows the shooter to keep shells in the magazine while ejecting a shell from the chamber without the magazine feeding another round in.

Beyond these, and several other shared qualities, the Gold range presents a targeted array of models. The Gold Rifled Deer Hunter, for example, has a 56cm (22in) rifled barrel for hunting with heavy slugs. By contrast, the Gold Micro is a shotgun for young shooters, with reduced weight and dimensions. There are also several 10-gauge models, such as the Gold NWTF Turkey Series. In terms of finish, some models feature standard wood, others black composite materials, while others have Mossy Oak® Break-Up™ camouflage. The very breadth of the series means that almost any shooter can find a semi-automatic that suits them from the Gold range.

The Browning Gold Hunter has particularly caught on with wildfowlers and pigeon shooters.

Fabarm Lion H35 Azur

$$

Listings at the time of writing detail 14 different models of Lion gun. The H35 Azur ticks most of the boxes when it comes to selecting a good general gun for field or shore.

SPECIFICATIONS: **Fabarm Lion H35 Azur**

GAUGE/CALIBRE: 12

BARREL LENGTH: 61cm (24in), 66cm (26in), 71cm (28in), 76cm (30in)

WEIGHT: up to 3kg (6.6lb)

MECHANISM: gas operated

CHOKES: interchangeable

FEATURES: fibre-optic receiver sight insert; PULSE®PISTON gas system

One of the first things to attract attention about the Azur is the green fibre-optic insert on the top of the receiver. Although shotgunning (apart from specialist hunting activities such as turkey shooting) generally does not require deliberate sighting of the gun (sighting tends to slow the swing of the gun, resulting in a miss behind the target), yet the peripheral vision must still have a strong sense of barrel alignment. The rear sight of the Azur corresponds with a luminous front sight, and provides useful feedback about the point of aim, particularly in low-light conditions. This feature is mainly aimed at wildfowlers, who typically will take most of their shots either as the sun breaks or sets, and the light conditions are usually very poor.

Broad specifications

A semi-automatic in today's market must cover several bases if it is to sell well. The Azur, for example,

The Fabarm Lion H35 Azur has a titanium-protected receiver for the ultimate in field durability. Both left- and right-handed versions of the gun are available, the former saving a left-hander being blasted by ejection.

has four different barrel lengths – 61cm (24in), 66cm (26in), 71cm (28in) and 76cm (30in). The barrel lengths ensure the gun's appeal to several camps, the shorter for woodland stalking and the longer for wildfowling.

Lion shotguns employ Fabarm's PULSE®PISTON technology in which, to use Fabarm's words, 'the polymer insert acts like a progressive brake, to perfectly regulate the speed of the reloading'. The result is a smooth recoil control and fast reloading time.

Light and durable

Fabarm has aimed for lightness and durability in all parts of the Azur. The use of aluminium in the receiver means that the Azur never exceeds 3kg (6.6lb), and at its lowest dips down to 2.8kg (6.16lb) – Fabarm claims it is 'the lightest semi-auto shotgun available on the worldwide market'.

The receiver, cocking handle and magazine cap are treated with the highly resilient PVD TITANIUM protection. Azurs are also very attractive semi-automatics. Adding the TRIWOOD™ 100 finish to the wood brings out a rich grain, and the receiver is decorated with subtle scrollwork, along with the H35 logo set in blue and white.

Fabarm Lion H38 Supergoose $$

The H38 Supergoose, as suggested in its name, is designed to tackle the most testing wildfowl shots. The central feature of this impressive weapon is a mighty 90cm (36in) barrel.

SPECIFICATIONS: Fabarm Lion H38 Supergoose

GAUGE/CALIBRE: 12	
BARREL LENGTH: 90cm (36in)	
WEIGHT: 3.45kg (7.59lb)	
MECHANISM: gas operated	
CHOKES: interchangeable	
FEATURES: PULSE®PISTON gas system; high-capacity magazine	

The Lion H38 includes gas-operated PULSE®PISTON technology to work the reloading mechanism.

Barrel length has a major effect on the handling of a shotgun, as mentioned in the introduction to the breech-loading guns chapter. For a start it pushes up the weight of the gun. For example, the Supergoose weighs 3.45kg (7.59lb), which is substantial for a semi-automatic gun, even though it is by no means excessive.

Weight, however, is not necessarily a negative in shotgunning. It is harder to maintain a smooth and fluid swing, so important for shotgunning, with a light and flighty short-barrelled weapon, whereas a long, heavy barrel generates a (hopefully) controlled momentum. Also, the lead picture with long-barrel guns tends to appear much narrower than with short-barrel guns, improving the so-called 'pointability' of the weapon. Such can be useful for goose shooting, where the extreme altitude and speed of flying geese traditionally requires long and difficult lead judgement.

Large capacity

Fabarm's Lion H38 series replaces the H368 series. Much about the new guns is the same as the old. The Fabarm PULSE®PISTON technology governs the gas-operated mechanism and the barrels are of the same type. What has changed is the shape of the frame and the fore-end. The Supergoose is also available in a composite material rather than wood, many shooters finding that this has greater durability for use in wildfowling conditions.

The Supergoose's magazine capacity is up to six 76mm (3in) shells or eight 70mm (2.75in) cartridges. Some wildfowlers might raise an eyebrow at the fact that the Supergoose does not come with an 89mm (3.5in) chamber, to provide loads matching the scale of the barrel. Many goose-shooting experts, however, do not feel that 89mm (3.5in) shells provide any definite killing advantage.

The new H38 Supergoose has an oil finish to the woodwork (as featured on this Hunter model), unlike the old H368 series, which had varnished wood.

Franchi 48AL

$–$$

With prices ranging from $700 to over $1000, the Franchi 48AL offers a high-quality gun within a good budget range. Although it is produced in Italy, Benelli USA are the 48AL's main importers into the United States.

The 48AL 28 gauge – this remarkable gun weighs in at only 2.45kg (5.4lb).

The 48AL 20 gauge with its classic English stock – an excellent general-purpose bird gun.

SPECIFICATIONS: **Franchi 48AL**

GAUGE/CALIBRE: 20, 28

BARREL LENGTH: 61cm (24in), 66cm (26in), 71cm (28in)

WEIGHT: up to 2.45kg (5.4lb)

MECHANISM: long recoil

CHOKES: interchangeable

FEATURES: extremely light; short-stock version

Unlike many semi-automatics on the market, which tend to lean towards gas as the preferred mode of operation, the Franchi 48AL uses a long-recoil action. When the gun is fired, the bolt and barrel travel backwards together under the force of recoil.

Once the pressure drops to an acceptable level the barrel and bolt unlock and the spent cartridge is ejected. The barrel returns forward, with the bolt following, picking up another cartridge and feeding it into the chamber.

The long-recoil method can be especially reliable, and the lack of a large gas-piston system helps to keep the guns slim and easy to handle.

Small-gauge guns

The Franchi 48AL is available in 20- and 28-gauge versions. The lack of a 12-gauge, while of concern to some, will not be of major consequence to the upland bird-shooting market the gun is aimed at – 20- and 28-gauge weapons are perfectly good shotguns for grouse, quail or the like. Franchi point out that the 28-gauge 48AL, which weighs only 2.45kg (5.4lb), stands as 'the lightest semi-auto on the market'. Even the heaviest gun in the range weighs a slight 2.95kg (5.7lb). Barrel lengths, depending on model, are 61cm (24in), 66cm (26in) and 71cm (28in), and the guns also come supplied with a set of three screw-in chokes: Improved Cylinder, Modified and Full. Magazine capacity for the 48AL is 4+1, and the guns are only chambered to fire 70mm (2.75in) cartridges.

The 48AL Deluxe version has an improved quality of wood, upgraded finish to the metal parts and a gold trigger. For additional portability when required, Franchi also make the 48AL in a short-stock version, which has only a 32cm (12.5in) length of pull (the distance between the end of the stock and the trigger).

Franchi I-12

$

With its inertia-driven operating system, similar to that of Benelli's Super Black Eagle, the Franchi I-12 offers a significant technological advance over already reliable guns like the 48AL.

SPECIFICATIONS: **Franchi I-12**

GAUGE/CALIBRE: 12

BARREL LENGTH: 61cm (24in), 66cm (26in), 71cm (28in)

WEIGHT: up to 3.5kg (7.7lb)

MECHANISM: inertia driven

CHOKES: interchangeable

FEATURES: fast cycling; two-part recoil pad

The I-12 differs from the 48AL because of its inertia-driven operating system. When the gun is fired, the free-floating bolt compresses a very short, strong inertia spring which, once the shot has left the barrel, then drives the bolt rearward, ejects the spent cartridge and cocks the hammer for the next shot. The system is known to be extremely fast and very reliable (the same system is used in many military-grade shotguns), and therefore the I-12 is very popular with those who demand a quick-firing semi-automatic shotgun, such as pigeon shooters and wildfowlers. Because it uses an inertia system, the I-12 is a very slender gun, the fore-end not having to cope with the bulk of a gas piston. The gun's ammunition capacity is four in the magazine plus one in the chamber.

Further advances

The I-12 is fitted with an advanced two-part recoil pad that has a special gel insert. On firing, the pad compresses and squashes, and so distributes the recoil over a greater area of the shooter's shoulder, reducing the perceived impact. Reviews from the shooting press do indicate that the pad has a genuine positive effect in reducing shoulder impact.

In terms of overall specifications, the I-12 has 61cm (24in), 66cm (26in) and 71cm (28in) barrels and is chambered for 70mm (2.75in) and 76mm (3in) cartridges. It weighs between 3.4 and 3.5kg (7.5 and 7.7lb). The receiver is drilled and tapped for a scope mounting.

Without a scope the shooter has a red bar luminous front sight and a gold bead midway along the rib. With a price tag of less than $700, the I-12 is a major lure for those wanting a semi-automatic in their gun cabinet.

12 gauge satin walnut – note the gun's two-part recoil part, designed to spread recoil energy over the shooter's shoulder.

This camo version of the I-12 shows why the gun is popular with people who take their hunting seriously.

Franchi 720

$

Reviews of the Franchi 720 often discuss its quick-shooting characteristics, a quality that makes it an ideal bird gun. It is also a sound purchase for those wanting a light 20-gauge semi-automatic shotgun.

SPECIFICATIONS: Franchi 720
GAUGE/CALIBRE: 20
BARREL LENGTH: 61cm (24in), 66cm (26in), 71cm (28in)
WEIGHT: up to 2.8kg (6.1lb)
MECHANISM: gas operated
CHOKES: interchangeable
FEATURES: ported barrel on Raptor model; rotating bolt head

The Franchi 720 is available in 20 gauge only. Although the 20-gauge calibre is treated by some as a poor relation to the ubiquitous 12 gauge, with the right cartridge type the 20 will give good service in many different shooting settings, from game shooting through to wildfowling. A 20-gauge gun is also, generally, lighter to transport during a day's shooting and its recoil is easy to handle, especially when fired through a gas-operated gun such as the 720. The 720 is certainly a light gun. In its heaviest configuration it weighs only 2.8kg (6.1lb), while the lightest version drops down to 2.7kg (5.9lb).

Franchi has designed the 720 in enough variants to satisfy most bird- and game-shooting activities. With its 76mm (3in) chambers it can take the magnum loads necessary for geese and turkey, and it also comes in two different types of photo-realistic camouflage to provide gun concealment. Overall length of the 720 is between 114cm (45in) and 124cm (49in), although a short-stock model, which takes the length down to 110cm (43.25in), is also available.

Solid lock

As with all Franchi semi-automatic shotguns, a rotating bolt head provides the locking mechanism. The bolt twists and locks into the barrel extension, providing an extremely solid engagement – most modern military rifles use rotating-bolt mechanisms. The cartridges are fed from the under-barrel magazine, which holds four cartridges plus one in the chamber.

Chokes on the 720 are interchangeable, with three chokes being provided – Improved Cylinder, Modified and Full. Barrel lengths range from 61cm (24in) up to 71cm (28in). Franchi have also produced the 720 Raptor version. This has a ported barrel to reduce muzzle flip and is aimed towards the clay-shooting market.

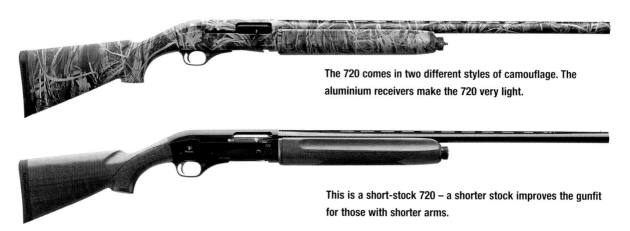

The 720 comes in two different styles of camouflage. The aluminium receivers make the 720 very light.

This is a short-stock 720 – a shorter stock improves the gunfit for those with shorter arms.

Hatsan Escort

$

The Escort is an affordable range of semi-automatic shotguns from the Hatsan concern of Turkey. Many of the shotguns occupy the sub-$500 region, but they offer enough quality to be serviceable field weapons.

SPECIFICATIONS: **Hatsan Escort AS**

GAUGE/CALIBRE: 12

BARREL LENGTH: 46cm (18in), 51cm (20in), 55cm (22in), 61cm (24in), 66cm (26in), 71cm (28in), 76cm (30in)

WEIGHT: (71cm/28in barrel) 3.2kg (7lb)

MECHANISM: gas operated

CHOKES: interchangeable

FEATURES: 76mm (3in) chambers; magazine cut-off

Depending on the model, Escort shotguns run through an unusually long list of barrel lengths: 46cm (18in), 51cm (20in), 55cm (22in), 61cm (24in), 66cm (26in), 71cm (28in) and 76cm (30in). At the heart of the gun is the 76mm (3in) chamber, and the Escort remains one of the cheapest entry-level magnum guns on the market.

Gas-operated

It is gas-operated, the gas system contained within the broad fore-end. The gun is locked on firing by a lug in the bolt, which is driven out to sit in a recess in the wall of the barrel extension. The gas system and the magazine feed are both reliable and functional. The author's test-firing of an Escort over several weeks of shooting produced only a single jam out of 500 rounds. The magazine also has a cut-off switch to allow the firing of a single shot without another round being reloaded.

Features

Although the Escort is a budget-gun range, it has many of the features essential for a successful hunting weapon. The barrels are made of nickel-chromium-molybdenum and the bores are plated with chrome. The receiver is made of a light alloy, meaning that the average weight of an Escort gun is 3.2kg (7lb). The magazine capacity on the basic AS model is 4+1. Interchangeable chokes are standard, either fitting flush or extended (the extended chokes come with the shorter barrel lengths). The chokes are also suitable for steel shot.

In terms of stocks, Escorts have either Turkish walnut woodwork or synthetic polymer versions. At the time of writing, eight separate models of the Escort are offered. These include the Escort Luxano, a higher-quality gun with an engraved receiver plate and a stock fitted with the TRIOPAD recoil pad, which also includes three spacers to allow the shooter to adjust stock length of pull.

The Hatsan Escort Magnum shows how the countries of Eastern Europe are more than able to take on the big Western producers in the sub-$1000 price category.

Ithaca Model 37

$

The Ithaca Model 37 has a history unmatched by almost any pump-action gun. It was first produced in 1937 and, albeit with many modern improvements, is still in production today.

SPECIFICATIONS: **Ithaca Model 37 Deerslayer**

GAUGE/CALIBRE:	12; rifled barrel
BARREL LENGTH:	61cm (24in), 66cm (26in)
WEIGHT:	4kg (9lb)
MECHANISM:	pump action
CHOKES:	fixed
FEATURES:	bottom ejection system

The Ithaca Company has, of recent years, gone through extreme commercial turbulence. The company went into liquidation at the end of 2005, but was bought up by new investors. Ithaca Guns USA now trades out of Ohio, and is still producing versions of the legendary Model 37.

At the time of writing the company website lists five different Model 37 series, based mostly around changes in colour/camouflage schemes and stock materials. The Model 37 Deerslayer is the foundation of the group. This is a 12-gauge pump-action gun equipped with either 70mm (2.75in) or 76mm (3in) chambers. The tubular under-barrel magazine holds four rounds.

Field and force

John Browning based the Model 37 upon a 1915 design, and his design led to the Model 37's bottom-

This Model 37 has a scope mounted on the receiver, probably suggesting the gun has a rifled barrel for slug shooting. In some regions deer hunting is only permitted with a slug gun.

ejection system, with cartridges being ejected out of the same port that is used for loading. Because of this, the Model 37 can be used ambidextrously. Model 37 guns are known for their rugged reliability, and so have found use amongst police and security forces over the decades.

Currently two models are made specifically for official roles: the Model 37 Law Enforcement, which features an extended eight-shot magazine and full military-style pistol grip, and the Model 37 Home Defense, which has the same extended magazine but a more traditional Monte Carlo stock.

Other models

Two other Model 37 types are worth noting. The Model 37 Turkeyslayer has a similar stock layout to the Law Enforcement model, but is covered in an unusual Realtree Hardwoods® camouflage colour scheme and is intended exactly for the purpose given in its name.

Finally, there is the Featherlight Model 37 Upland Gun, a slender gun in 12, 16 and 20 gauges, which is fitted with a simple bead sight instead of the front and rear rifle sights fitted to many other Model 37s.

Mossberg 500

$

Pump-action guns usually provide great durability, and with modern slide systems are little slower on the reload than many semi-automatic shotguns. The Mossberg 500 shotguns are a popular entry-level range.

SPECIFICATIONS: Mossberg 500 All-Purpose Field	
GAUGE/CALIBRE: 12, 20, .410	
BARREL LENGTH: 61cm (24in), 66cm (26in), 71cm (28in)	
WEIGHT: 3.4kg (7.5lb)	
MECHANISM: pump action	
CHOKES: fixed or Accu-Choke™ multichokes	
FEATURES: 76mm (3in) chambers; steel shot multichokes	

The Model 500 may be easily affordable, but Mossberg emphasizes that the gun has passed US Army military specification tests, probably the world's toughest proving examination of any weapon. Model 500 shotguns cross many different formats. The basic Model 500 is available in 12, 20 and .410 gauges, and all models come with 76mm (3in) chambers as standard.

Barrel lengths run from a compact 47cm (18.5in) through to 71cm (28in). Most of the Model 500 barrels are ported, helping to reduce recoil and muzzle flip and thereby facilitating more accurate rapid fire. A standard Model 500 holds five 70mm (2.75in) shells in its magazine and one in the chamber, the magazine capacity being reduced by one for 76mm (3in) shells.

Options and models

All versions of the Model 500 come with features such as ambidextrous safety switches and either fixed chokes or Accu-Choke™ multichokes (suitable for steel shot). Beyond these the Model 500 guns vary depending on model. Some versions differ principally in finish – the Model 500 Camo is covered entirely in Mossy Oak® Advantage camouflage, and also has the facility to mount a scope.

Designed more for security usage, the Model 500 Persuader has a nine-shot magazine, and has many Mossberg reliability features, such as an anti-jam elevator and dual extractors. Alternatively, for young or smaller shooters there is the Model 500 Bantam and Super Bantam (the latter is 20 gauge). These are designed to fit shooters of small frame, but also to take a full-size stock if growth demands it.

Two different patterns of camouflage are illustrated here for the Mossberg 500. The above is ideal for grassland shooting ...

... while this pattern is more suited to woodland. The sight configuration on this weapon makes it a purpose-designed turkey gun.

Mossberg 535 All Terrain Shotgun $

The Mossberg All Terrain Shotgun (ATS) is a new addition to the Model 500 series, rechambered to take shells up to 89mm (3.5in), thereby suiting the field or turkey shooter or the wildfowler wanting maximum power.

SPECIFICATIONS: **Mossberg 535 ATS Slugster**

GAUGE/CALIBRE: 12

BARREL LENGTH: 61cm (24in)

WEIGHT: 3.2kg (7lb)

MECHANISM: pump action

CHOKES: rifled barrel

FEATURES: 89mm (3.5in) chambers; adjustable rifle sights

Mossberg publicity describes the ATS as marking 'a new era for Mossberg pump action shotguns'. Essentially the gun is a fusion between the 500 series and 89mm (3.5in) chambered Model 835, another of Mossberg's popular models (see separate entry). The 535 is a 12-gauge only gun. Although it will take the mighty 89mm (3.5in) shells, it also handles 70mm (2.75in) and 76mm (3in) cartridges, with a magazine capacity of five for the 70mm (2.75in) rounds and one less for the larger cartridge sizes (the chamber also takes an additional cartridge). Barrel lengths are 55cm (22in), 61cm (24in) and 71cm (28in).

Versatile series

The 535 ATS series covers most bases for heavy-duty hunting. The six models listed at the time of writing are the Turkey, Waterfowl, Comb, All-Purpose Field, Tactical Turkey (which features a ported barrel) and Slugster. The last of these has a fully rifled bore for firing heavy slugs. Shotgun slugs, such as Rottweil's Brenneke and Remington's Buckhammer, are principally used for hunting heavy game such as deer and boar, and they have a considerable take-down power. They do not have the aerodynamic stability of rifle bullets, but they still have a respectable accuracy over 100–200m (328–656ft). Caution has to be taken over chokes, as severe damage to a barrel can result from shooting a slug down a tightly choked barrel, hence guns like the Slugster have fixed chokes whereas the Wildfowl model has the Accu-Choke™ multichokes for altering the shot pattern.

Many models of the 535 ATS have adjustable front and/or rear fibre-optic sights, being adjustable for both windage and elevation. As a further sight option the receivers are drilled and tapped for scope fittings.

As well as open sights the ATS can take a scope, which will principally appeal to deer or turkey hunters.

Fibre-optic sights are another sighting option on the ATS, mounted atop the wide-vent rib.

Mossberg 835 ULTIMAG

$

The Mossberg 835 ULTIMAG series is known for its solid reliability in the most arduous of outdoor conditions. Reviews of the 835 attest to its ability to soak up weather and punishment without malfunction.

Mossberg's Dual-Comb® stock system allows a quick change between combs to adjust for different sights.

SPECIFICATIONS: 835 ULTIMAG Thumbhole Turkey

GAUGE/CALIBRE: 12	
BARREL LENGTHS: 51cm (20in), 61cm (24in), 66cm (26in), 71cm (28in)	
WEIGHT: 3.5kg (7.75lb)	
MECHANISM: pump action	
CHOKES: Accu-Mag™ interchangeable	
FEATURES: 89mm (3.5in) chambers; over-bored barrels	

With either the 51cm (20in), 61cm (24in), 66cm (26in) or 71cm (28in) barrel, the Mossberg Model 835 delivers impressive power from its 89mm (3.5in) chambers. Mossberg is keen to point that that the 835 was specifically machined to take the force of the heaviest magnum loads, rather than simply tweaking an existing design. Recoil is managed by several systems, including ported barrels to redirect some of the gas expansion at the muzzle sideways instead of directly forwards (although this in no way affects muzzle velocity). Furthermore, the barrels are over-bored, principally to improve pattern characteristics regardless of the type of shot, but the process also reduces felt recoil. Chokes are interchangeable, and are of Mossberg's Accu-Mag™ variety, which are compatible with all forms of lead, steel and nontoxic shot.

Turkey gun

For turkey shooters, Mossberg has produced the 835 ULTIMAG Thumbhole Turkey gun. Turkey shooting is a distinctive form of hunting, the shooter needing a short gun that is convenient to handle from a sitting position and that delivers dense and accurate patterns to the head of the bird. The Thumbhole Turkey's stock and fore-end are purposely designed for extended comfort, and the camouflage covering is available in two different schemes: Realtree® Hardwoods® HD Green, and Mossy Oak® New Break-Up®, both of these providing ultrarealistic camouflage patterns that match some of the latest lines in camouflage clothing.

The laminate material used to construct the ULTIMAG's stock and fore-end is totally weatherproof.

Mossberg 935 Magnum Autoloader $

While much of Mossberg's reputation has been built upon pump-action guns, shooters also respect its auto-loaders. The 935 Magnum Autoloader utilizes the principles of the Model 835 pump action.

SPECIFICATIONS:

Mossberg Model 935 Magnum Autoloader

GAUGE/CALIBRE: 12

BARREL LENGTH: 61cm (24in), 66cm (26in), 71cm (28in)

WEIGHT: up to 3.5kg (7.75lb)

MECHANISM: gas operated

CHOKES: Accu-Mag™ interchangeable

FEATURES: 89mm (3.5in) chambers; over-bored barrels; fibre-optic adjustable sights

Several features of the 835 series are found in the 935 gun. The barrels are over-bored to improve patterns and reduce recoil, and the gun is chambered for 76mm (3in) and 89mm (3.5in) cartridges. Being a gas-operated semi-automatic, the 935 can handle the heavy magnum loads with confidence, particularly through Mossberg's self-regulating gas system. Such a system is common now on many premium-grade gas-operated semi-automatic shotguns – any gas that is surplus to the requirements of cycling the weapon is vented out of special piston ports. It also has the virtue of reducing the impact upon the moving parts of the gun, lessening wear and tear. Accu-Mag™ interchangeable chokes are provided with the Waterfowl models, three chokes being supplied: Improved Cylinder, Modified and Full.

Adjustable sights

Turkey models of the 935, as with the 835, come with adjustable fibre-optic sights. These are fully adjustable for windage and elevation, and the luminosity of the sights makes them ideal for acquiring targets in low-light conditions. The Turkey models also receive an Ulti-Full™ choke tube for dense killing patterns.

All 935 models have features that make them especially adapted for field use. The Uni-Line™ stock and receiver make for a seamless join between the two, resisting the elements and allowing a quick eye-rib alignment when mounting. The thumb-operated safety is set for ambidextrous use and is extremely quiet to avoid scaring sensitive quarry.

A new Mossberg gun comes with stock spacers to allow the shooter to customize the length of pull to his or her requirements.

The post-and-notch sight arrangement on this gun is mainly suited to turkey or deer shooting.

The 935 Magnum Autoloader takes 89mm (3.5in) shells, so when in a conventional shotgun arrangement it is a perfect wildfowling gun.

Remington 11-87

$

Remington's 11-87 is a major series of auto-loaders stretching between the $700 and $1000 price marks. It contains 14 different models, from a well-rounded clay and field gun through to a fully rifled deer gun.

SPECIFICATIONS: Remington 11-87 Premier

GAUGE/CALIBRE: 12	
BARREL LENGTH: 66cm (26in), 71cm (28in), 76cm (30in)	
WEIGHT: up to 3.5kg (7.75lb)	
MECHANISM: gas operated	
CHOKES: Remington Rem™ Choke interchangeable	
FEATURES: pressure-compensating gas system; 76mm (3in) chambers	

The foundation model of the 11-87 series is the 11-87 Premier. This 12-gauge semi-automatic shotgun has 66cm (26in), 71cm (28in) or 76cm (30in) barrels with 76mm (3in) chambers for those heavy hunting loads. The gun is fitted with Remington's patented pressure-compensating gas system, which permits switching between 70mm (2.75in) cartridges and 76mm (3in) cartridges without the need to make any adjustments to the gun. Therefore, as company publicity states, 'The same gun you use one day on the skeet range can be used the next day in the goose blind.' Stock wood on 11-87 Premier guns is walnut, and the stocks are fitted with solid rubber recoil pads.

Wide-ranging

The 11-87 Premier is a good general-purpose field and clay gun. Expanding beyond the Premier, however, we find guns to suit all manner of shooting purposes. Space here does not allow each model to be studied in turn, but the following are salient. The 11-87 Premier Super

Magnum and SPS Magnum (the latter has a black matte receiver and barrel) upgrade the power possibilities of the series, with chambers designed to accept 89mm (3.5in) cartridges (although, once again, no modifications are needed to switch between cartridge lengths).

The gas system on this gun regulates the amount of gas needed to cycle the weapon through an integral pressure relief valve, reducing the risk of stoppages and also limiting the amount of wear on bolts and pistons. The Premier Cantilever Deer has a 53cm (21in) rifled barrel for use with heavy slugs, and is fitted with sling swivels and sling. Another rifled barrel gun in the series is the Sportsman Deer.

The 11-87 is a well-tested design and the series should fulfil most hunting or field purposes. Using the Remington Rem™ Choke system also means that the patterns of any gun in the range can be adapted to different targets.

The self-regulation of the gas system results in a light and controllable shooting experience.

Remington 105CTi

$$

Newly introduced in 2006, the Remington 105CTi claims to be one of the most innovative semi-automatic shotguns on the market, designed to have the ultimate in soft recoil.

SPECIFICATIONS: **Remington 105CTi**

GAUGE/CALIBRE: 12

BARREL LENGTH: 66cm (26in), 71cm (28in)

WEIGHT: 3.2kg (7lb)

MECHANISM: gas operated

CHOKES: Remington ProBore™ interchangeable

FEATURES: titanium receiver; 'Double Down' ejector/feed; Rate Reduction System

The basic specifications of the 105CTi are fairly unsurprising. It is a 12-gauge shotgun with 66cm (26in) or 71cm (28in) barrels and 76mm (3in) chambers. The operating system is gas, and the average weight of the gun is a light 3.2kg (7lb). So why do Remington claim that the 105CTi 'is like nothing you've ever seen, felt or shot'? The problem with a light gun is that felt recoil can be very stern, especially when firing 76mm (3in) magnum

Recoil reduction is not just a matter of comfort with the 105CTi, it also allows for quicker, more accurate shooting.

cartridges. Remington points out, however, that the 105CTi has 'up to 48% less recoil than the competition'. This is partly achieved by the company's Rate Reduction System – an oil-filled cylinder in the stock that 'that absorbs shock and helps regulate bolt velocity'. Furthermore, the R3 recoil pad on the stock provides a further dramatic cushion against recoil.

Many innovations

The new features of the 105CTi do not end with recoil control. The receiver is constructed from aircraft-grade titanium with a carbon-fibre shell and TriNyte scratch-resistant coating, combining strength, lightness and environmental durability. Furthermore, Remington's 'Double Down' bottom feed and ejector mechanism allows for ambidextrous magazine loading, and ejects the spent shells downwards rather than into the shooter's peripheral vision. Trigger pulls are light and crisp owing to the Target Grade Trigger, which has a pull weight of between 1.6 and 1.8kg (3.5 and 4lb). The shot patterns produced by the over-bored barrels and lengthened forcing cones are excellent, and these also contribute to recoil reduction, as does the one-piece inertia sleeve. Even the barrel rib has received hi-tech investment. It is made from a compound of carbon and armamid, a light yet rigid and strong material that helps keep the weight of the gun down.

The 105CTi is steadily working its way into the market, but early reviews at the time of writing do indeed confirm the lightness of the gun's recoil, and it looks set to become a market leader in advanced semi-automatic shotgun technology.

Remington Model 1100

$

The Remington Model 1100 is another popular semi-automatic series in the Remington armoury. Although the series includes a field model, many of its guns are designed with the clay shooter in mind.

SPECIFICATIONS: Remington Model 1100 Sporting

GAUGE/CALIBRE:	12, 20, 28, .410
BARREL LENGTH:	68.5cm (27in), 71cm (28in)
WEIGHT:	(12 gauge) 3.6kg (8lb)
MECHANISM:	gas operated
CHOKES:	extended interchangeable
FEATURES:	.410 semi-automatic version

The Remington Model 1100 series appeals to every kind of shooter, from casual target shooters to dedicated hunters.

The basic Model 1100 Sporting is offered in 12, 20, 28 and .410 gauges. Barrel length for the 12 and 20 gauge is set at 71cm (28in) while the barrels for the 28 and .410 guns are 2.5cm (1in) shorter. Stock and fore-end are in a glossy American walnut and a sporting-clays type recoil pad is fitted. Being designed for clays, the 1100 Sporting models come with a set of four extended choke tubes: Skeet, Improved Cylinder, Light Modified, and Modified. The inclusion of a .410 model is astute because there are few .410 semi-auto weapons available on the international market. The Model 1100 Classic Field is also available in 16 gauge.

Latest models

The 1100 series has a dedicated skeet gun – the Model 1100 Tournament Skeet – which is a 12- or 20-gauge gun in 66cm (26in) barrel only, supplied with Skeet and Improved Cylinder chokes. There are also two new models gracing the series. The Model 1100 Competition has an over-bored 76cm (30in) barrel with a 10mm (0.39in) sporting rib with front and mid beads. All the major moving internal parts have been coated with nickel-Teflon to aid durability and smooth reciprocation. Finally, at the summit of the 1100 series is the Model 1100 G3. Chambered for either 70mm (2.75in) or 76mm (3in) cartridges, and available in either 12 or 20 gauge, the G3 has a carbon-steel receiver coated in Titanium PVD (Physical Vapour Deposition) for great damage resistance. The nickel-Teflon coating of the 1100 Competition is also present.

The Remington 1100 series is one of the company's most popular, and the retail prices stretch from around the $500 mark to over double that figure for some of the advanced models.

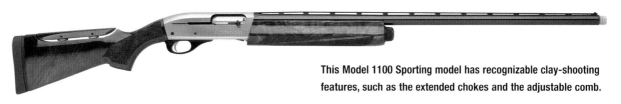

This Model 1100 Sporting model has recognizable clay-shooting features, such as the extended chokes and the adjustable comb.

Remington Model SP-10

$$

A 10-gauge shotgun is typically used for the heaviest types of bird shooting, such as taking on high-flying geese. Remington's SP-10 allows the shooter to deliver large amounts of shot to great distance.

SPECIFICATIONS: **Remington Model SP-10**

GAUGE/CALIBRE: 10	
BARREL LENGTH: 66cm (26in), 76cm (30in)	
WEIGHT: up to 5kg (11lb)	
MECHANISM: gas operated	
CHOKES: Remington Rem™ Choke interchangeable	
FEATURES: recoil-reduction system	

The SP-10 is capable of firing 10-gauge 89mm (3.5in) cartridges, which are some of the most formidable loads in shotgunning. With such lengthy rounds, the magazine only has a two-shell capacity, with space for another round in the chamber.

Two barrel lengths are available: 66cm (26in) for the Model SP-10 Magnum Camo and a much greater 76cm (30in) for the standard SP-10 Magnum. The heavy-duty barrels and parts of these guns make them hefty on the scales. The Magnum weighs an average of 5kg (11lb) and the Magnum Camo weighs 4.9kg (10.75lb).

Gun control

The weight of the SP-10 may put some off the gun, but for those with the strength to wield it the gun handles well, with a smooth swing. The weight also contributes to holding back the recoil, although Remington has also put many other innovations into the gun to help keep down its kick. The stainless steel gas-operating system features a moving cylinder to help soak up some of the recoil and this, combined with a deep recoil pad on the stock, gives what Remington claims is 'less perceived recoil than many 12-gauge magnums'.

The killing force of the SP-10 is not to be doubted, and Remington points out that on high-flying targets, 34 per cent more pellets are delivered onto the target than with a 12-gauge shell. Two Rem™ Choke interchangeable chokes are supplied in Full and Modified constrictions; the tighter choke patterns will give good performance at distance but close-range shots can result in destruction of the meat. Known for its reliability and power, the SP-10 is one of America's best-selling 10-gauge guns.

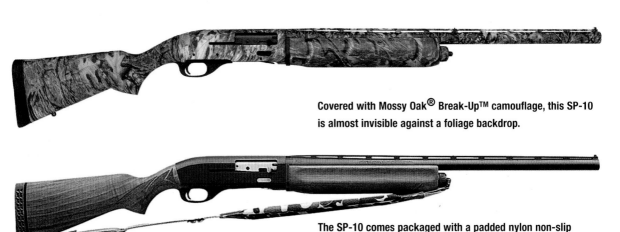

Covered with Mossy Oak® Break-Up™ camouflage, this SP-10 is almost invisible against a foliage backdrop.

The SP-10 comes packaged with a padded nylon non-slip Cordura carrying sling.

Weatherby SAS

$

The Weatherby company's rifles are already internationally popular, but they also produce the SAS range of semi-auto shotguns, which provide a cost-effective balance between affordability and quality.

SPECIFICATIONS: **Weatherby SAS Field**

GAUGE/CALIBRE: 12

BARREL LENGTH: 66cm (26in), 71cm (28in)

WEIGHT: up to 3.5kg (7.75lb)

MECHANISM: gas operated

CHOKES: IMC interchangeable

FEATURES: recoil-dampening system; easily removed trigger unit

At the time of writing there are five models in the Weatherby 12-gauge SAS series (the SAS abbreviation stands simply for Semi-Automatic Shotgun): Field, Synthetic, Break-Up™, Shadow-Grass and Slug Gun. All are gas-operated semi-autos, the gas system being a self-compensating type that adjusts itself for different loads and recoils. At the rear of the aircraft-grade alloy receiver is an integral dampening system, which further soaks up the kickback. The SAS series is chambered for 70mm (2.75in) and 76mm (3in) cartridges and the barrels are chromium-lined.

Interchangeable chokes

Weatherby provides every gun with three Integral Multi-choke system (IMC) interchangeable chokes, the constriction of chokes differing according to the specific model. The Field model, for example, has

The Weatherby SAS comes in several different varieties, including a slug gun and a version suited to sporting clays. Note here the HiViz front bead sight, which is luminous in low-light conditions.

Improved Cylinder, Modified and Full, while the camouflaged Break-Up™ has Modified, Full and Extra Full. Weatherby emphasizes that ported choke tubes are also available for sporting-clays enthusiasts.

Trigger unit

Cleaning a semi-automatic shotgun can be a fiddly business if the design does not allow easy access. The SAS guns all have a drop-out trigger system for quick maintenance. Two pins on the right side of the receiver are pushed in, and this allows the removal of the whole trigger unit. The unit is then simply snapped back into place. Such is a useful feature for those who have been using a gun on a muddy foreshore or riverbank.

The Field is the bedrock model of the series, and features a 66cm (26in) or 71cm (28in) barrel with a simple brass bead front sight and a weight of up to 3.5kg (7.75lb). It has a walnut stock, unlike the black injection-moulded stock of the Synthetic model. The Break-Up™ and Shadow Grass have different camouflaged colour schemes and the option of 61cm (24in) barrels, while the Slug Gun takes the barrel length down to 56cm (22in).

Prices for the Weatherby SAS range from around $700 up to $849.

Winchester Model 1300

$

The Winchester Model 1300's claim to fame is the extraordinary speed of its pump action. Winchester claims that three shots can be unleashed in just over half a second, making it the fastest pump on the market.

SPECIFICATIONS: **Winchester Model 1300 Black Shadow**

GAUGE/CALIBRE: 12, 20

BARREL LENGTH: 66cm (26in), 71cm (28in)

WEIGHT: average 3.2kg (7lb)

MECHANISM: pump action

CHOKES: Winchoke interchangeable

FEATURES: Speed Pump™ system

The speed of pump of the Model 1300 has made the gun extremely popular with wildfowlers, who appreciate its speed of reload when a flock of birds presents itself.

The Model 1300s belong to what Winchester designates its Speed Pump™ line of shotguns. The rapidity of the pump action is down to an inertia-assisted mechanism. As the gun is fired, the inertia generated by the recoil actually assists the rearwards pump of the slide, resulting in much faster reloading times. The importance of this fast reloading presents itself in several hunting situations, from the need to switch quickly between bird targets to taking on a running deer when the shooter has missed with the first shot. Indeed, Winchester also produce the Model 1300 in several different types of rifled-barrel deer gun. The Black Shadow Deer, for example, is a 12- or 20-gauge gun with a 56cm (22in) rifled barrel designed for firing sabot slugs. Non-glare finishes are applied to the external parts to reduce the chance of the deer spotting a glint in the wood.

Rotating bolt

The bolt head in the Model 1300 is of the rotating type, and has four lugs to provide a very stable and secure final lock before firing. This bolt is unlocked from the chamber a split second after the shell has been fired, allowing for an extremely smooth pump action. Recoil control is provided by, on some models, a Pachmayr® Decelerator® pad fitted to the stock.

Barrel lengths on the Model 1300 guns vary according to the type. At the upper end is a 71cm (28in) barrel for models such as the Black Shadow, dropping, as we have seen in the case of the Black Shadow Deer, down to 56cm (22in).

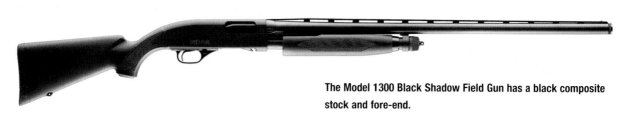

The Model 1300 Black Shadow Field Gun has a black composite stock and fore-end.

Winchester Model 1300 NWTF Short Turkey

$

Turkey shooting is a sport all of its own, requiring patience, excellent camouflage and the right gun. Winchester describes its NWTF Short Turkey as 'the most specialized turkey gun ever'.

SPECIFICATIONS:
Winchester Model 1300 NWTF Short Turkey

GAUGE/CALIBRE: 12	
BARREL LENGTH: 46cm (18in)	
WEIGHT: 2.9kg (6.5lb)	
MECHANISM: pump action	
CHOKES: interchangeable	
FEATURES: Speed Pump™ system	

Turkey shooting, unlike the quick snap shooting involved with walked-up bird shooting, often requires a more deliberate aiming process. The Model 1300 NWTF Short Turkey (the abbreviation stands for National Wild Turkey Federation, a conservation and hunting organization in the United States) has rifle-type front and rear sights, both with fibre-optic properties.

In low-light conditions, the rear sight presents two luminous dots straddling the V-notch, while the front sight is an elongated TRUGLO sight. The sights are fully adjustable. The receiver is also drilled and tapped for mounting a scope. As with other Model 1300 guns, the NWTF Short Turkey has the Speed Pump™ system for fast reloading, and the magazine capacity is four 76mm (3in) shells.

Tight chokes

Accuracy is demanded in turkey shooting because the size of the prey requires the dense patterns of tight chokes. An Extra-Long, Extra-Full Extended Turkey choke is provided as standard. For the purposes of camouflage, the whole gun is covered in the Mossy Oak® New Break-Up™ camouflage, which provides a photo-realistic woodland pattern that is extremely hard to distinguish against the woodland and grassland environments of the wild turkey.

The Short Turkey is just one of the specialist models within the Model 1300 range. The NRA (National Rifle Association) Defender, for example, is a security-type shotgun with a magazine capacity of seven cartridges plus one in the chamber. Designed for police use, it has a 46cm (18in) barrel that can take buckshot and rifled rounds. It is available in both 12 and 20 gauges. This gun also has a Combo option whereby a standard full stock and a pure pistol grip are provided.

The Short Turkey has only a 46cm (18in) barrel. Note also the ported muzzle to reduce muzzle flip.

Winchester Super X2

$–$$

The Winchester Super X2 is a new, advanced line of Winchester shotguns. Although the name alludes to the earlier, unsuccessful X1 series, the X2 are entirely different guns.

SPECIFICATIONS: **Winchester Super X2**

GAUGE/CALIBRE: 12

BARREL LENGTH: 61cm (24in), 66cm (26in), 71cm (28in), 76cm (30in)

WEIGHT: up to 3.6kg (8lb)

MECHANISM: gas operated

CHOKES: Invector™ or Invector-Plus™ interchangeable

FEATURES: Active Valve gas-regulation system

With his goose decoys in place, a hunter opens up with his Super X2, his dog at the ready.

The Super X2 series consists of a range of 12-gauge shotguns for field, clays or practical shotgunning competitions. One of the key features of the series is its extremely fast reloading times, courtesy of its Active Valve system, which self-regulates the amount of gas used to cycle the weapon. Speeds claimed by the manufacturer – 'the gas-operated Super X2 is the fastest gun around, capable of firing five shells in just over one half of a second' – are impressive. In practical terms, the Super X2 enables a shooter in any discipline to fire as quickly as he or she can pull the

trigger. The Super X2 is chambered for up to 89mm (3.5in) cartridges. Three of these or three 76mm (3in) shells can be held in the magazine, while the magazine has a four-shot capacity for 70mm (2.75in) cartridges. (A magazine plug is supplied to limit magazine capacity to two rounds if required.)

Easy clean

The magazine tube on the Super X2 is made of stainless steel. Powder residue buildup on the outside of the magazine tube can be a cleaning headache on many guns, but with the Super X2 the stainless steel is easily wiped clean. Winchester has paid attention to many other details of the guns. The safety mechanism is set just behind the trigger for easy operation by the trigger finger. The barrels, which come in 61cm (24in), 66cm (26in), 71cm (28in) or 76cm (30in) lengths, are over-bored, producing better patterns and helping to ameliorate the felt recoil. The X2 series also offers a Cantilever Deer slug gun.

Three Invector™ or Invector-Plus™ choke tubes are supplied: Improved Cylinder, Modified and Full.

Winchester Super X3

$–$$

The Super X3 series from Winchester maintains the company's reputation for being at the cutting edge of semi-automatic design. It is being marketed on the basis of its smooth-shooting characteristics and its durability.

SPECIFICATIONS: Winchester Super X3

GAUGE/CALIBRE: 12

BARREL LENGTH: 56cm (22in), 66cm (26in), 71cm (28in)

WEIGHT: up to 3.4kg (7.5lb)

MECHANISM: gas operated

CHOKES: Invector-Plus™ interchangeable

FEATURES: Active Valve gas-regulation system; weather-resistant finishes

In one test conducted by Winchester, 5000 rounds were fired through a Super X3 gun without a single malfunction. Such a test, while not necessarily replicating the conditions of private ownership or heavy field use, is nonetheless an impressive testimony to the Super X3's reliability.

Like the X2 and several other Winchester shotguns, the X3 uses the Active Valve technology in its gas system to regulate the amount of gas used to cycle the gun. X3s are 12-gauge guns, and the Active Valve system handles all manner of shells from light-loaded 70mm (2.75in) game cartridges through to powerful 89mm (3.5in) wildfowling shells. The recoil is not only controlled by the gas system. A high-tech Pachmayr® Decelerator® recoil pad is fitted to the stock, and the back-bored barrels also take away some of the kick, while also improving shot patterning.

Durability

The X3 has been built to withstand all manner of hard use. The Dura-Touch® Armour Coating (applied to the stock and fore-end) and Perma-Cote™ UT (Ultra Tough) finishes (applied to the metal) ensure that the gun is highly weather-resistant. This is especially important for wildfowlers, and for them

there is the Super X3 Waterfowl. This is rendered in Mossy Oak® New Shadow Grass® camouflage, to blend in perfectly with riverbank grasses, and the Dura-Touch® Armour Coating also increases hand adhesion on a wet gun. Another camouflaged gun is the Camo Field, which weighs around 3.4kg (7.5lb) and, like the Waterfowl model, has sling swivels for convenient carriage in the wild. X3 guns come supplied with three choke tubes, and prices range from around $950 to up to $1200.

All the parts of the Winchester Super X3 are given state-of-the-art weather-resistant finishes.

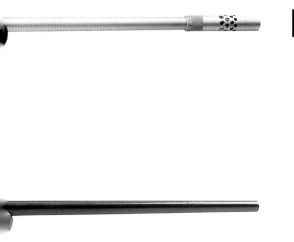

CHAPTER 3

BOLT & MANUAL ACTION RIFLES

This chapter moves away from the world of shotgunning, the principal focus of the last two chapters, into the world of bullet weapons. Here we will feature the classic hunting formats – bolt-action and lever-action guns – plus one or two single-shot models with other actions, such as falling block breech-loaders.

Bolt-action rifles remain popular for several simple reasons. They are, with the right sight (properly adjusted), the most accurate form of firearm. They also have relatively simple mechanisms, so rarely malfunction in the field.

Bolt-action rifles are the world's most popular firearms purchases. While the shotgun is the ideal gun for hunting small ground animals and birds at ranges of up to 50m (164ft), the rifle can take on far larger prey at much longer distances, with an accuracy within mere millimetres or centimetres of the point of aim. Although bolt-action mechanisms vary in construction from gun to gun, with signal differences in such features as number of locking lugs, type of extractor, method of feed, and overall build quality, all mechanisms perform the same job – a hand-operated bolt system loads, locks, fires and ejects the cartridge. In a lever-action gun, the rounds are pumped in from a tubular magazine via a lever set as part of the trigger guard. The big difference between rifles, however, tends to lie in calibre.

Calibre choice

The range of calibres available for rifles is truly vast. At the small end of the scale are the popular rimfire calibres, such as .22 Short (S), Long (L), and Long Rifle (LR). A .22 LR, one of the most popular rounds for bolt- and lever-action guns,

Having a rifle that breaks down and stores easily is the ultimate convenience. However, make sure you clean a gun well before such storage – a slightly damp gun will sweat in the case, encouraging corrosion.

has a bullet weight of below 40 grains, a muzzle velocity of around 320m/sec (1050ft/sec) and is useful for small game such as rabbits, foxes, and gophers at ranges of around 50m (164ft). At the absolute other extreme, a big-game centrefire cartridge, such as the massive .460 Weatherby Magnum, has a bullet weight of 500 grains, a muzzle velocity of 823m/sec (2700ft/sec), and could bring down a bull elephant at 500m (1640ft). The LAR Grizzly rifle fires a .50 BMG round that, in military use, has made kills well beyond 2000m (6561ft).

The important point is that you select a calibre of rifle appropriate to its intended use. For plinking, target shooting, or small-game hunting opt for a rimfire weapon in .17 or .22 calibre. (Be careful, however, of high-velocity rimfires such as the .17 HMR or .22 WRF Magnum. The velocity of these rounds will destroy a small animal at close range, and therefore they are better suited to ranges of up to and beyond 100m/328ft.)

For deer shooting, use a centrefire round. Such cartridges are larger, and therefore generate more powerful muzzle velocities and kinetic energy. Opinion varies on the entry-level calibre, but between .240 and .338 is a good bracket. Beyond this are the big-game

A hunting trip with a good bolt-action rifle can be a rewarding experience. Safety is central to the enjoyment. A standard .30-06 rifle will kill at distances of over 1.6km (1 mile), so any shot taken must have the target set against a solid backdrop to prevent the bullet's overflight.

calibres referred to earlier. These start with rounds like the .358 Norma Magnum and run up to the .600 Nitro (a 900-grain bullet), and are designed for the very largest animals, such as antelope, bear (although many of the deer calibres will handle these creatures at the appropriate range), and safari creatures. This run-through of the calibre selections available is very simplistic, and space does not allow a full consideration. Get expert consultation when buying a rifle, find the right calibre, and make sure that you can handle both gun and calibre well.

Good shooting

In this chapter we only consider the rifle, paying attention to sights purely in terms of whether the gun has open sights and/or what provision there is for scope mounting. A rifle, however, is only as accurate as its sight. There are three basic types of sight: open, aperture, and telescopic. Open sights are the least accurate but, generally speaking, the quickest to use. They tend to appeal to close-quarters woodland hunters, who might see a flash of prey through the trees and need to make a snap shot at ranges seldom more than 50m (164ft). Anything beyond this range will generally need a more advanced sighting system. Aperture sights are usually found on target rifles, and they give very accurate performance out to and beyond 100m (328ft). Yet as the small rear aperture sight has limited light transmission, they are rarely used on hunting weapons. Hunting rifles generally need telescopic sights. These come in numerous varieties and capabilities, but will give the shooter range capabilities that can comfortably stretch over several hundred metres (yards).

Of course, a good sight is also meaningless unless it is zeroed properly. This takes practice and training, as do all aspects of rifle shooting. Don't fall into the trap of thinking that a good sight is all that it takes to be a competent rifle shot. Rifle shooting, like all other forms of shooting, is an advanced practice and incorporates everything from fieldcraft to a decent understanding of ballistics. Aim to be a complete shooter, and you will discover much more about the passion of rifle shooting.

A rifle will not hunt for the hunter. To get into the position to take the shot, you will need good fieldcraft skills. Furthermore, you should only take the shot when confident of a clean kill.

Accuracy International Varmint $$$

The British Accuracy International Company has long been known for its military sniper rifles. It also produces a range of target and hunting rifles using the same precision engineering.

SPECIFICATIONS: **Accuracy International Varmint**

CALIBRE: .223–.308	
BARREL LENGTH: 66cm (26in)	
WEIGHT: up to 6kg (13.2lb)	
SIGHTS: provision for scope	
MECHANISM: bolt action, magazine fed	
FEATURES: match-grade barrels and triggers; adjustable stock	

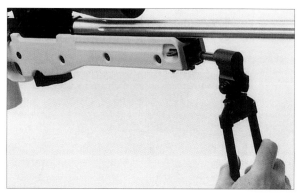

A highly adaptable weapon, the Varmint will take a bipod at the front of the fore-end.

The Varmint is a high-grade hunting rifle made with a view to superb levels of accuracy within the limits of the selected calibres. Available calibres for the Varmint are .223 up to .308, and the gun is fitted with a 66cm (26in) stainless-steel fluted match-grade barrel (the barrel flutes reduce the weight of what is usually the heaviest part of any rifle). Being based upon a military weapon, the Varmint has a higher magazine capacity than many other bolt-action weapons – it can carry eight rounds. The ammunition box is detachable, and cartridges within are staggered to reduce the depth of the box.

Precision trigger

Everything about the Varmint is designed towards the ultimate precision shot. The trigger, for example, is match grade, and has a two-stage design. Trigger pull weight itself ranges from 1.1 to 1.6kg (2.5 to 3.5lb), the weight being adjustable by the shooter. The bolt action is made to the highest tolerances, and development tests during production show that the action could fire 20,000 rounds without any serious malfunction. Nevertheless, Accuracy International makes all its parts interchangeable, and barrels can be swapped in a matter of minutes if necessary. Most other parts of the gun can be changed as well. The stock system is adjustable to fit the shooter, with spacers on the butt plate allowing the length of pull to be changed. (Stocks are available in various colours from grey through to olive drab.)

The Varmint is not fitted with iron sights as standard (although they could be an option), but with a precision scope it is a rifle with excellent hunting and target performance.

The Accuracy International Varmint is, in every element of its construction, built to produce near-perfect accuracy.

Anschütz Model 1417

$

Anschütz is best known for its large range of target and hunting rifles, including weapons that have helped shooters to triumph in Olympic-level competitions.

SPECIFICATIONS: Anschütz Model 1417	
CALIBRE: .22 LR	
BARREL LENGTH: 35.5cm (14in)	
WEIGHT: up to 2.5kg (5.5lb)	
SIGHTS: scope	
MECHANISM: bolt action, magazine fed	
FEATURES: adjustable trigger; free-floating barrel	

Anschütz specializes in small-calibre rifles, typically .22 LR and .22 Hornet, but it also chambers rifles for .17 and various other .22 calibres (as well as producing competition-grade air rifles). The range of styles within the Anschütz catalogue is extremely broad. At one end of the scale we have the Anschütz Model 1416, a classic-looking hunting rifle in .22 LR with iron sights, a beavertail fore-end, and a straight stock. These guns have folding rear leaf sights and pearl front beads, and they are known for their reliable bolt action, in which the bolt head is recessed to hold the cartridge securely. A gas-escape groove provides some security against backblast.

At the other end of the scale is the Anschütz 1827 Fortner, a .22 LR biathlon rifle with a straight–pull repeating action, a magazine holder mounted at the fore-end for spare magazines, a stock system that is adjustable in almost every direction, and a high-accuracy aperture sight.

Short rifle

Between these extremes lies a gun like the Model 1417, although as its name indicates it is closer to the 1416 series. The 1417 is essentially a .22 LR carbine, with a very short barrel of 35.5cm (14in) and the classic Anschütz bolt action. In this configuration it is obviously intended for very short-range (up to around 70m/300ft) vermin and game shooting. Despite the short length of the barrel, the free-floating design gives the gun its precision accuracy over the viable range. The trigger pull weight is screw adjustable. The only criticism that has occasionally emerged in personal reviews of the 1417 is a slightly weak ejection of spent shells, although no one felt this problem was sufficient to cause disappointment.

Above: The compact dimensions of the Model 1417 are apparent here, making it an ideal varmint gun.

The Model 1417 has a five-round detachable magazine curving out from in front of the trigger guard.

Anschütz 1700 Series

$–$$

Anschütz rifles have long been associated with superb levels of accuracy, and the 1700 series contains a top-quality range of .22 and .17 rifles for the dedicated competition shooter.

SPECIFICATIONS: **Anschütz Model 1700 series**

CALIBRE: .17 HMR, .22 LR, .22 Hornet, .222 Rem
BARREL LENGTH: 58cm (23in)
WEIGHT: up to 3.6kg (8lb)
SIGHTS: fixed rear adjustable and front ramp
MECHANISM: bolt action, magazine fed
FEATURES: match-grade barrels and triggers; Model 54 action

Every aspect of a 1700 series contributes towards the tightest and most consistent shot groupings. At the heart of the guns is the Model 54 action. This is composed of a dual-lug bolt, which has a recessed face to hold every cartridge head in a consistent position. A very positive claw extractor allows for an equally robust extraction. Anschütz company publicity also promises that a 'unique in line, very light firing-pin design gives the Anschütz 54 action the world's fastest lock time, and allows dry fire without damage'. Both of these features ingratiate the gun with the competition shooter, the first because a fast lock time limits the amount of time in which the accuracy can deviate between trigger pull and cartridge ignition, and the latter because dry-firing practice is useful in allowing the shooter to master breathing and posture without the expense of ammunition consumption.

The action is only one element of the Anschütz 1700's sophistication. Triggers are of match quality and are adjustable for weight of pull (they have to be adjusted by a gunsmith, however). The barrels are target grade and 'lapped to Olympic competition specifications'. The sights consist of a folding rear and front ramp. Such attention to accuracy pays off in groupings of 1.3–2.5cm (0.5–1in) over a range of 91m (298ft).

Match quality

The 1700 range is available in the popular .22 and .17 calibres – .17 HMR, .22 LR, .22 Hornet, and .222 Remington. Each gun in the range has the same action with differences in barrel weight (denoted by the suffix HB – Heavy Barrel) or stock type (the two basic stock types are Classic straight or Monte Carlo). Almost all the guns have 58cm (23in) barrels, although the Model 1712 Sporter Monte Carlo has a 55cm (21.6in) barrel.

A hunter takes a shot with a Model 1700 rifle, using a forked branch as an improvised monopod support.

ARMSCOR M1700

$

ARMSCOR Precision Inc. of Nevada offers the M1700 as a basic bolt-action rifle within a range of some rather more unusual weapon types.

SPECIFICATIONS: ARMSCOR M1700

CALIBRE: .17 HMR

BARREL LENGTH: 56cm (22in)

WEIGHT: 2.7kg (6lb)

SIGHTS: adjustable rear and front fibre-optic

MECHANISM: bolt action, magazine fed

FEATURES: blued or stainless-steel barrels

Although the .17 and .22 calibres are most popularly used in bolt- or lever-action rifles, ARMSCOR has not been backward in looking towards the entertainment value of these small and inexpensive calibres. Two of its popular ranges are the AK22 and the M1600.

The former is a direct AK47 copy set in a semi-automatic action and chambered for the .22 LR cartridge. It is fed from a diminutive 10-round magazine (a 30-round version is available), has a 46cm (18.25in) barrel length, and a weight of 3.18kg (7lb). In direct balance to the AK22 is the M1600, a .22 LR version of the US M16 rifle, again fed from a 10-round detachable magazine.

Such rifles are used for action-shooting sports, but with the sights properly set up could also be used for varmint control. The M1700, however, would be a much more conventional purchase for the light hunting and pest-control roles.

The M1700 is a simple workhorse rifle designed around an increasingly popular cartridge. The overall length of the gun is 103cm (40.5in), making it a compact hunting weapon for the right sort of prey.

High velocity

The M1700 is chambered for the .17 HMR (Hornady Magnum Rimfire). This round is currently one of the most popular rimfire cartridges on the market, and although small it produces an excellent results on prey up to and including fox size (at the right range).

Muzzle velocity of a 17-grain bullet is about 762m/sec (2500ft/sec), and the bullet tends to disintegrate on impact with the target, hence its respectable take-down power relative to bullet size. The M1700 takes five of these cartridges in its under-action box magazine.

Barrel and sights

The barrel length is 56cm (22in) to make an overall length of 103cm (40.5in). The finish is either blued or stainless steel. In terms of sights, the M1700 can take a scope, but comes with standard fixed sights, these being an adjustable rear sight combined with a fibre-optic front sight. With the combination of sights and the .17 HMR rounds, shots can be comfortably taken out to around (in some cases beyond) 100m (328ft).

In terms of safety, the M1700 has a simple thumb-operated trigger block device.

Blaser R93

$$–$$$

The Blaser R93 is a state-of-the-art hunting rifle, with almost euphoric reviews in the shooting press about its total reliability, its unbelievably smooth operation, and its undoubted accuracy.

SPECIFICATIONS: **Blaser R93**

CALIBRE: 15 calibres from .22-250 to .416 Rem Mag
BARREL LENGTH: standard calibres 56cm (22in), magnum calibres 64.7cm (25.5in)
WEIGHT: approx 3.18kg (7lb)
SIGHTS: ready for scope mount
MECHANISM: bolt action, magazine fed
FEATURES: straight-pull non-rotational bolt; free-floating barrel

On account of its easily interchanged barrel units, the R93 is effectively several rifles rather than one. Simply undoing two fastening screws allows the barrel to come off to be replaced by another; the bolt head also has to be replaced when switching between major calibre groups, but this is a simple process. The bolt-action system itself is the R93's major selling point. It is a straight-pull mechanism, removing the need for the physical rotation of the bolt and bolt handle and thereby improving both accuracy and fluidity of operation. The bolt is locked by a series of radial collet locking lugs which, when the bolt is closed, are forced out into a locking ring in the barrel extension. Furthermore, the feed system takes the cartridges straight from the magazine directly into the chamber without the need for a potentially bullet-damaging feed ramp. Such features, combined with Blaser's free-floating barrel, give superb accuracy.

Ultimate gun

Another seminal feature of the R93 is its ease of disassembly. Not only do the rifle and barrel come apart conveniently, but field tests have borne out Blaser's claim that disassembly does not affect the rifle's zero once it is reassembled. In some tests using .308 rounds the grouping at 91m (298ft) was 1.5cm (0.6in). Trigger pull is exceptionally crisp and light.

The R93 comes in numerous 'special editions', these affecting the type of stock, the furniture (such as sling swivels), the barrel set, and the calibres. The R93 Attaché, for example, has a black anodized action, a fluted barrel, and a titanium-nitrated bolt head. The R93 Safari, by contrast, has a heavy 64.7cm (25.5in) barrel to take the .375 H&H Mag or .416 Rem Mag cartridges it fires.

One press review described the R93 as the most innovative bolt-action rifle of the twentieth century.

BRNO 98

$

The CZ-BRNO 98 is a classic bolt-action design, a gun that utilizes the ageless Mauser action. Its ancestry in the Czech Republic stretches back over 100 years, and it is a solid workhorse of a rifle.

SPECIFICATIONS: BRNO 98

CALIBRE: 7 x 57, 7 x 64, 6.5 x 55SE, .234 Win, .270 Win, .308 Win, .30-06, 8 x 57JS, 9.3 x 62, .300 Win Mag, 7mm Rem Mag	
BARREL LENGTH: 60.5cm (23.8in)	
WEIGHT: approx 3.3kg (7.26lb)	
SIGHTS: adjustable rear, front ramp; fittings for scope	
MECHANISM: bolt action, magazine fed	
FEATURES: Mauser 98 action	

The Zbrojovka Brno (Brno Armoury) was created back in 1918, and has survived a turbulent history under Nazism, communism and democratic liberalism to retain its position as a manufacturer of fine firearms. Today the BRNO 98 is known for

The Mauser 98-type action is central to the BRNO 98, hence its reputation for reliability.

being a traditional Mauser-type bolt-action rifle of very high quality. It is available in 11 calibres in total: 7 x 57, 7 x 64, 6.5 x 55SE, .234 Win, .270 Win, .308 Win, .30-06, 8 x 57JS, 9.3 x 62, .300 Win Mag, and 7mm Rem Mag. The list of calibres puts the BRNO 98 firmly in line for being a good deer-gun purchase, while the magnum calibres give the capability to take on even larger game. As the Brno publicity states, the 98 is squarely 'designed for hunting'.

Sights and stock

The standard sights on the BRNO 98 are of an open type, with an adjustable rear sight and a front ramp sight, although the gun is ready to take a scope if preferred. Styling on the 98 depends on the sub-model, but all have the Bavarian-style curved stock made of European walnut. In terms of fore-end, there is either a half-length Schnabel fore-end, the same in a beavertail, or the full-length fore-end that reaches right up to the muzzle. Barrel length on all the guns is 60.5cm (23.8in) and total gun length is 104cm (41in).

Prices for the Brno rifles when exported to countries such as the United States remain very reasonable for the quality of the firearm. A basic 98 made in the standard calibres starts at around the $500 mark, but climbs up to nearly $1000 for some of the magnum calibre types.

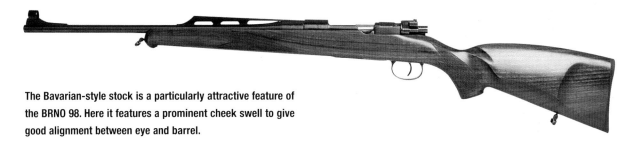

The Bavarian-style stock is a particularly attractive feature of the BRNO 98. Here it features a prominent cheek swell to give good alignment between eye and barrel.

Brown Savanna

$$$

The Ed Brown Savanna has received superb reviews in the shooting press. It is built for high-accuracy shooting with several .30 and .338 calibres.

SPECIFICATIONS: **Brown Savanna**

CALIBRE: .30-06, .300 Win Mag, and .300 Weatherby Mag
BARREL LENGTH: 61cm (24in)
WEIGHT: up to 3.6kg (8lb)
SIGHTS: drilled and tapped for scope
MECHANISM: bolt action, magazine fed
FEATURES: M704 Controlled Feed Action; match-grade barrels; fibreglass stock

Accuracy is as much about triggers as it is about barrels, actions, and ammunition. If a lock time is slow, a pull over-heavy or over-light, or with too much creep, accuracy will be compromised at some stage of the shot. Ed Brown uses Jewell triggers as the choice in many of its rifles, including the Savanna. These are adjustable without the user having to disassemble the rifle, and the pull weight can be taken up from an extremely light 0.3kg (0.5lb) – a pull weight that is only really suitable for bench-shooting at competition targets – up to a solid 1.8kg (4lb). Brown recommends a pull weight about midway in this range.

Common ingredients

The Savanna shares many of the features of other Brown rifles. It has the custom Controlled Action Feed, the Shilen barrel, and the McMillan fibreglass stock. In terms of calibre, the Savanna is chambered for .30-06, .300 Win Mag, and .300 Weatherby Mag. (As with all Brown rifles, the Savanna may be ordered in a wide range of other calibres

as a custom-build option, although this increases the price of the final gun.) For those guns chambered for the magnum round, a muzzle brake is fitted.

No fixed sights are provided with the Savanna; instead there are heavy-duty scope mounts that will make a stable foundation for a good-quality scope. Brown states that 'Our Savanna hunting rifle will normally shoot ½" to 1" at 100 yards [1cm–2.5cm at 91m] with tuned hand loads.' Press tests have indeed confirmed the great accuracy of the Savanna and other Brown rifles, and a Savanna is an ideal weapon for deer and other large game.

Brown's bolt action is one of the best in the business, and contributes to the Savanna's superb accuracy.

Browning A-Bolt

$

A total of 19 variants make up Browning's A-Bolt series, which promises 'custom rifle accuracy right out of the box'. The price is in the $700–$800 range.

SPECIFICATIONS: **Browning A-Bolt Stainless Stalker**

CALIBRE: wide range of calibres from .223 Rem up to .300 WSM

BARREL LENGTH: 56cm (22in), 58.4 (23in), 61cm (24in), 66cm (26in)

WEIGHT: up to 3.3kg (7.25lb)

SIGHTS: drilled and tapped for scope mount

MECHANISM: bolt action, magazine fed

FEATURES: non-bind bolt sleeve; chromed trigger sear; BOSS option

A-Bolt rifles go from varmint category calibres such as the .223 up to powerful .300 WSM, the range accounting for most of the popular cartridges in between. At the heart of the gun is the bolt action, which has been designed for speed of throw and great reliability. The bolt is wrapped for its entire length in a non-rotating bolt sleeve that features three guide ribs. The bolt itself has three locking lugs and when the bolt is opened the three lugs align with the sleeve ribs to bring about a very smooth re-cocking of the weapon. Furthermore, the bolt handle requires only 60 degrees of movement to unlock, so the action is both positive and fast.

Magazine capacity varies between three and five depending on the calibre – the magazine itself is detachable, but with a hinged aluminium floor plate. As a further refinement, the trigger sear is plated with chrome to provide a very crisp trigger pull. Trigger pull weight is also adjustable.

BOSS option

Select models of the A-Bolt series have the option of taking Browning's Ballistic Optimizing Shooting System (BOSS). This is an adjustable muzzle brake/weight; the weight is attached to the end of the A-Bolt's free-floating barrel and by adjusting its position on the barrel's screw thread the shooter can finely tune the vibrations and accuracy of the gun. Results for accuracy tend to be exceptional.

Models of the A-Bolt include the Hunter, Stalker, Medallion, Stainless Stalker, Composite Stalker, and Micro Hunter. Many of the models are available in left- and right-handed versions, and they come with drilled and tapped receivers ready to accept an optical sight.

The Browning A-Bolt is one of the world's most popular series of bolt-action hunting rifles. Its short bolt throw (only 60 degrees), good balance, wide range of calibres, durability and accessible price are the key reasons for its good sales.

Browning BL-22

$

The Browning BL-22 evokes the traditions of the West with its Henry-like appearance and its classic lever action. It is ideal for those wanting a light and tough field gun, especially young shooters.

SPECIFICATIONS: Browning BL-22 Grade I

CALIBRE: .22 S, .22 L .22 LR

BARREL LENGTH: 51cm (20in)

WEIGHT: up to 2.27kg (5lb)

SIGHTS: folding leaf rear, bead front

MECHANISM: lever action, tubular magazine

FEATURES: high magazine capacity; adjustable open sights

The basic BL-22 is the Grade I, which gives a good feel for the rest of the series (at the time of writing there are seven BL-22 models in total). It is a .22 rimfire weapon, chambered for .22 S, L and LR. Barrel length is a short 51cm (20in) and the overall finish is very plain and clean, with a blued receiver. Adjustable open sights are fitted – there is a bead front post and a folding-leaf rear sight – but the receiver is also grooved for scope mounts. With the open sights, shots of up to and over 50m (164ft) can be taken, while fitting a scope allows the shooter to utilize the full range of the .22 rounds.

Lever action

The BL-22 guns use lever action to cycle rounds in from the under-barrel tubular magazine. The total capacity of the magazine is 15 rounds of LR, 17 rounds of L, and an impressive 22 rounds of S, a capacity that not only makes the gun ideal for rapid-

The high capacity of the BL-22's under-barrel magazine makes it an ideal training gun for someone wanting to hone up their range skills. However, it is also perfectly suited to short-range varmint control.

fire varmint-shooting needs, but also for an enjoyable afternoon's plinking.

Lever-action guns can be difficult to use if the action is too long, as the gun has to be taken out of the shoulder to accommodate the movement. The lever action on the BL-22, however, is a very short 33 degrees and, as such, the gun would be good for those with small hands, or for those who want a very fast reload to switch quickly between targets without taking the gun from their shoulders. The trigger also moves with the lever to avoid trapped fingers.

Safety

Because the gun may be suitable for young shooters, safety is an important consideration in the design. The gun (as with all Browning firearms) comes with a trigger lock or other locking attachment. The gun's mechanism also prevents firing of the gun until the lever is swung up to rest, the breech has completely closed, and the trigger has been fully released.

Other models of the BL-22 take the finish to much higher levels. The Grade II, for example, has a gold-coloured trigger, while the Grade II Octagon features an attractive gold-engraved receiver.

Browning Eurobolt

$

The Browning Eurobolt has the same action as the A-Bolt series, but, as its name implies, its styling brings more of a European flavour to the table.

SPECIFICATIONS: Browning Eurobolt	
CALIBRE: .243 WSSM, .270 WSM, .300 WSM, 7 x 64, 7mmRM, .30-06	
BARREL LENGTH: 56cm (22in)	
SIGHTS: drilled and tapped for scope mount	
WEIGHT: approx 3kg (6.6lb)	
MECHANISM: bolt action, magazine fed	
FEATURES: short-rotation handle; 60-degree bolt rotation	

A sound suppressor, bipod and stock-mounted cartridge holder turn the Eurobolt here into a superb hunting setup for static position shooting.

The most distinctive feature of the Eurobolt is the shape of its stock, which is in the classic 'German' or 'Bavarian' style. The comb of the gun (the top of the stock that rests against the shooter's cheek) is pronouncedly curved, swelling up from the pistol grip to meet the face, then curving downwards quite sharply to the butt plate. The stock runs forward under the barrel to form a slender Schnabel fore-end. The whole appearance is poised and elegant, with a deep rich grain running through the walnut.

Hunting gun

The Eurobolt is principally a rifle for hunting deer and other large game, and the available calibres are: .243 WSSM, .270 WSM, .300 WSM, 7 x 64, 7mmRM, and the respected .30-06. These calibres handle all manner of sizeable creatures, with bullet weights of 100 to 180 grains and muzzle velocities straddling just either side of 914m/sec (3000ft/sec). Accuracy with these calibres is good for up to 300m (984ft). The minimum barrel length for any deer-hunting gun should be around 56cm (22in), which is the length provided with the Eurobolt. The Eurobolt also features a glass-bedded steel receiver. In terms of bolt, three lugs provide a very secure lock. Magazine capacity depends on the calibre, with the .243 gun holding three cartridges in the magazine and one in the chamber, while the .30-06 has a 4+1 arrangement.

To aid rapid cycling of the weapon, the Eurobolt's handle travels through only a 60-degree rotation, and the handle itself is dropped low against the stock to prevent its interference with sight of the target. No fixed sights are provided, but the receiver is drilled and tapped for a scope mount.

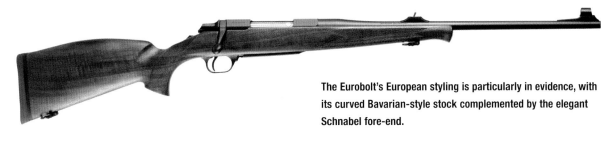

The Eurobolt's European styling is particularly in evidence, with its curved Bavarian-style stock complemented by the elegant Schnabel fore-end.

CZ 452 American

$

CZ has long been held in regard for its high-quality rimfire rifles. For less than $500 a shooter can have one of the CZ 452 range, available in a number of calibres and styles for light hunting.

SPECIFICATIONS: **CZ 452 American**

CALIBRE: .17 Mach, .17 HMR, .22 LR, .22 WMR	
BARREL LENGTH: 57cm (22.5in)	
WEIGHT: up to 2.68kg (5.9lb)	
SIGHTS: grooved receiver for scope mount	
MECHANISM: bolt action, magazine fed	
FEATURES: trigger adjustable for weight of pull; hammer-forged barrels	

Ceska Zbrojovka (CZ) was established in the early decades of the twentieth century in what is now the Czech Republic. Its existence today – having survived the violent turmoil of Eastern European history – is testimony to canny leadership and, more importantly, the high standards of its product line.

The 452 line is a range of rimfire bolt-action guns, chambered for various .22 and .17 cartridges. For example, the CZ 452 Varmint has the options of .22 LR, .22 WMR, .17 Mach, and .17 HMR. As with all the 452s, the Varmint's standard ammunition feed is a five-round detachable box, but a 10-round box is available, as are single-shot adapters.

Because the Varmint belongs to CZ's 'American' style of guns, no open sights are fitted (an optical scope is required). (Open sights are fitted on the Lux, Scout, and FS models of the 452.) CZ also produces a model of the 452 specifically called the 'American'.

This has a straight-comb stock and the top of the receiver has a dovetail groove for mounting the scope.

High-quality materials

Part of the reason for the popularity of CZ rimfire guns is the quality of the materials used in the construction of all the firearms in the series. Turkish walnut stocks are attractive, strong, and fitted to most of the 452 models. The exceptions to this rule are the 452 Style and 452 Silhouette, both of which are fitted with synthetic stocks. All 452 barrels are hammer-forged to give the guns exceptional accuracy over the range of the rounds.

The CZ 452 is a budget gun, but with the right sight will still deliver tight accuracy at up to 100m (328ft).

The trigger on the CZ 452 is adjustable for the weight of pull, a feature not commonly found on inexpensive rimfire guns.

CZ 527

$

The CZ 527 family has won numerous design and performance awards in its class of hunting rifle. Based on the redoubtable Mauser action, the guns are solid small-bore performers.

SPECIFICATIONS: **CZ 527 Varmint Kevlar**

CALIBRE: .204 Ruger, .223 Rem	
BARREL LENGTH: 61cm (24in)	
WEIGHT: up to 3.4kg (7.5lb)	
SIGHTS: provision for scope	
MECHANISM: bolt action, magazine fed	
FEATURES: Kevlar stock; micro Mauser action	

The cornerstone of the series is the CZ 527 Luxe, which retails in the United States for around $600. It comes in three calibres: .22 Hornet, .222 Rem., and .223 Rem. All of these calibres have five-round detachable box magazines that slot into the gun just in front of the trigger guard. The cartridges are fed into the gun via the bolt action, which utilizes a 'micro-length Mauser-style action'. The barrels are hammer-forged, and all come in 60cm (23.6in).

Fixed sights

Although the 527 naturally can take optical sights, the standard factory-supplied sights are fixed (the same applies to the 527 FS and the 527 Carbine), and feature a hooded front sight with an open and adjustable rear sight. In competent hands, such sights, properly zeroed, will give accurate performance for those who hunt fast-moving species (such as wild boar) in close-range wooded environments.

In terms of woodwork, the 527 Luxe, FS and Carbine have Turkish walnut stocks cut with a Bavarian pattern. However, the 527 is available in several different formats. The Carbine version already mentioned can be chambered for 7.62 x 39mm, and is a lighter gun, weighing in the region of 2.7kg (5.9lb). The standard .223 Rem Luxe weighs 2.8kg (6.2lb). The Varmint, Prestige, and American models all have American-type Monte Carlo stocks and no fixed sights.

Within the Varmint subdivision – which makes available .17 Rem and .204 Ruger – is the standard walnut-stocked Varmint and the Varmint Kevlar, the latter having an 'H-S precision Kevlar composite stock with an aluminium bedding block' (as described on the CZ website). Another Varmint type is the Varmint Laminated, which features a grey laminate stock.

The CZ 527 Varmint has an American-style Turkish walnut stock and a five-round detachable box magazine.

The Varmint Kevlar has an ultra-tough Kevlar composite stock with an aluminium bedding block.

CZ 550

$

For those wanting a rifle with a heavier calibre than the CZ 527 range, the 550 rifles offer good options. Nine different models are currently offered, reaching from .22-250 to .458 Win Mag.

SPECIFICATIONS: **CZ 550 Safari Magnum**

CALIBRE: .375 H&H Mag, .416 Rigby, .458 Win Mag

BARREL LENGTH: 63.5cm (25in)

WEIGHT: up to 4.3kg (9.4lb)

SIGHTS: Express open sights

MECHANISM: bolt action, magazine fed

FEATURES: Express sights; Mauser action; three-round magazine

CZ 550 guns are suited to a wide range of prey, from small deer up to the largest big game.

The CZ 550 series has good core features. A Mauser-style action is used, with the reliable feed and extraction of Mauser's claw extractor. The trigger mechanism can be single stage or single set, and the barrels are hammer-forged. As with the CZ 527 range, the CZ 550 rifles are split between 'European' and 'American' styles, the former having open sights and Bavarian-style Mannlicher stocks, while the American weapons require optical sights and have more western Monte Carlo-style stocks. The calibres contained in the series are wide-ranging, and include .22-250, 6.5 x 55, .30-06, .243 Win, and .308 Win.

On safari

At the most formidable end of the 550 range are guns like the Safari Magnum. It is chambered for some of the powerhouse big-game rounds: .375 H&H Mag, .416 Rigby, and .458 Win Mag. Magazine capacity for such large rounds is capacious, with three Rigby cartridges able to fit in the magazine alone. (The magazine is of the fixed type.) Big-game hunting requires very fast reactions and quick range judgement, so the Safari Magnum has Express sights fitted, which have folding leaves to switch quickly between ranges.

The CZ 550 Ultimate Hunting Rifle (UHR) is now complementing weapons such as the Safari Magnum. This, in the words of CZ USA, is 'a new CZ 550 based rifle in .300 Winchester Magnum that comes in at 8lbs [3.6kg], and includes a minute of angle accuracy guarantee to 1000 yards [914m]'. Naturally, such accuracy is not achievable with open sights, so the UHR comes with a Nightforce 5.5-22 scope.

As with many CZ guns, the 550 comes in a variety of contrasting stock configurations. Here is the 550 Safari Magnum with a European-style stock (as opposed to the straight American stock).

Dakota Model 76

$$$–$$$$$

The Dakota Company was founded in 1984, and the first rifle that the company made was the Dakota 76. It remains in production today as a popular and accurate hunting rifle in several different grades.

SPECIFICATIONS: **Dakota Model 76 Classic**

CALIBRE: over 20 calibres from .22-250 Rem to .416 Rem

BARREL LENGTH: 53.3cm (21in) to 58.4cm (23in)

WEIGHT: average 3.4kg (7.5lb)

SIGHTS: open sights with provision for scope

MECHANISM: bolt action, magazine fed

FEATURES: Mauser-type extractor; three-position safety

The Dakota Model 76 range guns all have the same Mauser-type extractor system, which is known for the stable feeding and ejection of every round. In the Dakota design 'the extractor, underneath the locking lug and positioned at the end of the bolt, opens fully to insure that the next round feeds smoothly' (Dakota publicity). Dakota has also included a three-position safety. In this mechanism the bolt can be operated even with the safety on, something that is an advantage for a hunter wanting to prepare for a shot, but who does not want to remove the safety.

The Classic is chambered for a vast selection of popular cartridge types (too many to list here), everything from the .22-250 Rem and .243 Win up to the potent .375 H&H Mag and .416 Rem. Magazine capacity naturally varies depending upon the cartridge type, holding three to five rounds. Dakota also emphasizes custom options in all its rifles.

The Model 76 is available in either left- or right-handed versions, with short, standard, or long actions, and with several different styles of finish and woodwork.

African and Safari

Aside from the Classic grades, Dakota also produces the Model 76 in Safari and African grades. Both grades have open fixed sights (they also have all necessary scope-fitting rails), the open sights being popular amongst bush and safari hunters. The African grade has a 61cm (24in) barrel and comes in .257 Roberts to .416 Rem plus .338 Lapua, .404 Jeffery, .416 Rigby, and .450 Dakota, and has a cartridge capacity of four rounds in its drop-belly magazine. The Safari has the same calibre range, but is slightly lighter and has a 58.4cm (23in) barrel. Other differences centre on the wood type and quality.

The Dakota 76 is a premium-class hunting rifle built around a Mauser-type action.

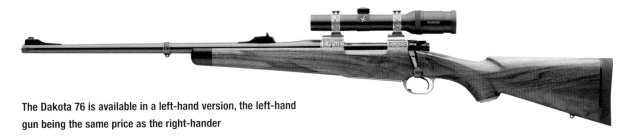

The Dakota 76 is available in a left-hand version, the left-hand gun being the same price as the right-hander

Dakota Model 97 Hunter

$$$

While the Model 76 stands as the defining Dakota bolt-action rifle, the Model 97 Hunter is a more affordable version that still incorporates many of the features of the 76.

SPECIFICATIONS: Dakota Model 97 Hunter

CALIBRE: from .25-06 Rem to .338 Win Mag	
BARREL LENGTH: 61cm (24in), 66cm (26in)	
WEIGHT: N/A	
SIGHTS: provision for scope	
MECHANISM: bolt action, magazine fed	
FEATURES: Mauser-type extractor; three-position safety	

The Model 97 Hunter shown here is in a stainless-steel finish with a fibreglass stock. As alternative to the synthetic stock, the Hunter is also available in English or Turkish walnut versions.

The Dakota website explains that the 'Model 97 Hunter was introduced in 1997 to reduce the base price on a Dakota'.

Despite the cost-reduction rationale, the Model 97 Hunter stands as a fine rifle in its own right, and the differences are as much to do with the economics of production as with design changes. The mechanical format is essentially the same between the two models.

Mauser extractor claw

The Model 97 has the Mauser-type extractor claw and the three-position safety of the 76. The trigger of the 97 is also fully adjustable. Dakota also states that 'We use the same barrels, walnut, oil finishing, bluing, checkering, break in, assembly range sight in, and rifle cases on both.' The differences lie more in fairly subtle details of machining around the receiver, although the bolt action has the same smooth travel.

Two versions

The Model 97 has two types: the Long-Range Hunter and the Deluxe Hunter. The Long-Range Hunter has a composite stock (XX Walnut is an option) whereas the Deluxe Hunter has a walnut stock as standard. Long-Range Hunter rifles also have free-floated barrel channels for enhanced distance accuracy. (The barrel lengths for both guns are either 61cm/24in or 66cm/26in.)

Calibres for the Model 97 are one of the many options facing a buyer of a Dakota rifle. At the smaller end of the range we have the .257 Roberts and .25-06 Rem, while at the other end of the scale there is the .300 and .338 Win Mag rounds. Various levels of wood upgrade are also optional, including fibreglass types.

Bolt-action catalogue

Dakota make several other types of bolt-action rifle. These include the small-calibre Predator, chambered in .20 and .223 calibres, and the Youth Hunter Rifle, specially designed for young shooters. Definitely not for youngsters is the Longbow Tactical Rifle, a military grade sniping/hunting rifle in .338 Lapua Mag.

Henry Acu-Bolt

$

While Henry's name is synonymous with under-lever rifles, it also produces small-calibre bolt-action rifles, its two main series being the Henry Mini Bolt .22 and the Acu-Bolt.

SPECIFICATIONS: **Henry Acu-Bolt**
CALIBRE: .17 HMR, .22 LR, .22 Mag
BARREL LENGTH: 51cm (20in)
WEIGHT: 1.9kg (4.25lb)
SIGHTS: x4 scope; Williams Fire Sights
MECHANISM: bolt action, single shot
FEATURES: Williams Fire Sights; stainless-steel barrel

The Acu-Bolt has a stainless-steel barrel and action set in a one-piece fibreglass stock.

The quality of Henry's bolt-action rifles is attested to by the fact that the Mini Bolt .22 is the Official Youth Rifle of the Olympic USA Shooting Team. The Acu-Bolt has a similar level of quality both in terms of finish and performance. It is a single-shot weapon, chambered for .22 LR, .22 Mag and .17 HMR. The bolt is made of stainless steel and has a very smooth feed. Acu-Bolt guns have semi-heavy stainless-steel 51cm (20in) barrels and the guns are known for being extremely accurate, hence they can appeal as much to target shooters as to field shooters.

They are also very light – average weight is 1.9kg (4.25lb). The weight makes the Acu-Bolt an ideal weapon for extended sessions of field shooting against small game (rabbits, hares, gophers, foxes, etc), and also for use by small-framed shooters or youngsters.

Sighting

Of course, a rifle is only as accurate as its sights. The Acu-Bolt includes a x4 scope as part of the package, this being mounted to the gun using a cantilever scope mount. However, it is also fitted with Williams Fire Sights for those not wanting to use a full-scale optical sight. The Williams sight consists of a rear peep sight and a luminous red front bead. The picture through the peep sight is aligned with the front bead, and used well such sights provide an extremely high degree of accuracy.

The Acu-Bolt is very durable. The fibreglass synthetic stock is of one piece and features a comfortable beavertail fore-end. Checkering on both the pistol grip and the fore-end give a steady grip.

Henry Big Boy

$

The Henry rifle is embedded in the history of the early United States, and the Henry Repeating Arms Company has revisited this history in its series of Big Boy lever-action guns.

SPECIFICATIONS: **Henry Big Boy**

CALIBRE: .357 Mag, .44 Mag, .45 Colt	
BARREL LENGTH: 51cm (20in)	
WEIGHT: 3.9kg (8.68lb)	
SIGHTS: open	
MECHANISM: lever action, magazine fed	
FEATURES: solid brass receiver; open sights	

The Henry Big Boy is so named after its calibres. While Henry's Golden Boy lever-action rifles are in various .22 and .17 calibres, and so meet the needs of varmint hunters, the Big Boy range is in .44 Magnum, .45 Colt, and .357 Magnum. These calibres make the Big Boy a serious rifle. Henry's website describes three particular groups who might be interested in the Big Boy: Wild West history enthusiasts, those who involve themselves in Cowboy Action Shooting, and big-game hunters.

Heavy build

The modern-day Henry Company has invested the Big Boy with historical authenticity. It has a 51cm (20in) octagonal barrel and a solid brass receiver. The latter, as Henry points out, means that the Big Boy 'is the first American made .44 Henry lever action featuring a solid brass receiver since the original Henry rifle of 1860'. (A brass barrel band and a brass butt plate are also standard features.)

A tubular magazine holds 10 of the .44 Mag rounds, giving the Big Boy serious game-shooting power. Press reviews of the Big Boy have noted how smooth and reliable the action is, with positive loading through an easy flick of the under-lever. Ejection is via a side port. Loading the Big Boy involves removing the brass loading tube, dropping in the rounds, and then replacing the tube.

Sights on the Big Boy consist of an adjustable marble semi-buckhorn rear sight with white diamond insert and brass beaded front sight. These sights give a good level of accuracy over around 50m (164ft). There are no scope mountings on the receiver, but Henry also sells cantilever scope mounts.

The Henry Big Boy will appeal to Wild West re-enactors but also to those simply wanting a heavy-duty field gun.

The Big Boy is a visually striking firearm, with a solid top brass receiver set between an American walnut stock and fore-end.

Heym Express Magnum

$$$$

The name of the Heym Express Magnum tells all there is to know about this gun – it is designed to handle the heaviest cartridges and take on the largest of the big-game creatures.

SPECIFICATIONS: Heym Express Magnum

CALIBRE: 19 different calibres from .300 Win Mag to .600 Nitro Express	
BARREL LENGTH: 61cm (24in)	
WEIGHT: 4.5kg (9.9lb)	
SIGHTS: fixed Express leaf sights; drilled and tapped for scope mount	
MECHANISM: bolt action, magazine fed	
FEATURES: bolt handle forms third lug; takes very heavy rounds	

Heym Waffenfabrik AG was formed in the 1860s and over its 150-year existence has specialized in hunting rifles and combination guns. Its combination-gun range has included many weapons beyond the usual one-smoothbore, one-rifled barrel set of typical combination weapons. Examples include the Heym 33 triple-barrelled gun (two smoothbore and one rifled) and the Model 37V quadruple-barrelled 'Vierling' gun (two smoothbore set side by side, with two rifled barrels stacked beneath). However, the Express Magnum is a more traditional single-barrel bolt-action rifle, based around a Mauser-type action.

Massive calibres

The Express Magnum is chambered in the largest practical big-game rounds known. These begin with the well-known cartridges such as the .300 Win Mag but then rise up to the .450 Rigby, the .500 Jeffrey, and even the prodigious .600 Nitro Express. (There has been a vogue over recent years to resurrect some of history's most formidable game calibres.) Big-game hunting has wandered towards such heavy shells because shots are often taken at close range and without time for considered aim – heavy shells give the greatest guarantee of a decisive take-down through their huge penetrative power.

The Express Magnum's bolt is of a two-lug locking design, with the bolt handle acting as a third lug when the bolt is closed. The magazine holds four or five rounds depending on the calibre. Fixed Express leaf sights and fixed front bead are provided as standard, but the receiver is also drilled and tapped for a scope mount. Big-game guns are necessarily heavy because they need substantial barrels, actions, and stocks to handle the recoil. The Express Magnum weighs in at around 4.5kg (9.9lb).

The solidity of the barrel and the action are evident in this photograph, and are necessary to handle the safari cartridges.

Heym SR21 Series

$$$

More and more hunting rifles, like the Heym SR21, are being offered today with interchangeable barrel units, thereby giving the owner several different rifles built around the same gun.

SPECIFICATIONS: **Heym SR21N**

CALIBRE: varies according to barrel/receiver unit used

BARREL LENGTH: 58cm (22.8in)

WEIGHT: N/A

SIGHTS: fixed sights; drilled and tapped for scope mount

MECHANISM: bolt action, magazine fed

FEATURES: interchangeable barrel/receiver unit

A close-up of the bolt-action system on the SR21 shows the three-position side-swing safety catch.

The SR21 series guns are in many ways fairly conventional, although extremely well-built, hunting rifles. They are bolt-action magazine-fed rifles that utilize a three-lug locking system on the bolt. (Heym publicity emphasizes the quietness of the bolt operation, something particularly important to any hunter of wily animals, such as deer.) In terms of sights, open sights are provided as standard fitment. These consist of a semi-buckhorn rear sight and a height-adjustable front sight. Depending on the calibre of rounds used, the detachable magazine will hold from two to five cartridges. A very positive three-position side-swing safety catch is set just behind the bolt handle at the end of the bolt sleeve, with a red dot and a white dot signifying the fire/safe positions. When the gun is cocked, the bolt handle also slots deeply into the stock woodwork for further secure lockup.

Barrel units

The versatility of the SR21 series is on account of its interchangeable barrel/receiver units. The receiver and barrel together are changed as single units, this ensuring that each barrel and action is totally suited to the calibre fired. The interchangeable barrel facility allows the SR21 to come in several different models and numerous different calibres. The calibres start at .22-250 Rem and climb up to 9.3 x 62. Stocks on the SR21s are of Monte Carlo styling and either left- or right-handed versions are available. Barrel length is set at 58cm (22.8in) for the N model and 61cm (24in) for the G model, and the overall length of the gun – depending on the type of barrel/receiver unit fitted – is around 111cm (43.7in).

Interchangeable barrel units allows the hunter to switch calibres to suit the target type.

Howa M1500 Series

$

The Howa M1500 series is a popular range of hunting rifles from the Howa Machinery Company Ltd, Japan. The company also makes barrels and receivers for Weatherby rifles.

SPECIFICATIONS: Howa M1500 Ultralight Mountain	
CALIBRE: .243 Win, .308 Win, 7mm-08	
BARREL LENGTH: 51cm (20in)	
WEIGHT: 2.9kg (6.4lb)	
SIGHTS: provided with scope mountings	
MECHANISM: bolt action, magazine fed	
FEATURES: three-position safety; barrelled actions available	

This Howa M1500 has been customized with a thumbhole stock and a bipod.

The Model 1500 rifles span the $500 to $800 price band, but their affordability is accompanied by the serious respect of the gun press. Reviews have noted the rifles' fine accuracy and user-friendly operation. One advantage of the series is that they can simply be bought as barrelled actions so that the shooter can customize the stock fittings to suit. However, outside these barrelled actions there are six basic types of M1500s: Lightning, Hunter, Ultralight, Varmint, Supreme, and the Howa/Hogue. Each type is available in blued or stainless-steel action, and some of the models have sub-models within them.

The action is common to all models. This consists of a twin-lug bolt with a large extractor claw. The barrel is free-floating and the magazine, which features a hinged floor plate, is loaded with cartridges through the receiver.

Hunting gun

A standard model of M1500 is the Lightning, available in calibres .204 Ruger, .223, .22-250, .243 Win, .25-06, 6.5 x 55, .270 Win, .308 Win, .30-06, 7mm Rem Mag, .300 Win Mag, .338 Win Mag, .270 WSM, and 7mm WSM. Two different barrel lengths, a 56cm (22in) and a 61cm (24in) for the magnum calibres, are sold.

It has a composite stock with a Realtree camo option and is provided with scope rings and bases (fixed sights are an option). All Model 1500s feature a three-position safety switch. This has the usual on and off positions, plus a second on position in which the bolt cannot be opened.

Stock variants

The M1500 Hunter rifles have traditional American walnut stocks, while the Ultralight Mountain and Ultralight Youth models are reduced-weight versions. Varmint models have heavy 61cm (24in) hammer-forged barrels, the Supreme guns have various laminated wood stocks, and the new Howa/Hogue features a Howa action married to a Hogue OverMolded™ stock.

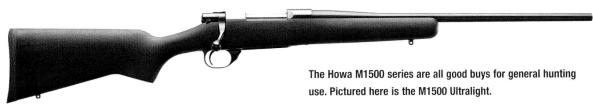

The Howa M1500 series are all good buys for general hunting use. Pictured here is the M1500 Ultralight.

Kimber 17 and 22 Rifles

$

Kimber's rimfire rifles offer a serious range of hunting weapons for rabbits, foxes, and other light game, but also have models purposely designed for target-competition sports.

SPECIFICATIONS: **Kimber 17 and 22 Hunter**

CALIBRE: .17 Mach, .22 LR	
BARREL LENGTH: 56cm (22in)	
WEIGHT: approx 2.95kg (6.5lb)	
SIGHTS: receiver drilled and tapped for scope mountings	
MECHANISM: bolt action, magazine fed	
FEATURES: three-position safety; free-floating barrel	

Kimber has eight rimfire bolt-action models in its collection – Hunter, Classic, Classic Varmint, Pro Varmint, Custom Classic, SuperAmerica, SVT, and HS. The Hunter is the bedrock of the series, available in either .17 Mach or .22 LR.

The action is a classic Mauser-type claw extractor backed by a match-grade chamber and a free-floated match-grade 56cm (22in) barrel. Such features almost guarantee a superb standard of accuracy, and are reflected in the price tag of around $800. No fixed sights are provided, and the receiver is drilled and tapped ready for a scope mount. A three-position wing switch provides safety.

Versatile range

The Hunter has many of the features of the other guns in the series. The Classic and Custom Classic have significant wood upgrades with AA- and AAA-grade walnut respectively. SuperAmerica models also have the AAA-grade walnut with a hand-rubbed oil finish, but also introduce finer checkering, an ebony fore-end tip and a polished blue finish. The Varmint models both have stainless-steel heavy fluted barrels (the Pro Varmint's flutes are black and the gun has a grey laminated stock). SVT stands for SuperVarmint/Target, and this high-quality rifle has a shorter 46cm (18.25in) stainless-steel barrel and a dramatically raised comb section on the stock for the serious target shooter.

Finally, the HS, which stands for Hunter Silhouette, is, in the words of the company, 'specifically designed for the demanding NRA Rimfire Silhouette Competition and can only be comfortably fired from a standing position'. The Kimber range offers a sound, high-quality investment for those wanting many years of service from their rimfire weapon.

Kimber produces some of the finest-quality rimfire rifles on the market. Here the shooter takes careful aim with the classic Hunter model.

Kimber Model 84M Classic

$–$$

A good hunting rifle for light- to medium-sized game should not be excessively heavy, or it will become a burden during a long day's shoot. The Kimber 84M is purposely designed to be easy to transport.

SPECIFICATIONS: **Kimber Model 84M Classic**

CALIBRE: 22-250 Rem, .243 Win, .260 Rem, 7mm-08 Rem, .308 Win	
BARREL LENGTH: 56cm (22in)	
WEIGHT: approx 2.6kg (5.8lb)	
SIGHTS: scope	
MECHANISM: bolt action, magazine fed	
FEATURES: three-position safety; free-floating barrel	

The Classic model is the Model 84M standard, and this weighs in at only 2.6kg (5.8lb). It is chambered for .22-250 Rem, .243 Win, .260 Rem, 7mm-08 Rem, and .308 Win, the calibres giving the 84M range a versatility from foxes through to deer and moose. The barrel length is 56cm (22in) and its overall length is 105cm (41.25in). Many of the features of the 84M are found in other Kimber rifles. It has the three-position safety switch that controls the cocking mechanism itself. There is an internal box magazine with a floor-plate release. The gun's action is the full-length Mauser claw extractor, which has gone down in history as one of the most reliable bolt-action mechanisms, and it is also bedded on aluminium pillars and fibreglass. Accuracy features include a free-floating barrel and a match-

grade trigger unit (this has a factory-set pull weight of 1.6–1.8kg/3.5–4lb). There are no fixed sights, just provision for a scope fitting on the receiver.

Multiple versions

The 84M is available in eight other versions besides the Classic – the Select Grade, SuperAmerica, Montana, Varmint, LongMaster Classic, ProVarmint, SVT, and LongMaster VT. Many of these models are defined by upgraded stock-wood quality or differences in stock finish/type. The Varmint and LongMaster guns have fluted stainless-steel barrels. Weight increases accompany some of the models beyond the Classic.

The LongMaster VT (Varmint/Target), for example, has a 66cm (26in) barrel and an overall length of 115.5cm (45.5in). With its walnut or kevlar/carbon-fibre stock, the LongMaster VT weighs a hefty 4.54kg (10lb), which makes it more suited to static long-range shooting rather than woodland snap shooting.

With an adjustable trigger and match-grade chamber, the Model 84M is designed to provide total shooting confidence.

Kimber Model 8400

$$

Kimber 8400 rifles are chambered in some of the most popular rifle hunting calibres, and break down into two categories – Winchester Short Magnum (WSM) or Standard and Magnum.

SPECIFICATIONS: Kimber 8400 Standard and Magnum Montana

CALIBRE: .25-06 Rem, .270 Win, .30-06, .300 Win Mag, .338 Win Mag

BARREL LENGTH: 61cm (24in), 66cm (26in)

WEIGHT: approx 3kg (6.6lb)

SIGHTS: provision for scope

MECHANISM: bolt action, magazine fed

FEATURES: kevlar composite stock; match-grade barrels, triggers and chambers

The WSM family of rounds are, as their name suggests, high-power rounds with short cartridge bodies. They are very accurate and powerful rounds (although the international jury is still out as to whether they offer any significant benefit over other standard rounds), but because of their dimensions

All barrels, chambers and triggers on the 8400 series are match grade in quality and performance.

they can work in rifles with short actions. The four WSM calibres are: .270 WSM, 7mm WSM, .300 WSM, and .325 WSM.

The first three categories will handle targets up to deer and antelope (although shots at extreme long range are better taken with standard magnum rounds), while the new .325 can take on large safari game or moose.

Magnum power

The Model 8400 WSM guns (Classic, Select Grade, SuperAmerica, and Montana) have Mauser actions and are available in all the WSM calibres. The Classic has a 61cm (24in) barrel, weighs approximately 3kg (6.6lb) and has a match-grade chamber. Different wood finishes define the other guns, while the Montana is fitted out with a grey kevlar composite stock.

The guns in the 8400 Standard and Magnum categories move away from the WSM calibres for more common cartridges. The Classic is chambered for .25-06 Rem, .270 Win, .30-06, .300 Win Mag, and .338 Win Mag. While the standard-calibre guns have 61cm (24in) barrels, the magnum guns take the barrel length up to 66cm (26in). Pachmayr® Decelerator® recoil pads are fitted to cushion against recoil. The Montana version is fitted with the kevlar composite stock option described above, whereas the SuperAmerica rifle has Grade AAA walnut. The capacity of the magazine, depending on the gun and the calibre, is four or five rounds. Prices for the 8400 series range from $1000 to $2000.

Krico Model 301

$

Krico is a German company with a history of firearms production reaching back into the nineteenth century, and in the years after World War II, it developed into a respected manufacturer of hunting rifles.

SPECIFICATIONS: **Krico Model 301**

CALIBRE: .17 HMR, .22 LR, .22 WRFM, .22 Hornet, .222 Rem	
BARREL LENGTH: 57cm (22.5in)	
WEIGHT: 3.2kg (7lb)	
SIGHTS: open sights; drilled and tapped for scope mount	
MECHANISM: bolt action, magazine fed	
FEATURES: adjustable open sights; hand-finished stock	

The Model 301 is a small-calibre bolt-action rifle, which is available in a range of popular .22 and .17 calibres: .17 HMR, .22 LR, .22 WRFM, .22 Hornet, and .222 Rem. The standard under-action magazine holds five rounds, but an optional 10-round magazine is also available. A 57cm (22.5in) barrel is standard, and the barrel is noticeably heavy for a small-gauge gun. For this reason the Model 301 covers several bases in terms of its possible use. It would be a highly accurate hunting rifle, robust enough to cope with the rigours of outdoor use, while it could also be used as a competition rifle for target shooting. Naturally, opting to use it for the latter requires different sights. An out-of-the-box 301 is equipped with open sights – a fixed front post and a rear sight featuring windage and elevation adjustment. However, it is also drilled and tapped to mount a scope. Single or double set triggers are available for the gun.

Standards of finish

The finish of the Model 301 is of a very high quality. The stock is cut in the curved Bavarian style frequently seen in German and Austrian guns, with the comb curving slightly downwards along its length. A cheek swelling on the stock also gives the shooter a very solid gun-to-face fit, although the stocks may need some alteration to fit individual shooters properly. The fore-end is of the Schnabel type, and the overall look of the gun is extremely slim and yet well balanced. Hand-finishing techniques bring out the grain of the walnut.

Krico makes a wide range of hunting and sporting firearms, including the Model 401 target/varmint rifle, the Model 902 hunting rifle (calibres up to .300 Win Mag), and several match firearms.

Although it is equipped with open sights as standard, a scope will bring out this gun's full potential.

The Krico 301 has a quality build throughout, particularly in its fine woodwork. There is also an option of having the rifle fitted with double set triggers.

Mannlicher Classic

$$–$$$

This fine hunting rifle is from the Steyr Mannlicher Company of Austria, one of Europe's premier producers of military and civilian firearms throughout the twentieth century to the present day.

SPECIFICATIONS: **Mannlicher Classic Full Stock**

CALIBRE: 11 calibres from .223 Rem to 9.3 x 62mm	
BARREL LENGTH: 51cm (20in)	
WEIGHT: approx 3.3kg (7.3lb)	
SIGHTS: fixed open sights; provision for scope	
MECHANISM: bolt action, magazine fed	
FEATURES: Safe Bolt System	

The Mannlicher Classic is seen here in the Full Stock version, which has the fore-end reaching right up the muzzle. One advantage of this is that the shooter can rest the fore-end on objects further away without scratching the barrel.

The name Mannlicher has almost as much of a cachet in European firearms history as the name Mauser, and although the guns have changed significantly, the quality of the firearms has not. The Classic is one of Steyr Mannlicher's premier hunting rifles.

High-level accuracy

The Classic rifle has received some excellent responses in the shooting press, especially for the great accuracy achievable with just the factory-fitted iron sights. These sights consist of nothing more than a simple ramp front sight and a V-notch rear sight, adjustable for windage and elevation. The reviewers also note the gun's total reliability, with a conspicuous lack of any sort of malfunction during rigorous test firings.

The Classic firearms feature Steyr Mannlicher's Safe Bolt System (SBS) as standard fitment. A bushing completely surrounds the bolt head, so that when the gun is locked the user has a further layer of protection from chamber gases. The body of the bolt also features an 'ice and residue groove' that prevents bolt bind in freezing, icy conditions. Both are welcome features for the serious shooter.

Three styles

The Mannlicher Classic is available in a particularly wide spectrum of calibres, from .223 Rem up to 9.3 x 62mm. The magazine capacity is four rounds for standard calibres, one less for magnum calibres. Styles of stock available for the Classic are Half Stock, Full Stock, and Mountain.

The Half Stock has a traditional layout, with the fore-end extending only halfway along the barrel. It also comes in two barrel lengths – 60cm (23.6in) and 65cm (25.6in) – the longer barrel reserved for rifles firing magnum rounds.

The Full Stock version runs the woodwork right to the muzzle in a traditional German style and has a shorter barrel, while the Mountain version has the Half Stock layout but with the shorter barrel of the Full Stock version.

Mannlicher Pro Hunter

$

'Undestroyable' is rarely a word you hear used about any gun. Steyr Mannlicher, however, use it in their publicity to describe parts of the Pro Hunter series of bolt-action rifles.

SPECIFICATIONS: Mannlicher Pro Hunter

CALIBRE: 14 calibres from .222 Rem to .300 Win Mag	
BARREL LENGTH: 60cm (23.6in), 65cm (25.6in)	
WEIGHT: up to 3.7kg (8.2lb)	
SIGHTS: provision for scope	
MECHANISM: bolt action, magazine fed	
FEATURES: Safe Bolt System; stock adjustable for LOP	

The Pro Hunter is a very modern rifle, which utilizes the latest in stock technology. A set of butt spacers is included to alter the length of pull.

The Pro Hunter is a serious range of rifles for tough outdoor use. All parts of the weapons are designed for both high accuracy in the final shot and for durability against environmental conditions. They are fitted out with a synthetic black or grey stock that is impervious to wet and cold (the stock can be reinforced with fibreglass as an option for additional cost). Stock stability is extremely important in a hunting rifle, because any warping in the stock material can affect the true straightness of the barrel or the seating of the action.

The length of pull (LOP) of the stock can also be adjusted simply by adding or removing the provided stock spacers – these take the LOP from around 32cm (12.8in) out to 35cm (13.8in). The magazine is made of a synthetic material, and a high-capacity 10-round adaptor is available for this. Regarding the word 'undestroyable', Steyr Mannlicher use it to refer to the 'matte metal surface finish [that] guarantees perfect anti-corrosion protection, as well as enhanced durability against mechanical strain'.

Stainless option

The Pro Hunter makes enough promises as to its durability without giving cause for concern, but a stainless-steel barrel option is available for those who want the ultimate in weather-defiance. Regarding its performance, the Pro Hunter is known for its solid four-lug locking and the crispness of its trigger pulls (the trigger is of a direct type, with a set trigger as an option).

Calibre options are typically wide, from .222 Rem up to .300 Win Mag. The barrel length of the standard calibre is 60cm (23.6in), while for the magnum calibres another 5cm (2in) of barrel length is added.

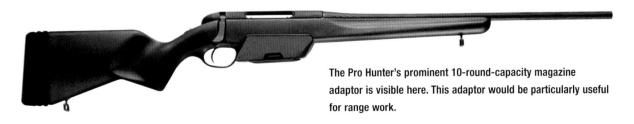

The Pro Hunter's prominent 10-round-capacity magazine adaptor is visible here. This adaptor would be particularly useful for range work.

Marlin XLR Series

$

Lever-action rifles are a traditional type of firearm that still have great popularity, particularly in the United States. Now a new ammunition type may fertilize that popularity even more.

SPECIFICATIONS: **Marlin 1895MXLR**

CALIBRE: .450 Marlin

BARREL LENGTH: 61cm (24in)

SIGHTS: fixed front and rear; tapped for scope mount

WEIGHT: up to 3.2kg (7lb)

MECHANISM: lever action, magazine fed

FEATURES: LEVERevolution ammunition; precision-fluted bolt

A long-standing concern about the use of lever-action guns lies in the way that the rounds are stacked bullet tip to primer. Pointed-tip bullets for lever-action guns have been generally avoided by manufacturers because of the danger of magazine chain fire, in which a bullet detonates the primer of the cartridge in front, thus setting off a highly destructive chain reaction.

However, the Hornady Company has developed the LEVERevolution, Flex-Tip™ rounds, designed specifically for lever-action guns. These are traditional Spitzer (pointed) rounds with a flexible red elastomer polymer tip that bends against the round in front of it during recoil or jarring, but immediately returns to shape for firing.

Terminal ballistic performance is also excellent, with little to distinguish the penetration and expansion capabilities from those of conventional ammunition. The availability of the new ammunition means that the under-lever rifle can now be used with confidence on a wider range of prey, including deer, bear and moose.

Traditional and modern

Marlin's XLR is, in the words of the company, 'built to take full advantage of the improvements gained with Hornady's new LEVEREVOLUTION ammunition'. Four models are offered, based on calibre: the 336XLR (.30/30), 444XLR (.444 Marlin), 1895XLR (.45/70 Gov't), and the 1895MXLR (.450 Marlin).

Taking the last of these as a typical example, we have a 61cm (24in) stainless-steel barrel with the lever-action feeding in from a four-round magazine. A precision-fluted bolt provides for reliable locking and ejection. Sights are an adjustable semi-buckhorn folding rear sight, with a brass-beaded hooded ramp front sight, as well as provision for a scope. Cartridges are side-ejected. In highly attractive wood finishes, the XLR series will very much appeal to the shooter who wants to blend tradition, modernity, and straight-up killing power.

The 1895XLR's under-barrel magazine takes four rounds of .450 Marlin. The gun also features quick-detachable swivel studs set just beneath the stock and at the front of the fore-end. For around $700 it is a good-value gun.

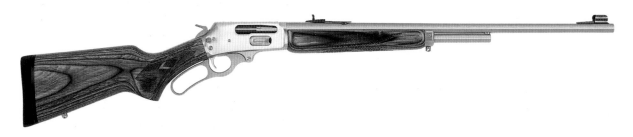

Marlin Model 980S

$

The .22 Long Rifle (LR) round is popular amongst new and experienced shooters alike, and the Marlin Model 980S is an excellent rimfire gun for basic pest control and hunting.

SPECIFICATIONS: Marlin Model 980S

CALIBRE: .22 LR	
BARREL LENGTH: 56cm (22in)	
WEIGHT: 2.7kg (6lb)	
SIGHTS: fixed front and rear; drilled and tapped for scope mount	
MECHANISM: bolt action, magazine fed	
FEATURES: T-900 Fire Control System	

Marlin produces an especially broad range of small-gauge rifles, and the quality of these firearms means the company commands strong sectors of the market. Its guns include automatic-loading .17 and .22 rifles such as the Model 60, Model 7000 and Model 717M2, a classic lever-action .22, the Golden 39A, and the rifle featured here, the Model 980S. This is a bolt-action rifle chambered only for .22 LR, the gun being fed from a seven-shot nickel-plated clip magazine. A thumb-operated switch provides safety, and the gun also has a red cocking indicator.

Fire Control System

Marlin rimfire rifles now all feature the T-900 Fire Control System, which Marlin promotes as an exceptional new trigger-system improvement over existing models. It has a wide, serrated trigger for positive trigger contact, a crisp single-stage trigger pull and a safety that acts upon the trigger itself.

The 980S is a budget gun from Marlin that has features more common on higher-end rifles. These features include an excellent trigger system, weatherproof stock and Micro-Groove® rifling.

Working gun

The 980S has much to recommend it in terms of operation, and of finish. Standards of finish are especially important in any sporting gun, as these weapons are generally exposed to harsh weather conditions. The stock, which features a Monte Carlo cheek piece, is fashioned from a black fibreglass-filled synthetic material, while the 56cm (22in) barrel is made of stainless steel.

The barrel features Micro-Groove® rifling that gives the gun great accuracy over the 100m (328ft) practical range of the rimfire round. Sights on the barrel are an adjustable semi-buckhorn folding rear sight corresponding with a ramped front sight (with an orange front sight post), and cutaway Wide-Scan™ hood.

The 980S overall is a compact gun, measuring 104cm (41in). Its weight is also kept to a manageable level – approximately 2.7kg (6lb). Nickel-plated swivel studs are also provided.

Value

One of the appealing factors about the 980S is its price. In its basic format it has an RRP of around $330, which makes it affordable on most budgets.

Mauser M98

$–$$

Many of the guns in this chapter are indebted to the Mauser 98 action. It is probably the finest general bolt-action operating system ever designed, known for its robust reliability.

SPECIFICATIONS: **Mauser M98 Basic**

CALIBRE: multiple calibres between .22-250 Rem and 9.3 x 62

BARREL LENGTH: 60cm (23.6in)

WEIGHT: 3.5kg (7.75lb)

SIGHTS: Express rear; brass bead front

MECHANISM: bolt action, magazine fed

FEATURES: classic Mauser action; three-position wing safety

Despite its venerable origins, the Mauser M98 is still a first-rate hunting rifle.

Paul Mauser's journey to create history's greatest bolt-action mechanism began in the 1880s, and on 5 April 1898 the design of his 8 x 57 Model 98 rifle was finally approved for official production. The Model 1898 went on to equip the German army through the two World Wars, and in total around 100 million rifles with Mauser 98 actions have been produced to the present day.

The current Model 98 brings with it the full weight of the Mauser tradition. Unlike the original 98, it is available in almost every mainstream calibre from .22-250 Rem through to 9.3 x 62. Mauser also makes clear that other calibres not listed can be manufactured upon request. The basic gun has a three-lug bolt, the action being machined out of one piece of solid high-grade steel. It is also fitted with a three-position wing safety switch.

The rear sights are of the Express type, with a brass bead front sight. The barrel length is 60cm (23.6in), which contributes to an overall length of 113cm (44.5in).

Magnum option

Mauser actions are extremely solid, and they have been used on some of the world's great big-game guns. With this in mind Mauser have also brought out the Model 98 Magnum. This is chambered for .375 H&H, .338 Lapua Mag, .416 Rigby, .450 Dakota, .458 Lott, and .500 Jeffrey. A Rigby-style peep sight is standard, matched by a Safari front sight with a white-enamel inlet to give a visible sight in low-light shooting.

The woodwork on the M98 is rosewood, and it is hand-finished with oil rubbing to give the wood a deep lustre.

Merkel KR1

$$$

The Merkel company is best known for its shotguns and break-barrel guns. Now it has introduced an advanced bolt-action gun into its range – the KR1 – which is already receiving extremely favourable reviews in the shooting press.

SPECIFICATIONS: **Merkel KR1**

CALIBRE: 13 different calibres from .243 Win to .300 Win

BARREL LENGTH: 51.5cm (20.25in), 56.6cm (22.25in), 61.5cm (24.25in)

WEIGHT: approx 2.9kg (6.38lb) depending on calibre

SIGHTS: mounting for scope

MECHANISM: bolt action, magazine fed

FEATURES: switch-barrel facility

The principal selling point of the KR1 is its calibre-change options. Barrel groups can be switched easily to shift calibres from standard rounds such as the .243 Win up to magnum cartridges like the .300 Win Mag and the .300 WSM. The barrel is secured into place with just two hex screws, making the change of barrels straightforward and uncomplicated. The magazine box insert is also changed with the barrel to ensure reliable round feed.

Currently the KR1 can take 13 different calibres, separated into three classes: standard, magnum and extended range.

One of the problems traditionally associated with switch-barrel guns is that the changeover affects the accuracy of the sight. Merkel has worked hard, however, to ensure that the scope mounting is very solid to minimize disruption, although it is probably more advisable to have a scope mount for each barrel to ensure maximum accuracy.

Accurate shot

The KR1 follows a fairly standard bolt-action layout, with a rotary-head bolt featuring six locking lugs turning into the barrel extension. A locking housing wraps around the receiver to protect the mechanism from the ingress of dirt. The gun also has a single set trigger that gives extremely crisp performance whether the set is used or not. In terms of shooting performance, the KR1 has produced very impressive groupings under test conditions, with groups of under 2.5cm (1in) at 200m (656ft).

The Merkel KT1's barrel-switch facility is likely to make it a popular firearm. It comes in three grades of finish (Standard, Premium, Luxury) and 13 calibres.

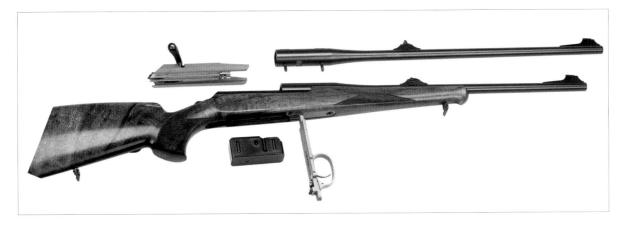

Remington Model Five

$

Remington's Model Five is a new rimfire addition to the Remington catalogue. Introduced in 2006, the Model Five is a five-shot weapon chambered for .22 LR and .22 WMR.

SPECIFICATIONS: **Remington Model Five**

CALIBRE: .22 LR, .22 WMR
BARREL LENGTH: 56cm (22in)
WEIGHT: up to 3.1kg (6.75lb)
SIGHTS: open sights as standard; receiver grooved for scope
MECHANISM: bolt action, magazine fed
FEATURES: detachable magazine

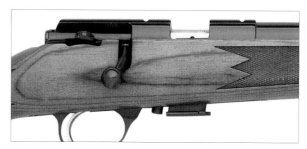

The Remington Model Five has a detachable magazine that carries five rounds of .22 ammunition.

Despite the emotional power of a large centrefire rifle, rimfire weapons remain extremely popular across the world. A .22 rimfire round, depending on the type, will give a good hunting performance out to a maximum of 100m (328ft). In addition, it has the advantage of being cheap to purchase. In countries that have strict firearms licensing laws, it is much easier to obtain a .22 rimfire weapon than is the case with a centrefire gun.

Powerful round

Remington markets the Model Five as 'a solid choice for the seasoned small-game hunters and target shooters, and beginners alike', covering many bases with one weapon. It is chambered for two different popular .22 calibres – .22 LR and .22 WMR. The former is better known for its qualities than the latter. The .22 Winchester Magnum Rimfire (WMR) adds greater power than the .22 LR – it carries a higher velocity and much greater terminal energy.

In fact, its power precludes its use against small game at close ranges, as these animals will probably be blown apart by the shock waves.

The Model Five holds five .22 rounds in its detachable box magazine, which sits in front of the trigger guard. It has a 56cm (22in) blued barrel and an overall length of 103.5cm (40.75in). The bolt action is the same one that Remington uses on many of its centrefire rifles, and gives a smooth and trouble-free performance (with all the proper cleaning and maintenance).

The stock is of a brown laminate, and it is fitted with a basic rubber recoil pad. Open sights are standard, with an adjustable rear sight, but the receiver is also grooved to take a scope.

The overall design of the Remington Model Five is classic and clean. The stock is fitted with a basic recoil pad, although recoil from the .22 rounds is minimal anyway.

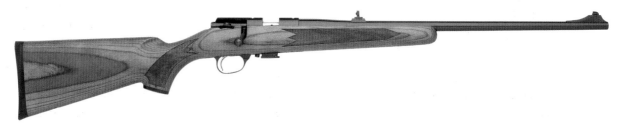

Remington Model 700

$–$$

The Model 700 denotes an extensive series of bolt-action rifles from Remington, all centrefire weapons in a variety of popular calibres and with price tags to suit most wallets.

SPECIFICATIONS: Remington Model 700 BDL

CALIBRE: .17 Rem, .222 Rem, .223 Rem, .22-250 Rem, .243 Win, .25-06 Rem, .270 Win, 7mm Rem Mag, 7mm Rem Ultra Mag, .30-06, .300 Win Mag, .300 Rem Ultra Mag

BARREL LENGTH: 56cm (22in), 61cm (24in), 66cm (26in)

WEIGHT: up to 3.45kg (7.6lb)

SIGHTS: receiver drilled and tapped for scope mount

MECHANISM: bolt action, magazine fed

FEATURES: hinged quick-release magazine floor plate; ramp front sight

The Model 700 range goes up to some heavy-duty safari weapons firing up to .375 H&H Mag.

The Model 700 is a venerable series of rifles, having laid its foundations back in the 1950s. It has since become one of the world's most popular brands of bolt-action rifle, and has been produced literally in the millions. The Model 700 BDL serves well to introduce the series. It is a magazine-fed bolt-action gun in calibres designed to meet the most popular of hunting requirements. Calibres currently listed on the Remington website include .17 Remington, .222 and .223 Remington, .243 Winchester, 7mm Rem Mag, .30-06, and .300 Rem Ultra Mag. The gun's

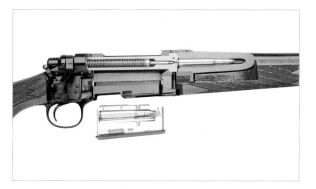

A cutaway diagram showing the Model 700's action, with the barrel lugs locked into place.

bolt action is fed from a magazine that features a hinged quick-release floor plate, and which holds five rounds of the smallest calibre down to three rounds of the .300 Rem Ultra Mag. The whole design is structured around strength and reliability. The receiver is, in Remington's words, 'machined from solid-steel bar stock resulting in uniformity and strength' and the firm also points out that the 'recessed bolt face locks up inside the counter-bored breech of the barrel, which is surrounded by the receiver, forming "three rings of steel" enclosing the cartridge case head for unparalleled strength'. American walnut woodwork gives the Model 700 BDL a classic appearance.

Every hunter

Model 700 rifles are produced in enough varieties to suit almost every hunting requirement. At the time of writing, models listed include the Model 700 Mountain Rifle DM (the DM standing for 'Detachable Magazine'), the Model 700 SPS (Special Purpose Synthetic) with an ergonomically improved synthetic stock and a recoil-reducing R3® stock pad, and the Model 700 Sendero SF II, which has, amongst other features, a 66cm (26in) heavy-contour barrel, which is fluted to assist rapid barrel cooling.

Remington Model 798

$

In the Model 798, Remington re-creates a rifle built around the classic Mauser 98 action, one of the most successful bolt-action types in history, known for its easy-working reliability.

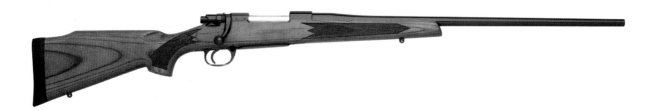

SPECIFICATIONS: Remington Model 798

CALIBRE: .243 Win, .308 Win, .30-06, .270 Win, 7mm Rem Mag, .300 Win Mag, .375 H&H Mag, .458 Win Mag

BARREL LENGTH: 56cm (22in), 61cm (24in), 66cm (26in)

WEIGHT: average 3.18kg (7lb)

SIGHTS: receiver drilled and tapped for scope mounts

MECHANISM: bolt action, magazine fed

FEATURES: Mauser 98 action; solid steel hinged floor-plate magazine

Mauser's famous bolt-action system was introduced back in 1898. The bolt featured three locking lugs (two set on the bolt head and a third positioned to the rear of the bolt), with the bolt handle an integral part of the bolt itself.

A powerful non-rotating claw extractor also gave crisp control to both loading and ejection. The 98 action not only became standard in German army rifles, but it has been directly used or subtly copied in thousands of rifles to the present day. Little wonder that some have referred to it as 'the greatest bolt-action ever developed'.

Remington's return

The Model 798 will appeal to those wanting the sense of tradition, but also those who like the undoubted reliability of the Mauser action in their

One of the strengths of the Remington Model 798 is the range of calibres available. For light deer hunting the gun starts with the .243 Win, going up to the mighty .458 Win Mag for taking on the heaviest land game.

hunting rifle. The available calibres are as follows: .243 Win, .308 Win, .30-06, .270 Win, 7mm Rem Mag, .300 Win Mag, .375 H&H Mag, .458 Win Mag, with barrel lengths of 56cm (22in), 61cm (24in), and 66cm (26in). A recoil pad is fitted at the end of the laminated stock, and the stock comb is raised to give a solid platform for the aiming eye.

Model 798s also come with a solid steel hinged floor-plate magazine. A safety switch is located just to the right of the receiver behind the bolt handle. The shooter can also tell whether the gun is cocked or not by looking at the rear of the bolt: if the gun is cocked the firing-pin mechanism is protruding.

Alongside the Model 798, Remington has also produced the Model 799, a short-action version in mainly .22 family calibres but also in 7.62 x 39.

Layout

The Model 798 has a reassuringly familiar look about it, with a plain brown laminated stock. The overall length of the gun varies depending on the barrel, but ranges from 107cm (42.25in) up to 117cm (46.25in). Prices range from around the $600 mark up to just over $800.

Remington XR-100 Rangemaster $

The XR-100 Rangemaster is a new target rifle from Remington based around three small centrefire calibres. It is aimed at those who want competition-standard accuracy without overspending.

SPECIFICATIONS: **Remington XR-100 Rangemaster**

CALIBRE: .204 Ruger, .223 Remington, .22-250 Remington

BARREL LENGTH: 66cm (26in)

WEIGHT: average 4kg (9lb)

SIGHTS: receiver drilled and tapped for scope mounts

MECHANISM: bolt action, single shot

FEATURES: adjustable trigger pull; thumbhole stock; vented fore-end

Fitted with a bipod, the Remington XR-100 Rangemaster is one of the most accurate medium-range single-shot rifles.

Surprisingly, the XR-100 Rangemaster's action is actually based upon that of the Remington XP-100 single-shot pistol, albeit longer and – according to some shooting reviews – incorporating a much easier bolt release. The Rangemaster is designed for either competition target shooting or accurate long-range varmint hunting. The available calibres are .204 Ruger, .223 Remington, and .22-250 Remington. These rounds offer very fast muzzle velocities, and can handle everything from foxes up to medium-sized deer. The .223, for example, has a muzzle velocity of around 914m/sec (3000ft/sec) based on a 55-grain bullet, while the .22-250 Remington adds another 244m/sec (800ft/sec) with a 50-grain bullet.

Heavyweight

The Rangemaster's accuracy is suggested by its weight – it weighs in at around 4kg (9lb). The 66cm (26in) long hammer-forged varmint-contour barrel accounts for much of this weight (heavy barrels are much more atmospherically stable than light barrels). Because the Rangemaster is a single-shot gun, the barrel has an extremely stable mounting, and the solid-bottom receiver offers great rigidity. Heat building up in the fore-end is a significant cause of lost accuracy – the distorting wood pulls on the barrel. Very expensive hunting rifles have 'free-floating' barrels (the barrel is not actually attached to the fore-end), but the Rangemaster has wide slots cut into the fore-end wood to help heat dissipate rapidly. The stock is also striking for its thumbhole design, giving the shooter a great deal of control over grip.

Trigger-pull is all-important in high-accuracy weapons, and the Rangemaster is fitted with a Model 40-X™ adjustable trigger.

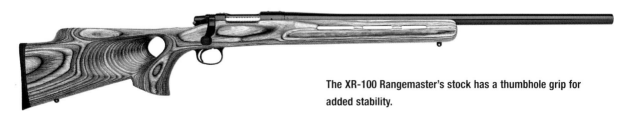

The XR-100 Rangemaster's stock has a thumbhole grip for added stability.

Robar Precision Hunter

$$$

Custom rifles may seem an unaffordable option for many hunters. Yet for those looking to spend up to $5000, custom gunshops such as Robar can produce a top-grade rifle to the customer's order.

SPECIFICATIONS: **Robar Precision Hunter**

CALIBRE: to order

BARREL LENGTH: dependent upon order

WEIGHT: dependent upon order

SIGHTS: dependent upon order

MECHANISM: bolt action

FEATURES: customized gun; free-floating barrel; options include muzzle brake, McMillan stock

Robar was started by Robert A. Barrkman, and today focuses on creating custom-made guns from scratch and on applying sophisticated finishes to weapons, including the Roguard polymer and the NP3 polytetra-fluorethylene coatings, both of which dramatically improve a weapon's resistance to weather, corrosion, and damage.

Precision customization

Because of the custom emphasis, any single gun cannot define the Precision Hunter weapons. Robar emphasize that its hunting rifles can be made for virtually any commercially available calibre the customer wants.

Muzzle brakes are frequently fitted, should the customer require very heavy calibres for large-game hunting (Robar makes weapons up to .50 BMG). These tend to consist of ports bored directly into the barrel at the muzzle, these dissipating some of the final muzzle blast out to the sides, thereby lessening the straight backward recoil.

Robar pays special attention to the quality of the barrels. They state that 'We use only match-grade barrels with contours and twists to suit your favorite bullet and caliber' and that 'All actions are fully accurized and blueprinted prior to barrel installation'. A precision-rebated match crown at the muzzle also enhances the accuracy of the weapon.

Although Robar can make stocks from fine grades of walnut, it also utilizes McMillan Fibreglass Stocks. These stocks are used by many in military and police service, and have the advantage of being totally resistant to damp and wet.

Nevertheless, Robar makes its Precision Hunter barrels free-floating to ensure total consistency shot after shot. Combined with the extremely high quality of finishing, a Robar Precision Hunter is a very durable and accurate investment for any shooter.

The fluted barrel on this gun is principally intended to both reduce the overall weight of the gun (the barrel is typically the heaviest part of a rifle) and to promote faster cooling.

Ruger No.1

$

While most of the rifles in this chapter are magazine-fed bolt-action or lever-action firearms, single-shot weapons still hold a considerable following for many hunters.

SPECIFICATIONS: **Ruger No.1 Standard**

CALIBRE: 16 calibres from .220 Swift to .338 Win	
BARREL LENGTH: 66cm (26in)	
WEIGHT: around 3.5kg (8lb)	
SIGHTS: provision for scope	
MECHANISM: bolt action, single shot	
FEATURES: lever-action falling-block mechanism	

Hunting with a single-shot weapon tends to produce a very different mindset than occurs when shooting with a repeating weapon. With a second shot rarely viable, the hunter must be extremely sure of his fieldcraft, targeting, ammunition, and weapon. Ruger's No.1 has actually been on sale since the 1960s, and it is an extremely solid gun that can be used by either the complete beginner (another group of shooters for whom single-shot rifles can be suitable) or the experienced hunter.

Falling block

The No.1 uses a hammerless falling-block that harks back to the Farquharson design of the nineteenth century, although with thoroughly modern updates and engineering. The value of this design is that it is immensely strong, which means that the No.1 can take cartridges ranging from .204 Ruger to .458 Lott.

To load the weapon, the lever latch is pressed and the under-lever is swung downwards to its fullest extent. This exposes the breech end of the chamber into which a cartridge is inserted. The lever is then raised back up to the closed position, a movement that closes and locks the breech block. After the gun is fired, operating the lever ejects the spent cartridge. (Note that the No.1 has a thumb-operated safety switch that should be used at all appropriate points during the firing and ejection cycle.)

The No.1 comes in a spectrum of different models, the principal differences being the shape/material of the stock, different weights of barrels and the use of stainless-steel barrels. The basic gun is the Standard, which comes in calibres from .204 Ruger to .338 Win Mag, has a 66cm (26in) barrel, and retails for around $1000. Medium Sporter No.1s are chambered purely in .45-70 Gov't, while the potent Tropical model takes four major big-game calibres from .375 H&H to .458 Lott. Other models include the Varminter, Stainless Standard, and International (the latter with a full-length fore-end).

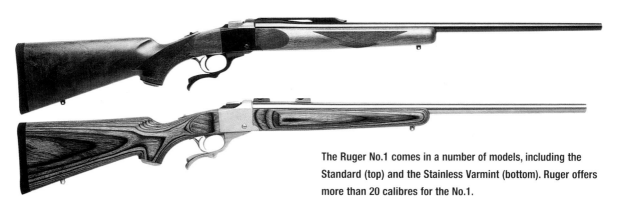

The Ruger No.1 comes in a number of models, including the Standard (top) and the Stainless Varmint (bottom). Ruger offers more than 20 calibres for the No.1.

Ruger M77 Mk II Series

$

The Ruger M77 Mk II rifles are available in more than 20 calibres, reflecting the trend in rifle design for one action being able to take different cartridges when simply re-barrelled.

SPECIFICATIONS: Ruger M77 Mk II Standard

CALIBRE: numerous calibres from .223 to .350 Win Mag	
BARREL LENGTH: 56cm (22in), 61cm (24in)	
WEIGHT: average 3.2kg (7lb)	
SIGHTS: receiver drilled and tapped for scope mounting	
MECHANISM: bolt action, magazine fed	
FEATURES: Mauser action; three-position safety	

M77 Mk II rifles can be bought in any of 12 models. All the rifles work on the same action – the ever-reliable Mauser-type action with controlled feed to give excellent seating in the chamber, smooth loading, and to reduce the risk of damaging rounds during the feed process. The bolt is a robust one-piece item, which is capable of handling the full spectrum of the M77 Mk II calibres, from .223 up to .350 Win Mag. Barrels are precision-hammer-forged, and the magazine has a steel-hinged floor plate. A floor-plate latch fitted just in front of the trigger guard prevents the accidental release of cartridges. All Mk IIs are fitted with three-position safeties, enabling the bolt to be locked when required.

Standard to specialized

The Standard is the core model within the Mk II series. This has a cut-checkered American walnut stock and blued surfaces, and is an attractive workhorse rifle with a barrel length of 56cm (22in) or 61cm (24in), depending on calibre. Beyond the Standard guns are some very different layouts and features. The All-Weather model has a stainless-steel barrel, receiver, bolt system and trigger, and combined with an impact-resistant synthetic stock it is a tough rifle for harsh-climate use. The All-Weather Ultralight is similar, but has a 51cm (20in) barrel and a weight of only 2.8kg (6.25lb).

Taking the barrel length down even further is the International model, which has a full-length stock (the fore-end reaches right up to the muzzle) and a 46cm (18in) barrel. There is even a 42cm (16.5in) barrel gun, the Target Grey Frontier, which has stainless-steel metalwork and a two-stage target trigger. By contrast, the Magnum gun increases the barrel to 58cm (23in) and is chambered for the classic big-game cartridges such as .375 H&H Mag.

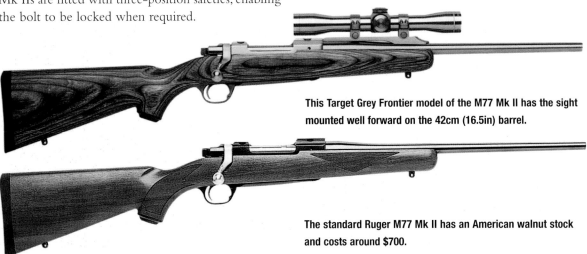

This Target Grey Frontier model of the M77 Mk II has the sight mounted well forward on the 42cm (16.5in) barrel.

The standard Ruger M77 Mk II has an American walnut stock and costs around $700.

Ruger Model 96

$

The Ruger 96 series offers rifles suitable, depending on the calibre, for hunting game from rabbits and squirrels up to larger quarry such as small woodland deer.

SPECIFICATIONS: **Ruger Model 96**

CALIBRE: .17 HMR, .22 WMR, .44 Magnum	
BARREL LENGTH: 47cm (18.5in)	
WEIGHT: 2.4–2.8kg (5.25–6.25lb)	
SIGHTS: open adjustable; integral scope mounts	
MECHANISM: lever action, magazine fed	
FEATURES: short-throw lever action; rotary magazine; dual extractors	

Lever-action guns have a genuine utility in hunting use. As with pump-action shotguns, lever-action weapons provide a robust reliability in the field while also allowing faster rates of fire than can be achieved with a bolt-action rifle. The Ruger 96 series offers a judicious selection of three calibres. For those who want the gun for plinking and small-game hunting, it can be bought in .17 HMR and .22 WMR rimfire calibres (the 96/17 and 96/22 models respectively). On the other hand, Ruger also make the 96 in .44 Magnum centrefire calibre (96/44), this providing take-down power for short-range deer shooting.

Useful hunter

The 96 series rifle is a lever-action gun, which requires only 54 degrees of movement from the lever to cycle the weapon. Ruger points to the 'enclosed action design', which prevents the ingress of wet, mud, and so on, into the action, and the dual extractors on the bolt, which add a further level of reliability in both chambering and extraction. The magazine is a rotary type that holds up to nine rounds for the .17 and .22 calibres, and four rounds for the .44 Magnum version. This magazine fits flush into the stock, thereby reducing the risk of magazine damage in the field.

All of the models have 47cm (18.5in) barrels, and they come with open sights as standard – a rear adjustable and a fixed front blade. Scope mounts, however, are integral with the receiver. The overall appearance of the guns is 'carbine' style, with a barrel band at the front and a plain hardwood stock that terminates in a curved Western-type butt plate.

The Ruger Model 96 has an integral scope mount in addition to open sights. Here the shooter has also fitted the gun with a bipod on the fore-end

Sako TRG 22

$$$

The TRG 22 is a pure accuracy weapon designed for either police officers or those wanting the most exacting competition standards in target sports.

SPECIFICATIONS: **Sako TRG 22**

CALIBRE: .308 Win (7.62 x 51 NATO)	
BARREL LENGTH: 66cm (26in)	
WEIGHT: average 4.7kg (10.25lb)	
SIGHTS: rails for scope mounting	
MECHANISM: bolt action, magazine fed	
FEATURES: fully adjustable stock; bipod fitting	

The TRG 22 has an arresting appearance. The composite stock is deeply cut down over the wrist, and the adjustability of the weapon is evident – the comb is adjustable for drop and cast and the butt plate is extendable to alter the length of pull. The stock material itself is a hard-wearing, weather-impervious composite, and the barrel has a completely free-floating arrangement in relation to the fore-end.

Long reach

The TRG 22 is capable of pinpoint accuracy up to 300m (984ft), but is capable of decent groupings well beyond this range. It is chambered solely for the redoubtable .308 Win (also known as the 7.62 x 51 NATO) and it has a large (for a centrefire bolt-action rifle) magazine capacity of 10 rounds. Target-grade barrels are cold-hammer-forged, and these can be provided with a mirage-sling fitting to obscure heat radiation.

The three-lug bolt is particularly precise in feeding the rounds from the centreline of the magazine, and moving the bolt handle through only 60 degrees of turn operates the gun. Triggers can be adjusted for the pull-weight preference of the individual shooter. Naturally, there are no fixed sights, but the gun's 17mm (0.7in) rails will take all manner of professional scopes for either military or target shooting.

The adjustability of the TRG 22's skeleton stock is pronounced, being adjustable for both drop and length of pull. The stock can be folded along the side of the gun.

The TRG 22 can have an optional bipod fitted just in front of the fore-end, and this can be adjusted for height.

Sako Model 85

$$

Imported into the United States by Beretta USA, the Sako Model 85 is a new rifle from Sako of Finland introduced in 2006, which builds upon the design of the Sako Model 75.

SPECIFICATIONS: Sako Model 85 Hunter
CALIBRE: 13 calibres from .22-250 Rem to 7mm-08 Rem
BARREL LENGTH: 57cm (22.5in), 62cm (24.5in)
WEIGHT: 3.5kg (7.75lb)
SIGHTS: receiver grooved to accept scope
MECHANISM: bolt action, magazine fed
FEATURES: Total Control magazine latch system; adjustable trigger pull weight

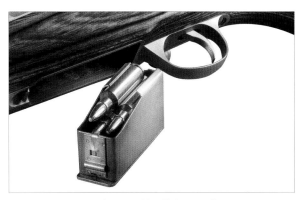

Four or five rounds of ammunition fit into the Sako 85's magazine in a staggered arrangement.

The Model 85 comes in three versions: Hunter, Grey Wolf, and Stainless Synthetic. Taking the Hunter as the baseline model, we find a gun available in a particularly broad swathe of calibres (13 in total), which include .22-250 Rem, .30-06 Springfield, .308 Win, 6.5 x 55, and 7mm WSM.

The magazine capacity for these rounds varies between four and five cartridges. The Sako 85 Grey Wolf contrasts, amongst other things, by having an all-stainless barrel and a grey laminated stock, while the Stainless Synthetic version has a synthetic stock with rubber inserts and a FinSoft recoil reduction system.

Technological innovation

Sako/Beretta publicity emphasizes several key features of the Model 85 rifles. For example, the rifle (as with many other rifle manufacturers) comes with a 91.44m 2.5cm (300ft 1in) accuracy guarantee as out-of-the-box performance. 'Controlled-round feeding' is another common feature, although some gun press reviews have questioned whether this is entirely effective in preventing double-feed jams, and whether the system differs significantly from many push-feed bolt actions.

Model 85s all have a Total Control magazine latch system. The guns have a detachable box magazine, and this has to be pushed up into the rifle before the magazine-release catch can be depressed. However, top loading through the loading/ejection port is also straightforward, and many may prefer to keep their loading activities to this method alone. Other features present in the Model 85 series include adjustable trigger pull weight and free-floating barrels.

Sako is entering a highly competitive field with the Model 85, and it remains to be seen whether the gun will be able to gain a toehold in the market.

This Sako 85 model has a stainless finish. The stock can be either walnut or synthetic.

Sako Quad

$–$$

The Sako Quad has caused quite a stir in the gun world, and it looks set to become a big seller. At first glance in looks like a fairly conventional bolt-action rifle.

SPECIFICATIONS: **Sako Quad**

CALIBRE: .17 HMR, .17 Mach 2, .22 LR, .22 WMR	
BARREL LENGTH: 56cm (22in)	
WEIGHT: 2.6kg (5.75lb)	
SIGHTS: provision for scope	
MECHANISM: bolt action, magazine fed	
FEATURES: Interchangeable barrel sets	

However, the real innovation of the Sako Quad lies in its ability to re-calibre itself through quick and easy barrel changes.

Barrel switch

The Sako Quad takes advantage of the fact that four of the world's most popular rimfire calibres – .22 LR, .22 WMR, .17 HMR and .17 Mach 2 – all share the same diameter of case head. With this in mind, Sako created a single rifle that has four interchangeable barrel sets for quick and easy calibre changes. Each barrel has a colour-coded ring denoting the calibre, and barrel change consists of nothing more than loosening the fitted barrel using a provided key, taking it out, slotting in a new barrel, and retightening the key. (The barrels are free-floated, so there is no difficulty in separating them from the fore-end.)

Four guns

Essentially the Quad is four guns in one. To buy the rifle with all four barrels costs around $1700; to buy the rifle with just one barrel fitted costs just under $1000. The performance of the Quad is typical of Sako – tight consistent patterns (even when the barrels are changed constantly) and a smooth 50-degree bolt throw. The five-shot magazine is detachable and comes in two versions, one for the .22 LR and .17 Mach 2, and the other for the remaining two calibres. For safety, the magazines will only feed when matched with the correct barrel.

By allowing the changing of barrel sets, the Sako Quad offers the shooter four guns for the price of one high-quality bolt-action rifle.

The Sako Quad can be fitted with a variety of telescopic sights for target practice.

Sauer S90

$$

The Sauer & Sohn company has over 200 years of history behind it, and the bolt-action mechanism on the Sauer 90 illustrates the sophistication of its engineering.

SPECIFICATIONS: **Sauer S90 Standard**

CALIBRE: 17 calibres from .25-06 Rem to .375 H&H Mag

BARREL LENGTH: 60cm (23.5in), 65cm (26in)

WEIGHT: up to 3.9kg (8.58lb)

SIGHTS: open rear adjustable, front post; scope mounting

MECHANISM: bolt action, magazine fed

FEATURES: Sauer bolt action; set trigger function; 60-degree handle movement

A bolt-action rifle is essentially defined by its bolt mechanism, and the Sauer 90 system is designed for the total precision placement of a cartridge in the chamber. Company publicity describes the mechanism thus: 'The patented SAUER 90 breech system does not rotate when opening or locking the bolt. The mechanism is regulated by three breeches at the back of the bolt, which sink into the bolt when the handle is raised and then turn up again when the bolt is locked.' This mechanism avoids the rotational movement of a cartridge case in the chamber before and after firing, thereby protecting the integrity of the chamber and of the cartridge itself. The Sauer 90 also requires only a minimum of rotation to operate – the bolt handle goes through only 60 degrees of angular movement to cycle the action (the gun is fed from a three- or four-round magazine).

Safety features

Sauer places significant emphasis on safety in its firearms design. The Sauer 90 has a signal-pin feature that allows the shooter to identify if the gun is cocked by a simple visual check or, if light conditions are low, by touch. The set trigger of the Sauer 90 is also taken off the set position whenever the bolt is opened. (Note that the Sauer 90 has a direct trigger, which also has a set control that enables the shooter to vary the pull weight in different situations.) Safe mode is implemented via a simple switch on the wrist of the stock. The S90 comes in several models divided into two basic types. The Standard model has a conventional Half Stock layout while the Stutzen model has the Full Stock configuration.

A woodland hunter takes aim with a Sauer 90. Sauer enjoys strong sales in both Europe and the United States.

The Sauer 90 has only 60 degrees of bolt movement to cycle the action. A low-turn bolt permits faster shooting and also less chance of knocking the scope out of alignment.

Sauer S202

$$–$$$

Modularity is an increasingly popular term in the field of hunting rifles. As is the case with the S202, it refers to the shooter's ability to mix and match rifle components to fit his need.

SPECIFICATIONS: **Sauer S202 Standard**

CALIBRE: 22 calibres from .223 Rem to .300 Wby Mag
BARREL LENGTH: 51cm (20in), 56cm (22in), 60cm (23.5in)
WEIGHT: up to 3.5kg (7.7lb)
SIGHTS: open rear adjustable, front post; provision for scope
MECHANISM: bolt action, magazine fed
FEATURES: modular design; six-lug bolt

In a sense there is no such thing as a basic S202. The number of optional components that a shooter can choose from when purchasing this rifle make the gun both personal and adaptable. Components currently listed by the Sauer website are: 5 fore-ends; 5 butt stocks; 3 stock materials; 10 wood grades; 8 bolts; 3 triggers; 11 receivers; 10 barrel contours; 5 barrel lengths; 4 surface finishes; 3 sights; and 23 calibres.

Despite the multiple possibilities involved in this choice, there are some common factors in every S202 put together. All the barrels are made from Krupp steel and are cold-hammer-forged for great accuracy. These barrels are free-floating, not being in contact with the two-piece stock. The bolts, although they differ in scale according to calibre, feature six locking lugs. Triggers are direct with an adjustable set function. The magazine is detachable and holds from two to five rounds depending on calibre selected.

'Standard models'

Although the S202 can be put together in dozens of different configurations, the rifles are also sold in 10 different models, with the Standard model also being subdivided into other models on the basis of finish. The main Standard model has a 51cm (20in), 56cm (22in), or 60cm (23.5in) barrel, a weight of between 3.3 and 3.5kg (7.2 and 7.7lb) and has calibres from .223 Rem to .458 Lott. Beyond this the models vary quite considerably in appearance.

The Stutzen model, for example, has a short bolt action and a full-length fore-end. (One of the advantages of this layout is that in mountainous or wooded terrain the gun can be rested on an object and the barrel will always be protected from contact.) Alternatively, the Wolverine model has a fluted varmint barrel and adjustable comb on the stock. The Synthetic Classic has a two-piece non-slip synthetic stock.

The ability to change components easily on a rifle is of great advantage to an all-round hunter. The shooter should check, however, that changing a part does not require a licence modification (in countries where a licence is needed).

Sig-Sauer SSG 3000

$$$$

For those with up to $5000 to spend on the ultimate target rifle – one used by police marksman as a sniper tool – the Sig-Sauer SSG 3000 might be a first choice.

SPECIFICATIONS: **Sig-Sauer SSG 3000**

CALIBRE: 7.62 x 51mm
BARREL LENGTH: 60cm (23.5in)
SIGHTS: integrated scope rail
WEIGHT: around 6kg (13lb) with scope
MECHANISM: bolt action, magazine fed
FEATURES: bipod; flash suppressor/muzzle brake; set trigger pull

There is little argument that the SSG 3000 is principally a sniper weapon, designed for precision shots in the hands of professional law enforcers and military professionals. However, the weapon is on sale to the general public in several countries, including the United States, and will appeal to those who want to test themselves at targets over particularly challenging ranges.

The rifle's military purpose is attested to by its single calibre – 7.62 x 51 NATO (.308 Win). Precision accuracy is built into every feature of the gun. The stock and butt plate are fully adjustable to provide a customized fit with the shooter. A bipod at the front of the fore-end provides a permanent stable firing position. The heavy barrel features a flash suppressor/muzzle break for controlled recoil and a reduced firing signature.

Stable foundation

The integrity of the barrel, bolts, and receiver are vital to an effective sniper weapon. In the SSG 3000's case, the bolt is of a six-lug design to give a very precise and controlled lock with the barrel. The receiver is machined from a single block of steel for great structural integrity.

Trigger pull is set by the user, there being two take-up weights. Lock time is extremely fast through using a very light and short firing pin, as well as a fundamentally fast mechanism.

The SSG 3000 can take many optional extras, including night-vision devices and even fabric heat slings over the barrel to prevent heat rising off the barrel distorting the shooter's vision and disturbing the perfect shot.

The SSG 3000 has some of the typical features of a sniper weapon – very heavy barrel, adjustable stock dimensions, and integral bipod support.

Savage Model Mk 1 GY Youth

$

Finding the right gun for a young and inexperienced shooter can be problematic, but the Savage Mk 1 GY Youth model ticks many of the right boxes in terms of layout and performance.

SPECIFICATIONS: Savage Model Mk 1 GY Youth

CALIBRE: .22 S, .22 L, .22 LR	
BARREL LENGTH: 48cm (19in)	
WEIGHT: 2.27kg (5lb)	
SIGHTS: open	
MECHANISM: bolt action, single shot	
FEATURES: AccuTrigger system	

The Savage Model Mk 1 GY Youth is simplicity itself. While there is little sophistication about the rifle it does everything a basic rifle needs to do – shoots accurately and with consistent reliability, even in young hands.

Young shooters typically need to learn the basics of shooting over open sights before progressing onto scope shooting, and the Youth gun comes with a standard adjustable-notch rear sight and a front post sight.

Young shooters face a unique range of concerns by comparison with adult beginners. Principally, their physical control over a gun is dictated by their size, age and strength, hence most guns aimed at a young market are necessarily light with easily managed recoil.

Purpose-designed

The Youth gun can be bought in .22 S, .22 L, or .22 LR. All of these calibres are suitable for young shots, producing almost no recoil on firing and having rounds with limited range (but still respectable power for varmint control). The overall dimensions of the gun are compact: the barrel is 48cm (19in) long, which contributes to a total gun length of 94cm (37in). Weight is a mere 2.27kg (5lb), light enough for a small-framed adolescent shooter, and there is a 32cm (12.5in) length of pull.

AccuTrigger

Although the Youth rifle is a fairly basic weapon – its price tag comes in at less than $200 – special attention has been paid to the trigger mechanism. The rifle is fitted with Savage's new AccuTrigger, an advanced trigger system designed to improve the control over the trigger and its safety. The AccuTrigger allows the shooter to adjust the pull weight of the trigger without having to take the gun to a professional gunsmith.

However, an AccuRelease system integrated with the trigger means that even on the lightest setting the gun will not fire if it is dropped or jarred – a finger needs to depress the AccuRelease before the sear is allowed to function. This feature alone will make the Mk 1 GY Youth appeal to many experienced shooters who want to be reassured about safety when teaching a youngster to shoot.

Savage 14 Classic

$

The Classic series of rifles from Savage provides a group of good all-round hunting rifles with simple styling but the latest in Savage rifle technology.

SPECIFICATIONS: Savage 14 Classic

CALIBRE: .22-250 Rem, .243 Win, .308 Win	
BARREL LENGTH: 56cm (22in), 61cm (24in)	
WEIGHT: up to 3.4kg (7.5lb)	
SIGHTS: drilled and tapped for scope mounts	
MECHANISM: bolt action, magazine fed	
FEATURES: AccuTrigger system, short action	

There are three principal variants of the Classic series, these in turn being subdivided by whether the rifle falls into the long- or short-action category. The models 14 Classic, 14 American Classic, and 14 Euro Classic are all short-action rifles, while the 114 Classic, 114 American Classic, and 114 Euro Classic belong to the long-action category. Choosing which type of gun to buy depends much on what you want to use the gun for.

Short/long

The definition of a short or long action can vary slightly depending on the manufacturer, but as a general rule short actions take cartridges of up to 7.1cm (2.8in) in total length, while the cartridges for long-action guns can be up to 8.6cm (3.4in).

Short-action guns have some technical advantages in principle over the long-action weapons, in that they are quicker to operate (mainly because the shooter does not have to take his head off the stock to cycle the weapon) and are lighter. The advantage of long-action guns resides with the type of cartridges that can be used.

The Classic rifles all have walnut stocks with rubber recoil pads as well as blued barrels, and they are fitted with the AccuTrigger system discussed above in relation to the Savage Model Mk 1 GY Youth. The calibres accepted by the guns vary according to their short- or long-action status. The 14 Classic, for example, takes .22-250 Rem, .243 Win, and .308 Win. The 114 Classic, however, takes .270 Win, .30-06 Spfld, 7mm Rem Mag, and 300 Win Mag. Ammunition is fed from a conventional box magazine, which holds between two and four rounds depending on calibre.

Classic style

The Classic, American Classic, and Euro Classic are also defined by the style of the stock. The 14/114 Classic rifles have Monte Carlo cheek pieces, while the American Classic goes for a straight-comb stock. Euro Classic guns also have Monte Carlo stocks, but a different finish to the woodwork and also adjustable open sights – the other rifles are only configured to take scopes.

The Savage 14 Classic has a good trigger system and comes in a useful range of calibres. It therefore makes a ideal first hunting rifle for deer and other game.

Savage Model 210F Slug Warrior $

The Slug Warrior is purposely designed to fire heavy 12-gauge slugs in close-range hunting. It is a potent weapon against deer and other game.

SPECIFICATIONS: **Savage Model 210F Slug Warrior**

CALIBRE: 12-gauge slugs

BARREL LENGTH: 61cm (24in)

WEIGHT: 3.4kg (7.5lb)

SIGHTS: drilled and tapped for scope mounts

MECHANISM: bolt action, magazine fed

FEATURES: free-floating barrel; controlled round feed

The Slug Warrior is here rendered in a camouflage across the stock and fore-end. The size of the 12-gauge rounds is indicated by the projecting magazine body, which holds two cartridges with one in the chamber.

The rationale behind slug shooting still generates some controversy amongst the international shooting community. Firing a heavy, solid slug from a smoothbore weapon will never approach the accuracy of a bullet from a rifled weapon, even though some of the modern precision slugs can create some reasonable groups.

Slug cautions

However, even the best slugs should not be fired at quarry more than 100m (328ft) away, and half that distance is probably more realistic. Ironically, as the gun writer Chuck Hawks points out in his excellent article 'Shotgun Slugs' (http://www.chuckhawks.com/shotgun_slugs.htm), even though slugs are mandatory for deer hunting in some US hunting grounds because of safety concerns regarding bullet overflight, slugs are actually much more likely to smash through foliage and therefore endanger other

proximate hunters. Many of the high-velocity bullets fired from conventional rifles will often disintegrate or quickly lose momentum if passing through foliage or other woodland obstacles.

Bolt-action slugs

Bearing in mind such reservations, the Model 210F is a well-designed bolt-action slug gun. It is designed for 76mm (3in) 12-gauge shells, and it has a magazine capacity of two rounds, plus one in the chamber. The barrel, unusually for many smoothbore weapons, is free-floating to enhance the accuracy of the gun. A controlled round feed mechanism ensures the smooth loading of the large 12-gauge shells and an oversized bolt handle aids manual loading.

The Slug Warrior's stock is made from a black synthetic material, and the gun is also available in a Realtree camouflage version for the ultimate in concealment. There are no open sights on the gun, but the receiver is drilled and tapped for a scope mount. The power of a 12-gauge slug gun is formidable, and the Slug Warrior features a recoil pad on the stock to soak up some of the kick. For the standard shotgun-shell version of this gun, see the next entry.

Savage Model 210FT Turkey Gun $

The Savage Model 210FT Turkey Gun has one hunting purpose, and press reviews of the gun in action acknowledge it as a capable turkey killer within the range of its 76mm (3in) shells.

SPECIFICATIONS: Savage Model 210FT Turkey Gun

CALIBRE: 12-gauge	
BARREL LENGTH: 61cm (24in)	
WEIGHT: 3.4kg (7.5lb)	
SIGHTS: open; drilled and tapped for scope mounts	
MECHANISM: bolt action, magazine fed	
FEATURES: interchangeable chokes; controlled round feed	

Bolt-action shotguns are not common weapons, and by far the majority of turkey-hunting guns are semi-auto shotguns or break-action guns. However, the Savage Turkey Gun is well designed for its purpose. Like its slug gun counterpart, it has a 61cm (24in) barrel, the difference in this case being the interchangeable choke tube. Only one choke tube is supplied with the gun – a tightly bored choke suitable for turkey shooting – but the 210FT will also take standard choke tubes from several other makes of 12-gauge shotgun.

Sighting

As turkey hunting involves aimed rather than instinctively pointed shots, the 210FT has open sights as standard. The sights are very simple – a rear V-notch corresponding with a simple brass bead front sight. These sights may in themselves be sufficient for turkey shooting, as the range of a standard 76mm (3in) 12-gauge shell is only around 30–40m (98–131ft). However, turkey shooting also requires some precision to target the right part of the bird, or spot it amongst the foliage in the first place. The 210FT receiver is also drilled and tapped for a scope mount, and the 60-degree of rotation means that operating the bolt handle stays well clear of a scope.

Recoil-handling

To handle its 12-gauge loads, the 210FT has a very substantial bolt action, the bolt alone weighing just under 0.7kg (1.5lb). The bolt head rotates to lock before firing, and dual extractors and a powerful ejection spring ensure positive removal of the spent cartridges. As with the Slug Warrior, the Turkey Gun is fed from a two-shell-capacity box magazine. The stock of the 210FT is fitted with a recoil pad and the standard colour scheme is camouflage.

Other guns in Savage's 'Specialty' series include two combination rifle/shotgun models (the Model 24F-20 and Model 24F-12), which are break-barrel guns with one rifled barrel and a smoothbore barrel in either 12 or 20 gauge.

This side view of the Savage Model 210FT Turkey Gun shows the basic sight arrangment along the barrel. The camouflage finish is essential for turkey hunting, the wild turkey being one of nature's most easily alarmed animals.

Tikka T3

$

The Tikka T3 series is one of the most highly respected ranges of bolt-action rifles in the world, with models ranging from a classic Hunter through to a military-grade sniper rifle.

SPECIFICATIONS: Tikka T3 Hunter

CALIBRE: 19 different calibres from .222 Rem to .338 Win Mag

BARREL LENGTH: 52cm (20.5in), 62cm (24.4in)

WEIGHT: up to 3.2kg (7lb)

SIGHTS: receiver drilled and tapped for scope mounts, and integral scope rail

MECHANISM: bolt action, magazine fed

FEATURES: single set trigger option; free-floating barrel

The Tikka T3 has built up a faithful following of users, who are rarely let down by this firearm.

All Tikka T3 rifles are built around the same action. The bolt has a counter-bored head and double locking lugs, and is operated by a 70-degree movement from the bolt handle. A recoil lug channels more of the recoil into the T3's stock to take stresses out of the bolt system and improve accuracy. When cycling the weapon, the bolt throw (the distance between fully open and fully closed) varies according to the length of the cartridge case.

Regarding triggers, the T3 series' are machined from aluminium alloy and are hand-finished. Trigger pulls are crisp and lock times are fast, but there is also an option for a single set trigger – the trigger is first pushed forward to give an extremely light pull weight. Two types of precision barrel are available for the T3s, either a stainless-steel barrel or a chrome-molybdenum version. Both have hand-crowned muzzles.

Models

Most T3s come without open sights or provision for mounting a scope. The Battue and Battue Light models, however, have fibre-optic Truglo sights, the rear sight being ramped up with two fluorescent dots straddling the view of the front bead. The Battue and the Battue Light are just two guns in the T3 series. Outside the basic Hunter model (see specifications) the models include the Lite (which has a fibreglass-reinforced polymer stock) and the Camo Stainless (with stainless barrel and camouflage stock).

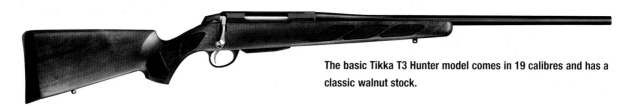

The basic Tikka T3 Hunter model comes in 19 calibres and has a classic walnut stock.

Voere Model 2155

$

The Voere Company began life in 1948 as a small engineering company in Germany, launching its manufacture of rifles in 1955 and growing to become an innovative and skilled firearms developer.

SPECIFICATIONS: Voere Model 2155

CALIBRE: 13 different calibres from .22-250 to .308 Win	
BARREL LENGTH: 60–65cm (23.6–25.6in)	
WEIGHT: 3.3kg (7lb)	
SIGHTS: open rear leaf and front post; receiver drilled and tapped for scope mounts	
MECHANISM: bolt action, magazine fed	
FEATURES: multiple trigger options; Bavarian-style stock; top tang safety	

A sight rail such as this one is an option for scope mounting, being quickly attached and very stable.

The Model 2155 is one of Voere's bedrock models. What we have is a high-quality centrefire bolt-action rifle available in a total of 13 calibres, these ranging from .22-250 up to .308 Win. The rounds are loaded into a clip magazine that sits flush with the stock, the cartridge capacity being three to five rounds depending on the calibre. A hinged floor plate allows easy access to the magazine. Barrel length of the Model 2155 varies according to preference, ranging between 60 and 65cm (23.6 and 25.6in), and the overall length of the gun extending up to 118.5cm (46.75in). The bolt is locked by two locking lugs.

Safe and fire

Voere make fine trigger mechanisms, and the 2155 comes with multiple options for trigger units. A two-stage trigger is standard, but further options (based on company website information at the time of writing) include adjustable one-stage, double set, single-stage, Match two-stage, and direct. A top tang safety switch provides reassuring protection against accidental discharge, it locking the sear itself.

In terms of overall appearance, the Model 2155 has a very slender and refined appearance. Its oil-finished walnut stock has a Bavarian-style comb and a Schnabel-type fore-end. A synthetic stock is also available, and both stock types come fitted with a rubber recoil pad. Open sights are provided as standard, but the receiver is drilled and tapped for a scope mount. The weight of the gun is 3.3kg (7lb).

Voere also make the Model 2165, which is like the 2155 except with improved grades of finish and either a double-set or adjustable single-stage trigger.

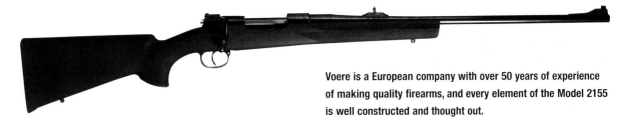

Voere is a European company with over 50 years of experience of making quality firearms, and every element of the Model 2155 is well constructed and thought out.

Voere Model Tirolerin

$

The Voere Model Tirolerin could be termed a 'traveller's rifle' owing to its modular design and the facility for the shooter to break it down into a backpack.

SPECIFICATIONS: Voere Model Tirolerin

CALIBRE: multiple calibres from .223 Rem to 9.3 x 62	
BARREL LENGTH: optional	
WEIGHT: average 3kg (6.6lb)	
SIGHTS: open rear leaf and front post; receiver drilled and tapped for scope mounts	
MECHANISM: bolt action, magazine fed	
FEATURES: modular rifle; two-row magazine	

With its modular construction, the Tirolerin breaks down easily into its constituent parts for transportation.

As is typical of Voere hunting rifles, the Model Tirolerin comes in an extremely wide range of calibre options reaching from small high-velocity rounds, like the .223 Rem (5.56mm), up to heavy deer-hunting shells, such as the 9.3 x 62. Modularity is the key word in the Tirolerin's construction. It is built for quick and easy hand disassembly in the field. Without tools, the shooter can take off and change the stock, remove the barrel, and even change the calibre of the weapon through swapping the barrel and the bolt head.

Solid construction

Although the Tirolerin is effectively a breakdown weapon, it should not be confused with some of the light, skeletal survival rifles on the market. Various stocks are available. The company lists some of the options as 'an elegant stock/workhorse stock for rough conditions/match stock for target shooting' – but all are made in high-quality walnut. Voere also emphasizes that no plastic is used in the construction of the rifle, only top-quality metals.

The specifications of the Tirolerin vary according to the type of options selected. However, the gun centres around a Voere bolt action fed from a two-row high-capacity clip magazine. The weight of the gun is around 3kg (6.6lb), another factor that lifts it out of the category of survival rifle.

As a practical and well-designed hunting weapon for trips in which ease of transportation is important, the Tirolerin is a good choice, especially as the modular barrel selection allows the shooter to shift between calibres.

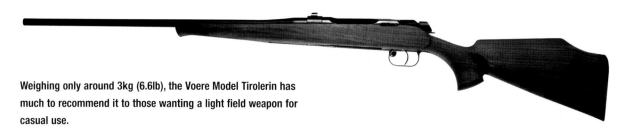

Weighing only around 3kg (6.6lb), the Voere Model Tirolerin has much to recommend it to those wanting a light field weapon for casual use.

Walther KK 300

$$$

The Walther name has been synonymous with high-quality European firearms since the early part of the twentieth century, and the KK 300 is a top-end target rifle for superlative competition performance.

SPECIFICATIONS: **Walther KK 300**

CALIBRE: .22 LR	
BARREL LENGTH: 65cm (25.5in)	
WEIGHT: 5.9kg (13lb)	
SIGHTS: aperture rear sight and front post	
MECHANISM: bolt action	
FEATURES: stock fully adjustable; match-grade components	

Walther has been particularly well known for its military outputs, particularly its famous PP/PPK pistol. Its hi-tech weapons today include the G22 semi-automatic rifle and the P22 and P99 semi-automatic handguns, plus a wide range of target air rifles, air pistols, and small-bore rifles. The KK 300 rifle has adjustability at every level of its construction – competition shooters customize their weapons until they are the perfect body fit.

There are three different sizes of pistol grip (the KK 300 has a true pistol grip rather than being part of the flow of the stock). The stock itself is adjustable for every conceivable dimension and comfort, including drop, cast, length of pull, and shoulder fit. A hook arm provides stability for various disciplines, and the gun can be set up for prone, kneeling, or free-standing disciplines. All the settings can be locked in place for easy setup at a competition.

The KK 300 is a small-bore competition rifle in the .22 LR calibre. The trigger and action in particular have been designed for a light pull and an incredibly fast lock time. Trigger pull is fully adjustable, the range being 70–130g (2.5–4.6oz). The length of the match-grade barrel comes to 65cm (25.5in) and the total weight is 5.9kg (13lb). The rifle is set for use with an aperture sight that, in trained hands and in combination with the rifle's inherent accuracy, will give tiny groups at ranges of up to 100m (328ft).

The KK 300 comes in two models. The Alutec has a light metal stock while the Universal model has a larger beechwood stock that retains stock adjustability but has a more conventional appearance.

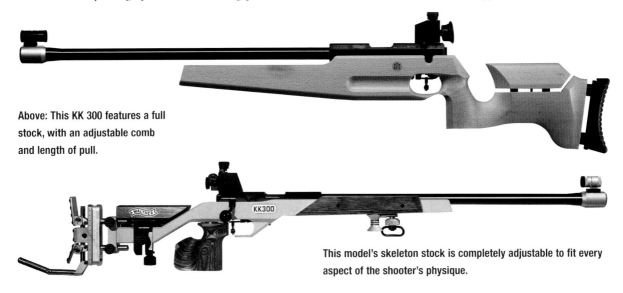

Above: This KK 300 features a full stock, with an adjustable comb and length of pull.

This model's skeleton stock is completely adjustable to fit every aspect of the shooter's physique.

Weatherby Mark V

$–$$

The Weatherby Mark V series is a legend amongst US rifle owners. Its extremely tough Mark V bolt system is a superb example of firearms craftsmanship.

SPECIFICATIONS: **Weatherby Mark V Deluxe**

CALIBRE: eight magnum calibres from .257 Wby Mag to .460 Wby Mag

BARREL LENGTH: 66cm (26in), 71cm (28in)

WEIGHT: 3.8–4.5kg (8.5–10lb)

SIGHTS: provision for scope

MECHANISM: bolt action, magazine fed

FEATURES: Mark V action; cocking indicator; good safety features

The Mark V action was introduced all the way back in 1957 by Roy Weatherby, and in an improved form is still fitted into the Mark V rifles today. In its essence, the action consists of a six- or nine-lug bolt, which is fluted to aid cooling and prevent bolt bind, but also features three gas ports to control the gas pressure and vent excess gas away from the shooter's face in the case of a cartridge rupture. This, combined with the Mark V's 'three rings of steel' that surround the cartridge, allow the gun to take on heavy magnum loads, which run up to .375 H&H Mag and .430 Weatherby Mag.

Safe action

Weatherby balances the power of the Mark V with a good range of safety systems. The safety mechanism provides direct striker intervention – a thumb-operated safety switch locks the firing pin and bolt and also disengages the sear to make both trigger and action dead while the safety is on. A cocking indicator also clearly shows whether the gun is ready to fire or not. Using the Mark V is made particularly pleasant by only 54 degrees of bolt rotation being needed to cycle the gun and feed in shells from the magazine.

The Mark V comes in many different models, calibres and configurations far too numerous to list here. There are Mark Vs with stainless-steel barrels and various types and colours of synthetic stocks. Most unusual is the Mark V Compact Firing Platform (CFP). This has a pure pistol grip forming the Fibermark® composite stock, and is basically a bolt-action two-handed pistol used for various forms of hunting. It has a 41cm (16in) barrel and is available in .223, .22-250, .243, and 7mm-08.

The hunting handgun market is becoming particularly popular in the United States, although it remains to be seen whether such weapons can deliver the consistent clean kills which are necessary for ethical hunting.

The Mark V Compact Firing Platform is essentially a two-handed handgun version of the Mark V rifle.

The Weatherby Mark V series has much variety in terms of stock and metal finish. This gun features an injection-moulded synthetic stock.

Weatherby Vanguard

$

The Weatherby Vanguard promises the ultimate in hunting accuracy and, according to Weatherby, is 'perhaps the finest rifle value on the market today'.

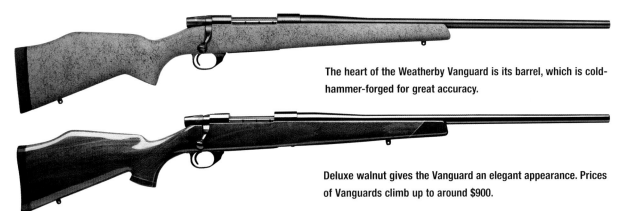

The heart of the Weatherby Vanguard is its barrel, which is cold-hammer-forged for great accuracy.

Deluxe walnut gives the Vanguard an elegant appearance. Prices of Vanguards climb up to around $900.

SPECIFICATIONS: Weatherby Vanguard Sporter

CALIBRE: 13 calibres from .22-250 Rem to .338 Win Mag	
BARREL LENGTH: 61cm (24in)	
WEIGHT: up to 3.5kg (7.75lb)	
SIGHTS: receiver drilled and tapped for scope mount	
MECHANISM: bolt action, magazine fed	
FEATURES: fluted bolt; trigger adjustable for let-off weight	

Vanguard rifles first entered the Weatherby catalogue in 1970, and they are popular amongst hunters wanting the reliability that generally comes with the Weatherby marque. All the guns in the series are built around the same two-lug bolt action. The sophisticated bolt has a fluted body, thereby reducing the weight of the bolt and also helping prevent bolt-binding after firing. The bolt also has three gas ports as a safety measure. These allow the lateral escape of gases should a cartridge rupture. At the end of the bolt a fully enclosing sleeve gives further protection against ruptured-cartridge blowback, and the sleeve also features a cocking indicator.

The Vanguard barrels are cold-hammer-forged, and company confidence in these barrels is great. Website publicity claims that the barrels produce a 'guaranteed 1½in [4cm] or better three-shot group at 100 yards [91.5m] when used with premium (non-Weatherby calibers) or Weatherby factory ammunition'. Triggers are also fully adjustable for let-off weight.

Vanguard models

The Vanguard Sporter model is typical of the range. It comes in 13 popular calibres ranging from .22-250 Rem up to .338 Win Mag and a barrel length of 61cm (24in). Its magazine capacity is three or five rounds depending on the calibre and it weighs in at around 3.5kg (7.75lb). Other models, such as the Synthetic and Stainless, vary in the stock and metal materials used, while others adopt noticeably different formats.

The Vanguard Sub-Moa Varmint, for example, is chambered only for .223 Rem, .22-250 Rem, and .308 Win and has a one-piece, hand-laminated tan Monte Carlo composite stock with vents around the fore-end. Prices for Weatherby Vanguard guns start at around $400.

Winchester Model 1885

$$

The Winchester Model 1885 is a single-shot, falling-block design weapon with an historical design and appearance. It should appeal to those who want a whole tradition behind their rifle.

SPECIFICATIONS: **Winchester 1885 High Wall Hunter**

CALIBRE: .22-250 Rem, .223 Rem, .325 WSM, 7mm WSM, .270 WSM, .300 WSM	
BARREL LENGTH: 71cm (28in)	
WEIGHT: 3.8kg (8.5lb)	
SIGHTS: barrel drilled and tapped for scope mounts	
MECHANISM: lever action, single shot, falling-block system	
FEATURES: multi-directional ejection; adjustable trigger	

The falling-block design, introduced back in the nineteenth century, conferred several advantages. First, it was extremely reliable, and able to absorb much punishment before malfunction. Second, it was able to handle extremely powerful cartridges, hence, as Winchester point out, 'The Model 1885 has been chambered in more calibers than any other rifle in history, simply because the falling-block design is the strongest, most time-tested and accurate action ever invented.'

Winchester's 1885 comes in two versions – the High Wall Hunter and Low Wall Hunter. To take the former first, the High Wall Hunter is chambered for

six different calibres – .22-250 Rem, .223 Rem, .325 WSM, 7mm WSM, .270 WSM, and .300 WSM. It has a 71cm (28in) octagonal barrel, which is of a free-floating design (the barrel does not actually touch the wood of the fore-end) that contributes towards the gun's great accuracy. The weight of an unloaded gun is around 3.8kg (8.5lb).

Modern features

Despite its traditional appearance, the Model 1885 is a thoroughly modern firearm in its features. Its trigger pull can be adjusted between 1.6 and 2.3kg (3.5 and 5lb). The user can choose the direction in which the gun ejects its shells, or can opt for the spent shell to be retained inside the gun for removal by hand. For controlling the recoil of the bigger rounds, a Pachmayr® Decelerator® recoil pad is fitted. The receiver is drilled and tapped for a scope mount.

The Low Wall is much the same as the High Wall, except that it has shorter dimensions, comes chambered for .17 Mach 2 or .17 HMR, and has open iron sights fitted. The Low Wall's receiver is also case-coloured, and the gun is as attractive as it is accurate.

The Winchester 1885 Centennial High Wall Hunter, emblazoned with a Winchester motif on the receiver.

The High Wall Hunter retails at just over $1000 and is available in six different calibres.

Winchester Model 70

$–$$

The Model 70 is yet another classic design renewed by Winchester. After a long evolution beginning in the 1930s, the new Model 70 consists of a series of high-quality bolt-action rifles.

SPECIFICATIONS:
Winchester Model 70 Classic Super Grade III

CALIBRE: .22-250 Rem, .270 Win, .270 WSM, .30-06 Springfield, .300 WSM, .325 WSM, .338 Win Mag, 7mm WSM

BARREL LENGTH: 61cm (24in), 66cm (26in)

WEIGHT: up to 3.7kg (8.2lb)

SIGHTS: receiver drilled and tapped for scope mount

MECHANISM: bolt action, magazine fed

FEATURES: Controlled Round Feed; Pachmayr® Decelerator® recoil pad

The Model 70 features excellent recoil-reduction technology to dramatically reduce the impact of the shot. Some models have two sling swivels on the fore-end.

Fifteen different versions of the Model 70 are listed on the Winchester website at the time of writing, although all are united by a core body of features. Winchester promotes the Controlled Round Feed mechanism as the core of the rifle. This involves a large claw on the bolt grabbing the rim of a fed round and guiding it directly into the chamber. Controlled feeding has fewer problems with rounds jamming than in systems that simply push the round into the chamber. Short and super-short actions are also available.

Diversity

The Winchester Model 70 Classic Sporter III is the bedrock of the Model 70 series. It is chambered for nine popular calibres, including .25-06 Rem, .30-06 Springfield, .338 Win Mag, and 7mm WSM. Two different barrel lengths are available – 61cm (24in) and 66cm (26in) – and the magazine capacity varies between three and five rounds depending on the calibre. The rifle is designed entirely for use with a scope, there being no fixed sights, and the receiver is drilled and tapped for a scope mounting.

Beyond the Classic the Model 70 goes through a series of other configurations for different hunting styles. The Stealth II, for example, is a long-range varmint rifle with a 66cm (26in) heavy-target barrel and a non-glare composite stock. The Model 70 Safari Express, by contrast, is chambered for three big-game calibres (including .375 H&H Mag and .458 Win Mag), has iron sights (hooded front blade, adjustable Express-style rear), and extra recoil fittings to handle the powerful loads.

Other models express equal standards of quality. The Model 70 has been branded as the 'Rifleman's Rifle', and although that title has looked uncertain at times as Winchester reinvented the Model 70, most critics now applaud the gun's design and performance.

Winchester Model 94

$

The Winchester 94 is a piece of American history. Its under-lever action has been in use now for well over 100 years, and is still going strong in the hands of hunters and collectors alike.

SPECIFICATIONS: **Winchester Model 94 Legacy 24**

CALIBRE: .30-30 Win, .357 Mag, .44 Rem Mag, .45 Colt	
BARREL LENGTH: 61cm (24in)	
WEIGHT: up to 3kg (6.7lb)	
SIGHTS: drilled and tapped for scope mounts	
MECHANISM: lever action, tubular magazine	
FEATURES: full-length magazine	

A boy takes instruction in shooting using a Model 94. The 9422 rimfire rifles are particularly suitable for young shots.

In the Legacy version – one of 13 variant models of the 94 produced by Winchester – we find a .30-30 Win or .38-55 Win rifle with an octagonal 66cm (26in) barrel, open sights, a curved cowboy-style butt plate, and the classic Winchester lever action, known for its reliability. Using this foundation, Winchester has created a broad range of types, many with only subtle differences from the Legacy, while others are more substantially different. The Model 94 Timber Scout, for example, has only a 46cm (18in) barrel with quick-detach scope mounts for when the shooter wants to make a rapid switch to the open sights. Regardless of the model, however, the Model 94 action remains constant.

Rimfire rifle

The Winchester Model 9422 is a .22 rimfire gun set in the evocative style of the Henry/Winchester under-lever rifle, and complementing Winchester's standard Model 94 range. It is chambered for three types of .22 cartridge – .22 L, .22 LR and .22 WMR. The gun primarily appeals to those who want a high-capacity varmint rifle – the 9422 can hold up to 15 rounds (depending on the calibre) in its tubular magazine – or to those wanting to teach young ones the principles and practices of shooting.

At the time of writing Winchester was announcing the final discontinuation of the 9422 series, but was undertaking a commemorative run of the firearms. Five tribute models are being produced, each based around the standard 94 action but with differences in styling and finish.

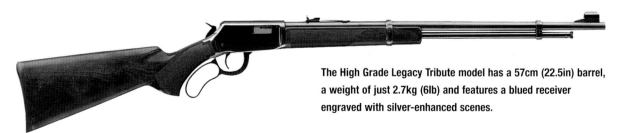

The High Grade Legacy Tribute model has a 57cm (22.5in) barrel, a weight of just 2.7kg (6lb) and features a blued receiver engraved with silver-enhanced scenes.

Winchester Wildcat Bolt Action 22 $

Winchester claim that the Wildcat Bolt Action 22 'may possibly be the best bolt-action 22 value in history'. With the gun having a price tag of around $230, that claim may well be justified.

SPECIFICATIONS: Winchester Wildcat Bolt Action 22

CALIBRE: .22 LR

BARREL LENGTH: 53cm (21in)

WEIGHT: up to 2kg (4.5lb)

SIGHTS: open adjustable; drilled and tapped for scope mount

MECHANISM: bolt action, magazine fed (detachable)

FEATURES: four magazines supplied; micro-adjustable rear sight

The Winchester Wildcat is chambered for the popular .22 Long Rifle round. Long Rifle rounds give an accurate performance over 100m (328ft), although they can actually fly for up to 1.6km (1 mile), and so have to be respected. The Wildcat Bolt Action 22 publicity promises that 'With correct loads and a little skill, you'll cover your groups at 25 yards [23m] with a dime, and a quarter will take you out to 50 yards [46m].'

One of the other great benefits of the .22 LR is the cheapness of the ammunition, and a whole day can be spent plinking without too excessive a cost.

The 53cm (21in) Sporter barrel with a semi-target chamber imparts accuracy. For sights, the Wildcat comes fitted with an open type. The front sight is a simple fixed post, while the rear sight is micro-adjustable to enable the shooter to create good close groups at appropriate range. Naturally, provision is made for the mounting of a scope.

Affordability is an important consideration when buying a rimfire rifle, especially as a rimfire is often a shooter's first gun, bought when not wanting to make a huge outlay. The Wildcat Bolt Action 22 is tremendous value at sub-$250, yet does full justice to the .22 LR round.

Magazine system

Impressively for the small cost of the gun, the Wildcat comes supplied with four magazines. These are three 10-round magazines and one five-round magazine, and such good capacity will make the gun popular with target shooters who don't want to reload too often. A forward magazine release allows the box to be easily removed, the magazine simply dropping out into the hand.

Trigger system

The Wildcat's two-stage trigger has received special attention to give it a crisp pull, and for maintenance the bolt is designed to be stripped easily.

In terms of overall finish, the Wildcat has a full stock with a substantial comb, deep checkering on the pistol grip (which also features a composite pistol grip cap), and a Schnabel fore-end. Internally, the Wildcat has a polished bore and precision rifling, and a semi-target chamber to ensure a respectable out-of-the-box accuracy. The complete look is one that is more familiar on larger-calibre rifles, so the Wildcat should be a popular model.

Semi-auto rifles range from the familar-looking hunting guns –
such as the Remington M750 at the top – through to full-on
military-style designs such as the Colt Match Target (bottom).

CHAPTER 4

SEMI-AUTOMATIC RIFLES

In civilian-market catalogues and books, semi-automatic rifles tend to occupy a much smaller percentage of the pages than do bolt- or lever-action weapons. One of the reasons for this is legal.

The citizens of many countries, including the United States (within a state-variable and complex history of legislation), can own a magazine-fed rifle that automatically loads the next round after a shot is fired. However, in many other countries, these firearms are often classified as assault rifles, and are therefore banned from the hands of anyone but a soldier or police officer.

For example, the massacre in 1987 of 16 people in the English town of Hungerford by Michael Ryan, who was armed with an AK47, led the British government to ban the ownership of centrefire semi-automatic rifles. Furthermore, many countries (and certain US states) prohibit the use of semi-automatic rifles for deer hunting or similar types of hunting.

The second factor in the relatively small number of semi-automatic rifles bought is the common perception (not necessarily always accurate) that a semi-automatic rifle does not offer the hunting accuracy of a bolt-action weapon. The debate is ongoing, but it should be borne in mind that there are a good number of semi-automatic police and military-sniper rifles out there, all calibrated for the greatest demands on accuracy.

Rimfire/centrefire

So what is the position of the semi-automatic rifle today? Calibre can be an indication. A great many semi-automatic rifles are small-calibre rimfire weapons. These often use a blowback mechanism (the bolt and barrel are not locked together, the pressure of the firing gases on the cartridge pushing back the bolt to cycle the weapon) and are cheap to produce. Rimfires are generally used for plinking, target shooting, small-game hunting, and, indeed, any form of shooting that can use up plenty of cartridges at relatively short ranges.

Having a semi-automatic means that the hunter can, say, take on a colony of rabbits without having to crank a bolt handle between each shot and further alert the targets.

Yet even on larger game the semi-automatic can have a place. Centrefire semi-automatics tend almost always to be gas-operated firearms. The gas system absorbs much of the recoil generated by the powerful centrefire cartridges, and so makes for more controllable multiple shots. All shooters have in their

time only wounded an animal with their first shot, and having a rapid follow-up shot can reduce the chance of the animal escaping wounded into the undergrowth. Good-quality semi-automatics, such as the Benelli R1, control the recoil to such an extent that an aimed follow-up shot can be taken within a second of the first round being fired.

The key word here is 'aimed'. Semi-automatics in themselves are fine hunting weapons; the main problem with them is they can be both dangerous and unsporting in the wrong hands. As long as the hunter exercises self-control, is well trained, and takes care that he or she only pulls the trigger when the aim is good and the picture of the target is clear, then the fire capabilities of the gun do not really matter. If, however, the shooter sprays fire in the general direction of a target, hoping for at least one terminal strike, that is unacceptable.

When firing a semi-automatic rifle, keep a keen awareness of your backdrop at all times. While your first shot's overflight might go safely into a bank of earth, if taken quickly on the swing, the second shot might inadvertently be taken when there is nothing but clear blue sky behind the target. Use the semi-automatic rifle with the same disciplined mentality as a single-shot gun, and any arguments against its use should disappear.

The Walther G22 is a strange-looking gun. It uses state-of-the-art materials to create a precision tool for hunting or target shooting. It is made entirely of steel and polymer and comes in only one model – the .22-calibre Long Rifle.

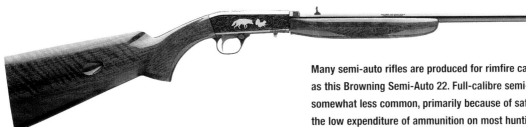

Many semi-auto rifles are produced for rimfire calibres – such as this Browning Semi-Auto 22. Full-calibre semi-autos are somewhat less common, primarily because of safety factors and the low expenditure of ammunition on most hunting trips.

Unusual types

While bolt-action rifles all tend to come in a recognizable format, semi-automatic rifles have some more outlandish specimens. Many of these are civilian versions of military weapons. The Barrett M82A1, for example, is a .50 BMG semi-automatic recoil-operated sniper rifle, its massive box magazine holding 10 of the huge rounds. The Bushmaster XM15 rifles and several other similar makes are effectively US military M16 assault rifles without the full-automatic facility and some of the military fitment.

Military-style semi-automatic guns have to be treated with caution, because, when used in hunting formats, they can give shooters a bad press. This is especially the case if the shooter goes over the top when accessorizing – a 30-round magazine of 7.62mm ammunition just isn't needed on a hunting trip when you might see only a single deer, if you're lucky. However, in growing sports such as practical shooting, or for long-range target shooting or home defence, they have their place.

Prices of semi-automatic rifles vary widely from a couple of hundred dollars for a cheap rimfire through to the $7000 needed to buy a new Barrett. As always, the rule is buy the best quality of gun you can for the exact purpose you require.

The 5.56mm M16 rifle has not only been one of the most successful military weapons of all time, it also enjoys strong civilian sales through a number of different makes and models. They are particularly used for target and practical shooting and home defence.

Barrett M82A1

$$$$

Firing the Barrett M82A1 is an experience never forgotten. Yet although it fires the awesome .50 BMG round, it is still a semi-automatic rifle, in contrast to many other .50-calibre rifles.

SPECIFICATIONS: **Barrett M82A1**

CALIBRE: .50 BMG	
BARREL LENGTH: 74cm (29in)	
WEIGHT: 13kg (28.5lb)	
SIGHTS: backup folding iron sights; mountings for scope	
MECHANISM: short-recoil operated	
FEATURES: 10-round box magazine; muzzle brake	

The Barrett M82A1 works on the principle of short recoil, the barrel recoiling about 25mm (1in) on firing to provide the momentum for the bolt to continue rearwards, eject the spent cartridge, then return forwards to strip another round from the magazine and load it in the chamber. (The bolt is of a three-lug type.)

Massive power

The Barrett is an extremely large weapon in all its dimensions. It is 145cm (57in) long and weighs an impressive 13kg (28.5lb). The 10-round detachable box magazine, when fully loaded, also ups the weight significantly. Such length and weight necessitate the adjustable bipod on the front part of the fore-end, and the gun comes with a folding carry handle to aid transportation. A detachable rear monopod also sits beneath the stock.

Firing experience

The blast from the weapon on firing is formidable. A US Marine artillery captain with the author during a test firing said the back blast was not dissimilar to that of an artillery piece. A large muzzle brake at the front controls some of the recoil, and the recoil experience is more of a giant controlled push rather than a painful impact.

An extensive recoil pad on the butt plate soaks up further recoil. Folding iron sights are provided on the Barrett as a backup, but with the .50-calibre rounds capable of ranges beyond 2000m (6561ft), a powerful scope is fairly essential. The top of the receiver is fitted with mounts for a scope.

The Barrett is a specialist weapon that has found its principal use in the ranks of the US military as a sniper rifle, mainly designed for anti-materiel sniping. Its price tag in excess of $7000 also prohibits many from investing in this weapon, but for those that do it is the centre of attention on any shooting range.

The Barrett M82A1 was originally designed, and is still used, as a military anti-materiel rifle. Note the powerful muzzle brake to control some of the recoil and flash.

Benelli R1

$$

Benelli prides itself on the light recoil and fast reload of its R1 rifles. With advanced features throughout its construction, the R1 stands as one of the most capable hunting semi-automatics on the market.

SPECIFICATIONS: **Benelli R1**

CALIBRE: .30-06 Springfield, .270 WSM, .300 WSM, .300 Win Mag, .308 Win

BARREL LENGTH: 51cm (20in), 56cm (22in), 61cm (24in)

WEIGHT: up to 3.3kg (7.3lb)

SIGHTS: Picatinny rail mounting for scope

MECHANISM: gas operated

FEATURES: fast reload; ComforTech™ recoil-dampening stock; Grip-Tight™ texture

The R1 is chambered for .30-06 Springfield, .270 WSM, .300 WSM, .300 Win Mag, and .308 Win, these being loaded and locked into the chamber by Benelli's rotary bolt-head system. Benelli has also given the R1 system interchangeable barrels, so the shooter can quickly and conveniently switch between calibres.

The rounds are fed up into the gun from a three- or four-round (depending on calibre) detachable box magazine, which is contoured to continue the flow of the fore-end. The ARGO (Auto-Regulating Gas-Operated) system is purposely designed for very fast cycling (the gas port is set much closer to the breech than is commonly found on semi-automatic rifles), and Benelli claims that the R1 can reload as much as

51 per cent faster than some other semi-automatic rifles. Nevertheless, the three lugs on the rotary bolt ensure a very stable lock before the shot is taken.

Form and function

Fast reload is only part of what the R1 offers. The ComforTech™ recoil-dampening stock also dramatically reduces felt recoil by up to 50 per cent over a standard weapon to allow for very quick recovery between shots. This system has gel pads on the butt plate and the comb and within the stock that soak up the recoil and, according to manufacturer's claims, reduces muzzle climb by up to 20 per cent. The stock and fore-end are also covered with Benelli's Grip-Tight™ texture to give a superb level of hand adhesion even in wet conditions.

In terms of sights, the R1 comes with a Picatinny rail scope base for the shooter to fit his own scope. The R1 is one of the most impressive semi-automatic rifles on the market, and the shooting press to date has given little but favourable reports to this gun. With a retail price of just over $1000, it looks set to become an extremely popular model.

Few semi-auto rifles pack in as much technological advancement as the Benelli R1, from first-class recoil control to ultrafast reloading.

Browning BAR

$–$$

The Browning BAR rifles hold the dominant position in the auto-loading rifle market, a position obtained through the quality of construction and the popularity of the available calibres.

SPECIFICATIONS: **Browning BAR Long Trac**

CALIBRE: .270 Win, .30-06 Springfield, 7mm Rem. Mag, .300 Win Mag

BARREL LENGTH: 56cm (22in), 61cm (24in)

WEIGHT: up to 3.4kg (7.5lb)

SIGHTS: receiver drilled and tapped for scope

MECHANISM: gas operated

FEATURES: BOSS system option

There are four basic models in the BAR range: the Long Trac and Short Trac (representing long-action and short-action rifles respectively), the Safari model, and the new Stalker model. Differences between the models are mainly to do with construction and finish. The Safari model has a scroll-engraved ordnance steel receiver, while the other three models have plain aluminium alloy receivers.

Composite stock

The composite stocks of stalker guns are also rendered in a matte black finish, whereas the Short Trac and Long Trac come in either natural wood or Mossy Oak® New Break-Up® camouflage. Across the guns the available calibres include .243 Win, .25-06, .30-06 Springfield, .270 Win, .270 WSM, 7mm WSM, 7mm Mag, 7mm Rem Mag, .300 Win Mag, .308, and .338 Win Mag. This selection of calibres

Browning BAR guns make good woodland hunting weapons, particularly when one shot might not be enough on a fleeting target. This BAR is fitted with open sights, but most BAR models will easily take a scope.

covers almost all the bases for hunters who want to take on everything from deer through to moose and safari game.

Core features

BAR rifles are gas-operated auto-loaders. The bolt locks into the barrel via seven lugs on its head and the bolt face is also recessed to grip the end of the cartridge very firmly, thus ensuring controlled feeding and a stable seating in the chamber. BAR rifles are known for their accuracy, and this can be further improved through the option of the Ballistic Optimizing Shooting System (BOSS). This is essentially an adjustable muzzle brake/weight system that can be configured to tune out vibrations, which can impair accuracy, hence improving the stability of the bullet flight. (Browning also make the BOSS CR system, which has the weight-adjusting features but without the muzzle brake.) Recoil control in the BAR guns is also excellent.

All of the BAR rifles have receivers that are drilled and tapped for scope mounts, but the Lightweight Stalker model comes with open sights as standard. These consist of a rear click-adjustable sight corresponding with a hooded front bead.

Browning Semi-Automatic 22

$–$$

The Browning SA-22 is a rifle with real field utility for around $500. It is a light, reliable weapon ideally suited to varmint hunting or survival use.

SPECIFICATIONS: **Browning Semi-Automatic 22**

CALIBRE: .22 LR

BARREL LENGTH: 49cm (19.25in)

WEIGHT: 2.3kg (5.1lb)

SIGHTS: open sights; optional scope bases

MECHANISM: blowback operated

FEATURES: 11-round tubular magazine; breakdown design; cross-bolt safety

The SA-22 is chambered for the ever-popular .22 LR calibre, one of the most practical calibres for those wanting to take small game at ranges of under 100m (328ft). Shooting press reports on the now venerable SA-22 (it has been produced since 1965) have been extremely favourable, reviewers noting its reliability, its light weight and convenient dimensions, and its workaday accuracy.

A popular feature of the SA-22 is its 11-shot magazine capacity (the rounds are loaded in through the butt stock), a capacity that appeals to those who want to enjoy some rapid-fire plinking or who want to be confident of not running out of rounds when a quick-fire target opportunity appears. Operation is particularly simple: the magazine rod assembly is removed, the rounds are just dropped into the tubular magazine, and the magazine rod is replaced. Finally the bolt is cycled by hand and the gun is ready to go. In terms of its dimensions, the SA-22 has a 49cm (19.25in) barrel with an overall length of 94cm (37in). It weighs a mere 2.3kg (5.1lb), making it suitable for use by youngsters wanting their first semi-automatic rifle.

Convenient breaking-down

The SA-22 can be quickly and conveniently broken down into two parts at the point just in front of the receiver. This feature makes the gun extremely handy for storage and transportation. However, it also presents a potential problem for maintaining the zero of sights on reassembly. Browning deals with this by placing the open sights purely on the barrel, so they are not affected by disassembly of the gun. Furthermore, the scope fittings are also located on the barrel. Safety is very important in any gun, but especially semi-automatics, and the SA-22 has a cross-bolt safety fitted just in front of the trigger guard.

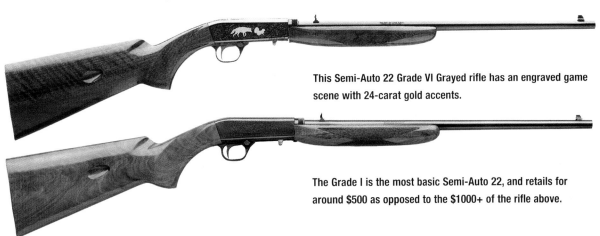

This Semi-Auto 22 Grade VI Grayed rifle has an engraved game scene with 24-carat gold accents.

The Grade I is the most basic Semi-Auto 22, and retails for around $500 as opposed to the $1000+ of the rifle above.

Browning Buck Mark

$

The Browning Buck Mark has one of the most unusual appearances of any auto-loading rifle, it actually being a rifle redesign of Browning's Buck Mark pistol.

SPECIFICATIONS: **Browning Buck Mark Semi-Automatic Rifle**

CALIBRE: .22 LR	
BARREL LENGTH: 46cm (18in)	
WEIGHT: up to 2.4kg (5.25lb)	
SIGHTS: fibre-optic sights; rail mounting for scope	
MECHANISM: blowback operated	
FEATURES: 10-round magazine; two types of barrel	

The Buck Mark pistol is a popular .22 LR 10-shot auto handgun for target shooting or light hunting. Its rifle counterpart retains the same blowback-action mechanism, blowback generally being a reliable and relatively inexpensive method of auto-loading – the Buck Mark rifle sells for around $500. The Buck Mark pistol becomes a rifle through two principal changes. A walnut or laminated hardwood stock is fitted to the back of the gun on metal braces that extend from the rear of the receiver and the bottom of the pistol grip. At the other end of the gun, there

is an obvious change in barrel configuration. Two different 46cm (18in) barrels are available for the Buck Mark. The first is the tapered sporter-weight barrel for the Sporter models. For Target models, there is a heavy steel bull or alloy-sleeved barrel. The crowns of all the barrels are recessed; this shields them from damage that could impair accuracy.

Handling

Because it has pistol grip along with a full fore-end, the Buck Mark handles somewhere between a pistol and a rifle. Its accuracy, however, is not in doubt. The sporter model has a Truglo®/Marble's® adjustable fibre-optic sight for quick target acquisition, and the guns can take scopes via an integral rail scope mount. The design also means that the shooter has an extremely light weapon, with the Sporter versions weighing only 1.9kg (4.1lb) while the Target guns are a little heavier at around 2.4kg (5.25lb). As such the Buck Mark rifle allows for the very quick acquisition of targets and, with its 10-round detachable box magazine, for quick shooting.

This is the Buck Mark FLD Target Gray Laminate Rifle. Note the lack of open sights, but the provision of a scope rail.

The Buck Mark Sporter Rifle has adjustable fibre-optic sights as well as a scope rail, and an oil-finished walnut stock.

Bushmaster XM15 Rifles

$–$$

For those wanting a military-grade weapon for practical shooting, quick-fire hunting or for home defence, the Bushmaster XM15/AR15 series of rifles is often the first port of call.

SPECIFICATIONS: Bushmaster A2/A3 20in Rifle
CALIBRE: .223 Rem
BARREL LENGTH: 51cm (20in)
WEIGHT: 3.8kg (8.27lb) without magazine
SIGHTS: A2 Dual Aperture Rear Sight; scopes can be fitted
MECHANISM: gas operated
FEATURES: chrome-lined bores and chambers; manganese phosphate coated

The Bushmaster XM15/AR15 family is an extensive group of weapons that are civilian/law enforcement versions of the US forces' M16 assault rifle. Apart from selective-fire differences, such as the absence of full-automatic/burst settings seen on military weapons, and some more subtle differences in fitment, the Bushmaster weapons are in most ways identical to the military specifications.

The basic configuration of the XM15 family is a gas-operated .223 Rem (5.56mm) calibre semi-automatic rifle or carbine. Bores and chambers are lined with chrome, and the standard heavy-profile barrels have rifling that imparts one twist every 22cm (9in). This rifling, in the company's words, 'gives optimum accuracy results with a broad range of ammunition, and will stabilize bullets up to 75 grains'.

All metal parts are finished with a military-grade protective manganese phosphate finish for excellent anti-corrosion protection. Sights are the A2 Dual Aperture Rear Sight, which offers the ability to switch between quick-firing target acquisition and more deliberate aimed shots using a flip-up sight.

Bushmasters are popular with those who appreciate military-grade reliability in a hunting weapon.

Extensive family

The XM15 family is big – counting the Carbon 15 series of rifles and pistols, there are over 30 different variants. A good example of a 'standard' XM15 would be the Bushmaster A2 20in Rifle. This has a 51cm (20in) barrel, a weight of 3.8kg (8.27lb) and comes supplied with a 10-round box magazine – other magazines are available that go up to a 40-round version (multiple magazines can also be held together using magazine holders).

By contrast, the Bushmaster Superlight with Stubb Stock has only a 41cm (16in) barrel, an overall length of only 79cm (31.25in) and weighs 2.63kg (5.8lb). (All weights here are given without the magazine.) Other models include guns with tele-stocks, free-floating or stainless-steel barrels, skeleton stocks, and other configurations, and they are an attractive family for those wanting a military-proven weapon.

Colt Match Target HBAR

$$

Competing for its share of the AR15-type market is the Match Target series from Colt, Colt being the original manufacturer of the military AR15/M16. Colt states that the guns are 'ideal for hunting, plinking, and competition shooting'.

SPECIFICATIONS: Colt Match Target HBAR

CALIBRE: .223 Rem

BARREL LENGTH: 51cm (20in)

WEIGHT: 3.6kg (8lb)

SIGHTS: adjustable open sights; flat receiver for scope mounting

MECHANISM: gas operated

FEATURES: chrome-lined bores and chambers; compensator as option

The early days of the AR15/M16 were extremely troubled, with major reliability issues during the conflict in Vietnam leading to a loss of confidence in the rifle for many years. Evolving improvements, however, have transformed the rifle into a first-rate weapon, with excellent reliability figures as long as the gun receives its recommended cleaning programme and proper cooling-time allowances.

Colt's Match Target HBAR has received excellent press reviews for its range performance, firing many thousands of rounds without malfunction. My own personal experience with Colt AR15s also bears this out.

Accurate assault rifle

The Match Target HBAR (Heavy Barrel) follows the standard AR15 layout. It is chambered for the .223 Rem (5.56mm), and fires these through a 51cm (20in) barrel. The standard sights are a front post adjustable for elevation and a click-adjustable rear aperture sight, which give respectable accuracy out to 100m (328ft).

With a good scope fitted (the Colt guns have flat receivers to allow for easy scope mounting) the accuracy of the .223 Rem round can be taken out to two or three times this distance, and the Match Target HBAR is designed to give competition-level accuracy.

Choice of models

Four models of the Match Target HBAR are listed, each of which has subtle variations in fitment, such as whether a muzzle compensator is included or not. The Match Target M4, however, is a carbine-type version with a metal military-style butt stock. There is also the Colt Accurized rifle, this having a free-floating 61cm (24in) stainless-steel heavy barrel for optimal range accuracy (it is configured to take a scope as standard).

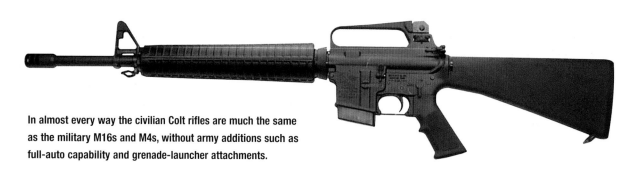

In almost every way the civilian Colt rifles are much the same as the military M16s and M4s, without army additions such as full-auto capability and grenade-launcher attachments.

CZ 511

$

The CZ 511 is a basic rimfire semi-automatic, which has, in CZ's words, been 'resurrected' because of its popularity. It does exactly what someone wants from a rimfire repeater – works consistently and gives accurate result.

SPECIFICATIONS: CZ 511

CALIBRE: .22 LR

BARREL LENGTH: 53cm (21in)

WEIGHT: 2.6kg (5.9lb)

SIGHTS: adjustable open sights; dovetail groove for scope mounting

MECHANISM: blowback

FEATURES: eight-round detachable magazine

The CZ 511 is a blowback weapon chambered for .22 LR. Blowback systems are ideal for small-calibre weapons, such as the 511, because the bolt does not have to be too large to restrain the power of the small cartridge, and blowback is also known for its reliability.

A further factor in the mix is that blowback is cheap to manufacture compared with gas-operated systems – a 511 can be picked up for around $350. Basic dimensions of the 511 are a barrel length of 53cm (21in), an overall length of 98cm (38.5in), and a weight of 2.6kg (5.9lb).

Small report

In spite of its budget price tag, the 511 has much to recommend it as a small game hunting rifle or

Acknowledging the fairly low power and limited range of the .22 LR round, the CZ 511 has open sights as standard, with an adjustable rear leaf corresponding with a hooded post at the front of the gun.

plinking gun. The hammer-forged barrel is fitted into either a beechwood (on the Standard model) or walnut stock (on the Luxe model), the comb of the stock curving in a 'German' style.

Open sights are fitted as standard on all CZ 511s. The rear sight is of a flip-over type with two leaves, the first calibrated out to 50m (164ft) while the second is set to 100m (328ft). The magazine is a detachable box that holds a total of eight rounds of the .22 LR ammunition.

The overall length of a CZ 511 is compact enough for it to be comfortably handled by someone of small frame, or a child under instruction.

Subsonic shells

The noise signature of any .22 LR gun is not great, but the 511 can also come in a version designed for subsonic shells. Furthermore, the 511 has the option of a threaded muzzle to take a sound moderator. In this configuration the rifle is very quiet indeed, and is ideal for hunting animals such as rabbits, when the hunter does not want to disturb other animals too much with the gun's report.

Les Baer Custom Ultimate AR.223 $$$

The Les Baer AR.223 Super Varmint offers competition-level accuracy and superb levels of engineering in a gas-operated semi-automatic rifle with prices ranging between $2000 and $3000.

SPECIFICATIONS:
Les Baer Custom Ultimate AR.223 Super Varmint

CALIBRE: .223 Rem

BARREL LENGTH: 46cm (18in), 51cm (20in), 56cm (22in), 61cm (24in)

WEIGHT: 5kg (11lb)

SIGHTS: Picatinny rail for scope mounting

MECHANISM: gas operated

FEATURES: match-grade barrel; precision machining throughout; bipod attachment; Bear Coat™ finish

At the time of writing, the Les Baer website says 'We'll guarantee that our Super Varmint Model will shoot ½ MOA groups!' – indeed, a shooting test by Wayne van Zwoll in *Guns & Ammo* (March 2005) confirmed the accuracy of this .223 semi-automatic rifle. Tests in other shooting magazines produced similar results.

The Super Varmint is built around an LBC Bench Rest 416 R barrel. This is a precision-rifled barrel, and is available in 46cm (18in), 51cm (20in), 56cm (22in), and 61cm (24in) lengths. It is made of stainless steel and there is an option of the barrel taking the Bear Coat™ finish. This contains Teflon® and is applied to much of the rest of the gun.

Every part of the action is similarly precision-machined, producing a wonderfully solid and smooth feed and ejection cycle (the carrier, bolt, and the extractor are all chromed). The firing pin is made from titanium and the gas block is made from aluminium.

Trigger happy

The Jewell two-stage trigger is another feature emphasized by Les Baer and by the shooting critics. Trigger pull is very smooth with a final crisp snap and a total pull weight of just under 1.4kg (3lb). Naturally such an accurate rifle does not feature open sights. Instead a Picatinny flat top rail is provided that will allow the shooter to fit any manner of custom optics. The gun will also take a bipod, which is fitted to a stud at the front of the rifle and has legs with adjustable heights.

Les Baer make several other models of the .223 semi-automatic rifle, all with the same attention to detail and quality, and they are much respected by target shooters, hunters, and law-enforcement officers alike.

Although the Les Baer gun is a semi-auto, its level of accuracy would challenge most bolt-action guns.

Marlin Model 60

$

New Marlin Model 60 rifles can be bought for under $200, even with a x4 scope fitted at the factory. This affordability puts them amongst them United States' bestselling auto-loading rifles.

SPECIFICATIONS: Marlin Model 60

CALIBRE: .22 LR

BARREL LENGTH: 48cm (19in)

WEIGHT: 2.5kg (5.5lb)

SIGHTS: adjustable open sights; receiver grooved for scope mounting

MECHANISM: blowback

FEATURES: 14-round tubular magazine; automatic last-shot bolt hold-open device

The Model 60 has not only sold well across the United States. Developed in 1960 from the earlier Model 99, it has gone on to become the most popular .22 LR rifle in the world, favoured by both hunters and casual target shooters alike. Nevertheless, the Model 60 is in the typical format of many budget rimfire repeaters.

Details

It is chambered for the ubiquitous .22 LR and works on a blowback principle. In terms of dimensions, it has a 48cm (19in) barrel, an overall length of 95cm (37.5in), and a weight of 2.5kg (5.5lb). So far, a very familiar rimfire weapon. The Model 60 is so popular both because of the quality of its build and the

A basic Marlin Model 60 can be picked up for under $200. The long under-barrel magazine is visible here, and this holds 14 .22 LR rounds, making the Model 60 a terrific plinking gun.

collection of small features that it has, which add up to make an impressive gun. In total, the Model 60 can hold 14 .22 LR rounds in its under-barrel tubular magazine, an impressive magazine capacity by anybody's standards. The magazine tube is also made of brass, therefore resisting any of the corrosion problems that can accompany steel. The barrel has Marlin's Micro-Groove® rifling, with a total of 16 grooves imparting great accuracy to the small-calibre round.

Young guns

Useful in a gun commonly used by young shots, the Model 60 also has an automatic bolt hold-open feature when the last round in the magazine has been fired (the bolt locks open at the halfway point so the shooter can see that the chamber is clear).

The sights are open type, with an adjustable rear and a ramped front post. The gun also features a Monte Carlo walnut-finished stock, with the Mar-Shield® finish to protect the weapon against the climate. When such features are combined with great reliability, it is not surprising that the Model 60 retains the place that it does.

Marlin Model 7000

$

The Model 7000 is a rimfire repeater upgraded from the Model 60 considered previously. The calibre is the same, but the gun is designed for much greater levels of accurate shooting.

SPECIFICATIONS: **Marlin Model 7000**

CALIBRE: .22 LR	
BARREL LENGTH: 46cm (18in)	
WEIGHT: 2.4kg (5.25lb)	
SIGHTS: receiver grooved for scope mount	
MECHANISM: blowback	
FEATURES: 10-round box magazine; automatic last-shot bolt hold-open device; heavy target barrel	

T he heart of the Model 7000 is the same blowback action used on the Model 60. It is also chambered in the .22 LR calibre. It has a cross-bolt safety and side ejection and the automatic last-shot bolt hold-open device. However, the gun looks very different to the Model 60 and has a price tag of around $250. So where is the little extra money going?

Ammunition feed

An immediate difference from the Model 60 is the magazine, which is a 10-round detachable nickel-plated box.

The barrel itself is also one of the major changes in the Model 7000. It is a substantial 46cm (18in) heavy target barrel turned out with Marlin's Micro-

The Model 7000 does not come with open sights. Because of its emphasis on accuracy, scope mounting rings are standard.

Groove® rifling to make a superb platform for accuracy, good for building up the tight groupings that win competitions. The muzzle of the barrel is also recessed to protect it from incurring any accuracy-impairing damage. Such features are extremely welcome in a budget gun, and the recessed muzzle is not always found on far more expensive rifles.

Stock and fittings

Because of the Model 7000's emphasis on high-level accuracy, no open sights are fitted to the gun. Instead the receiver is grooved for a scope and scope mounting rings are provided. Unlike the wooden stock of the Model 60, the Model 7000 has a black fibreglass-filled synthetic stock, which is extremely durable and environmentally stable. The checkering is moulded into the surface of the stock itself.

Despite the more substantial appearance of the Model 7000 when compared to the Model 60, it actually weighs only 2.4kg (5.25lb). As a super-accurate short-range hunting rifle the Model 7000 is an excellent investment for young shooter or experienced hunter alike.

Marlin Model 70PSS $

The Marlin Model 70PSS falls into the 'survival rifle' category. As Marlin says, it's a rifle to take with you when you're 'backpacking, boating, four-wheeling or just taking a hike'.

SPECIFICATIONS: Marlin Model 70PSS Stainless
CALIBRE: .22 LR
BARREL LENGTH: 41cm (16.25in)
WEIGHT: 1.5kg (3.25lb)
SIGHTS: open sights; receiver grooved for scope mount
MECHANISM: blowback
FEATURES: seven-round box magazine; automatic last-shot bolt hold-open device; easy disassembly

Survival rifles come with several different names, including 'trail gun' and 'wilderness gun'. All are intended to stand either as a substitute for taking a large and heavy rifle into the field, or as backup survival tool if a camping trip or other wilderness adventure goes wrong.

Wilderness gun

There is a basic set of criteria for a good survival rifle. First, it must be capable of being broken down and packed up small. This means that the gun can slot into a backpack or into some recess of a vehicle without taking up too much space. Second, it must weigh very little – it may have to be carried for days on end over many kilometres (miles). Third, it must be very tough to withstand continual exposure to the outdoor elements. Finally, the cartridge has to be just powerful enough to act as a genuine hunting round should an emergency arise.

Marlin's survivor

The Model 70PSS manages to satisfy all of these criteria. The barrel is easily separated from the receiver, and both of these parts fit into a convenient carrying case, which also has built-in flotation should the gun be dropped into water.

It is a lightweight gun, weighing only 1.5kg (3.25lb). In terms of its toughness, the barrel and receiver are made from stainless steel, one of the best metals for harsh-environment use. The stock is made from black fibreglass-filled polycarbonate, which is equally tough in shrugging off wet weather.

The 70PSS fires the redoubtable .22 LR round. This is a rimfire round, so carries little force for taking on larger prey such as deer. However, the .22 LR will perfectly happily despatch many of the small species that separate a person from life or death in a survival situation, ranging from small birds up to foxes. For around $300, it may be a wise investment for any group embarking for the wilderness.

The Marlin Model 70PSS is a practical rifle through and through. The sights consist of a post surrounded by a cutaway front hood and an adjustable rear sight.

Remington Model 597

$

The Remington Model 597 offers a series of rifles that go beyond the standard .22 LR calibre. They have a price range that extends from around $170 up to nearly $400.

SPECIFICATIONS: Remington Model 597

CALIBRE: .22 LR	
BARREL LENGTH: 51cm (20in)	
WEIGHT: 2.5kg (5.5lb)	
SIGHTS: open sights; receiver grooved for scope mount	
MECHANISM: blowback	
FEATURES: 10-round box magazine; automatic last-shot bolt hold-open device	

A cutaway of the Remington 597, showing the bolt group with firing pin, trigger group and the magazine feed.

The standard Remington Model 597 is a .22 LR rimfire auto-loader, working on a straightforward blowback mechanism and taking its feed from a staggered-stack detachable 10-shot box magazine. It has a 51cm (20in) barrel and a weight of 2.5kg (5.5lb). Where the series differs from most other rimfire repeaters, however, lies in what Remington feels are some distinctive improvements in the quality of the gun's build and design. It points to its 'proprietary bolt-guidance system', which has 'twin tool-steel guide rails' to ensure a very reliable and consistent standard of feed from magazine to chamber.

Furthermore, a Teflon®/nickel-plated coating is applied not only to the bolt but also to the hammer and sear, the application to the trigger parts resulting in a very crisp and predictable pull. As a safety feature, the bolt automatically holds itself open after the last round of the magazine has been fired.

Six versions

Six different versions of the Model 597 are listed at the time of writing. The Model 597 SS has similar specifications to the standard model, but is fitted with a stainless-steel barrel with a satin finish, which is also set in a free-floating arrangement with the fore-end. The LSS model retains this stainless-steel barrel, but replaces the synthetic stock with a laminated wooden stock, which gives a good contrast between the light of the plain wood and the dark of the grain.

A heavy-barrelled version of the 597 is provided, logically, in the 597 HB. The 597 Magnum and 597 Magnum LS HB change the calibre, being available in .17 HMR and .22 Win Mag. The magazine capacity of these weapons is eight shots rather than 10.

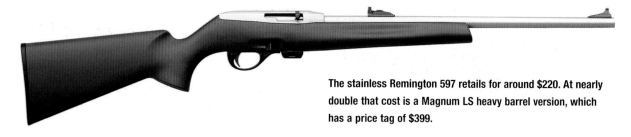

The stainless Remington 597 retails for around $220. At nearly double that cost is a Magnum LS heavy barrel version, which has a price tag of $399.

Remington Model 750 Woodmaster

$

The 750 Woodmaster is a powerful repeating rifle ideally suited to hunting elusive prey such as woodland deer and boar in close-quarters terrain, or for taking on packs of animals where a quick second shot is needed.

SPECIFICATIONS: Remington Model 750 Woodmaster

CALIBRE: .243 Win, .308 Win, .270 Win, .30-06 Sprg, .35 Whelen, .308 Win (Carbine), .30-06 Sprg (Carbine), .35 Whelen (Carbine)

BARREL LENGTH: 56cm (22in)

WEIGHT: up to 3.4kg (7.5lb)

SIGHTS: open sights; receiver drilled and tapped for scope mount

MECHANISM: gas operated

FEATURES: R4 recoil pad; American walnut stock

The Model 750 Woodmaster has a total of eight calibres in the series: .243 Win, .308 Win, .270 Win, .30-06 Sprg, .35 Whelen, .308 Win (Carbine), .30-06 Sprg (Carbine), and .35 Whelen (Carbine). The gun actually stands as a replacement for the wood-stocked Model 7400 series rifles, and indeed retains many of the features of that series.

Like the 7400, the 750 is a gas-operated weapon, and a gas system is ideal for any potentially rapid-fire hunting, as the gas piston and springwork soak up much of the recoil, allowing a shooter to get back on

to target more quickly for a second shot. Remington has also added the R3 recoil pad to the Model 750. This is an impressive bit of technology in its own right. Limbsaver's™ proprietary NAVCOM™ (Noise And Vibration Control Material) absorbs the initial shock, while at the same time air chambers inside the stock compress to further soften the recoil and spread it over a wider area of the shoulder.

Woodwork

Although the Model 7400 stock now only features in a fibreglass-reinforced synthetic material, the Woodmaster has an American walnut stock and fore-end, the stock featuring a Monte Carlo comb and the fore-end swelling prominently to provide a stable front grip.

The overall design is very flat and slim, with the recoil of the gun having a good 'in-line' relationship with the shoulder. Basic specifications for the Woodmaster are a 56cm (22in) barrel, adjustable open sights, and a weight of 3.4kg (7.5lb). The Carbine versions, however, take the barrel length down to 47cm (18.5in) and the weight down to 3.3kg (7.25lb).

The Woodmaster guns come with a satin walnut stock and open sights as standard. The overall length of the gun is 115cm (46.5in).

Ruger 10/22

$

Ruger make a particularly broad range of auto-loading rifles, including the 10/22 series, a versatile group of firearms chambered for the .22 LR or .22 WMR cartridge.

SPECIFICATIONS: **Ruger 10/22**

CALIBRE: .22 LR, .22 WMR

BARREL LENGTH: 41cm (16.1in), 47cm (18.5in), 51cm (20in)

WEIGHT: average 2.3kg (5lb)

SIGHTS: open sights; facilities for scope mount

MECHANISM: blowback

FEATURES: detachable rotary magazine; fibre-optic sights on some models

Although Ruger 10/22s are highly customizable using aftermarket parts, the basic model of this popular .22 LR series is plain and unassuming. With an American hardwood stock, the 10/22RR model has extremely clean lines, something aided by the detachable rotary magazine fitting flush into the stock (this magazine has a 10-round capacity). The barrel length on this particular model is 51cm (20in), but other models are available in 41cm (16.1in) and 47cm (18.5in) lengths. The mechanism of the 10/22, housed in the steel receiver, is a basic blowback and gives an extremely dependable performance. Ruger emphasizes that it has given the 10/22 a very short lock time on account of the 'high-speed, pivoted hammer'.

Stocks and magnums

While the basic shape of the stock on the 10/22 does not change, the material it is made in does. Brown, black and Jacaranda laminates are available, as are versions with black synthetic stocks or stocks made entirely from American walnut. Stainless-steel metal versions are also available. Open sights are provided on all 10/22s, some models having fibre-optic versions that are very suitable for shooting in low-light conditions. For around double the price tag (around $500 instead of around $250), a .22 WMR magnum version of the rifle is available (the 10/22RBM). This has scope rings fitted for easy scope mounting and a nine-round magazine capacity.

The 10/22 series has enjoyed a long-running popularity in the United States and abroad – bear in mind that they began production in 1968. The ability to customize the rifles with non-proprietary parts has further enhanced the appeal of these weapons.

The K10/22RPF model has a black synthetic stock and a stainless metal finish.

The 10/22-T has a heavy 51cm (20in) barrel and is designed purely for use with a scope, there being no open sights.

Ruger Mini 14

$

The Ruger Mini 14 is a centrefire rifle chambered for the .223 Rem (5.56mm) cartridge. It belongs to Ruger's 'Ranch Rifle' series of auto-loaders, giving a suggestion of its suitable usage.

SPECIFICATIONS: **Ruger Mini 14**

CALIBRE: .223 Rem

BARREL LENGTH: 47cm (18.5in)

WEIGHT: 2.9kg (6.4lb)

SIGHTS: integral scope bases; Ghost Ring aperture sights

MECHANISM: gas operated

FEATURES: Garand mechanism; recoil buffer system; sling swivels

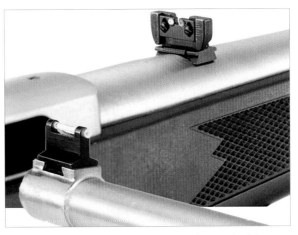

The Mini 14 can also be fitted with special fibre-optic sights, for greater accuracy.

The .223 Rem is high-velocity round that is also currently the NATO standard calibre for its assault rifles and small arms. Muzzle velocity for a 55-grain bullet is around 975m/sec (3200ft/sec), and with the proper grade of ammunition and the right scope accurate shots can be taken out to several hundred metres (yards). However, the .223 is not a deep-penetrating round – it tends to fragment on impact – so it is ideally used for varmint hunting and not on larger prey (although some authorities, not without controversy, feel that the round is appropriate for small deer).

The Mini 14 is a compact .223 Rem auto-loader retailing for up to around $800. It has a 47cm (18.5in) barrel and, being a centrefire weapon, is cycled via a fixed-piston gas mechanism. The breechbolt locking system is based on the legendary Garand rifle, so reliable function is rarely disturbed in the Mini 14.

Scope mounting

The Ranch Rifle series is, in Ruger's words, 'specifically designed for mounting today's scopes or other optical sighting systems'. This is achieved by setting the scope bases directly into the receiver, hence ensuring that they 'can never shoot loose'. The side-ejection system is also set to prevent empty shell interference with the scope, and Ruger also points in its publicity to its 'patented recoil buffer, which protects the scope from damage or shifting impact when the mechanism parts move automatically during firing'. Beyond the scope fittings, however, Ghost Ring aperture sights are also fitted.

The Mini 14 is available with either a hardwood stock or a black synthetic version. Sling swivels are provided as standard.

Ruger Mini 30 All-Weather

$

While the Mini 14 is a good rifle for varmint hunting, the Mini 30's heavier calibre gives the hunter a useful, portable and accurate auto-loading rifle suitable for medium-sized deer.

SPECIFICATIONS: **Ruger Mini 30 All-Weather**

CALIBRE: 7.62 x 39	
BARREL LENGTH: 47cm (18.5in)	
WEIGHT: 3.3kg (7.25lb)	
SIGHTS: integral scope bases; Ghost Ring aperture sights	
MECHANISM: gas operated	
FEATURES: detachable box magazine; all-weather synthetic stock; matte stainless barrel	

The Mini 30 All-Weather is chambered for the 7.62 x 39 round, a cartridge easily available on account of the fact that it is a standard round for the Russian AK series of rifles. The ballistic properties of this cartridge should not be over-estimated, but it provides for very confident shooting at ranges of 91.5–183m (300–600ft).

The specifications for the Mini 30 break down as follows, and are very similar to those for the Mini 14. The receiver and barrel are of a matte stainless finish, with the latter being 47cm (18.5in). The stock is made from a black synthetic material. Combined with the stainless metalwork, this feature is what lends the Mini 30 its 'All-Weather' name.

The magazine capacity is five rounds, these being set in a staggered arrangement in a detachable box magazine. The overall length of the gun is 95cm (37.5in) and its weight is 3.3kg (7.25lb). The gun has integral scope mounts in addition to the adjustable Ghost Ring aperture rear site, which is used in tandem with the front post site.

Carbines

Between the Mini 14 and the Mini 30, Ruger also manufactures two similar carbine models – the Deerfield® Carbine and the Carbine. The Deerfield®

Carbine looks very similar to the Mini 14/30, but is chambered for the .44 Magnum revolver cartridge. The Carbine, however, looks quite different, its stock being entirely in black synthetic material and its 10-round magazine projecting well beneath the trigger guard.

Built more for defence and combat sporting use, the Carbine has a short 41cm (16.25in) barrel and can be bought in either 9mm Parabellum or .40 SW.

The Ruger Mini 30 retails for around $800, and it is a popular home-defence weapon as well as a good sporting gun. Many police forces around the United States use Ruger Mini firearms as backup weapons, appreciating their portability and decent levels of firepower.

Savage Model 64G

$

With a suggested retail price tag of only $162, the Savage Model 64G is true bargain-quality rimfire repeater. Other guns in the series take the cost in either direction.

SPECIFICATIONS: Savage Model 64G

CALIBRE: .22 LR

BARREL LENGTH: 51cm (20.25in)

WEIGHT: 2.3kg (5lb)

SIGHTS: open sights; receiver grooved for scope

MECHANISM: blowback

FEATURES: 10-round detachable box magazine; thumb-operated safety

The Savage Model 64G is a classic .22 LR rimfire repeater. It has a walnut-finished hardwood stock that features a Monte Carlo comb for a snug fit against the shooter's cheek. The barrel is 51cm (20.25in) long and takes the open sights – an adjustable rear notch sight and a simple bead front post. The overall length of the gun is 101cm (40in).

A 10-round detachable magazine juts prominently out from beneath the receiver. A scope can be fitted to the grooved receiver, and the gun is a side-ejecting type to prevent interference between ejecting charges and the scope. In terms of safety, the 64G has a thumb-operated safety switch and a bolt hold-open device to allow the shooter to confirm an empty chamber. Good safety is especially important on a budget rimfire gun, as typically this type of weapon is popular amongst young shooters and those new to shooting.

The Savage 64 guns work on a simple blowback principle well suited to the low recoil produced by the .22 LR cartridges. This mechanism does not require the levels of maintainance required by gas-operated auto-loaders.

Budget variants

The 64G appeals to many shooters because of the good quality of its build and its extremely affordable price tag. Other guns in the series provide variations in the cost and different options for the shooter (all within the context, however, of the .22 LR calibre). The 64F replaces the wooden stock with a black synthetic material, and drops the suggested retail price down to an impressive $135.

Top model

By contrast, the 64FSS occupies the top of the Model 64 tree with a stainless finish and fibre-optic sights, these taking the value up to just over $200. Just shy of that price is the 64F Camo, which is completely rendered in Realtree Hardwoods® HD™ camouflage. The Savage 64FV is similar to most of the other versions of the 64 (particularly the 64F), but differs in having a heavy 53cm (21in) barrel with a recessed crown.

Savage also provides the Model 64 guns in packages with scopes. For those wanting a first gun or a cheap, practical varmint hunter, then the Model 64 rifles offer a good place to start.

Springfield M1 Garand

$$

Buy an M1 Garand, and you buy a piece of American firearms history. As the first standard-issue semi-automatic rifle in the world, it carried US forces through World War II and the initial postwar decades.

SPECIFICATIONS: Springfield M1 Garand

CALIBRE: .30-06, .308

BARREL LENGTH: 61cm (24in)

WEIGHT: 4.37kg (9.5lb)

SIGHTS: adjustable aperture rear sight; front post

MECHANISM: gas operated

FEATURES: eight-round magazine; original-style aperture sights

A US Marines sniper aims his M1 Garand rifle towards enemy lines, Korea 1951.

The US Army started to equip itself with the M1 Garand back in 1936. Although the switch from the venerable 1903 Springfield was a great culture shock for many, almost every US soldier grew to appreciate the solid reliability of the M1 as a combat weapon. Furthermore, the gas-operated semi-automatic action allowed the average US infantryman or marine to generate much higher levels of fire than were available to those with bolt-action rifles.

The Springfield Armory is still producing M1 rifles to the original US Army specifications. The relatively low cost (they retail for around $1400) makes availability sometimes a problem.

M1s are very solid and accurate rifles, the durability suggested by the 4.37kg (9.5lb) empty weight. Barrel length is 61cm (24in) and the overall length of the gun is 110cm (43.5in).

Eight-round feed

One of the quirkiest features of the M1 was its feed system – a clip of eight rounds inserted into the magazine via the open bolt. Once the gun was loaded, individual rounds could not be added to the clip – all had to be fired before reloading. In a combat situation, such a feature could be a real problem, but for today's civilian users it is more a feature of nostalgia. While the original M1 was available in only one calibre – .30-06 – Springfield's model gun is available in both .30-06 and .308. Sights on the M1 are as original – a military-grade rear aperture sight and a front post protected by metal guards. In spite of its heavy weight, the M1 is an accurate enough rifle to be used as a hunting tool.

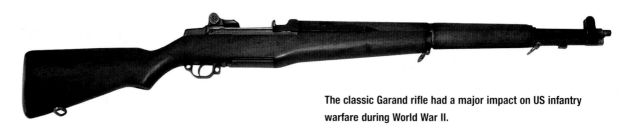

The classic Garand rifle had a major impact on US infantry warfare during World War II.

Springfield M1A

$$–$$$

The Springfield M1A is the civilian version of the M14 rifle, the weapon that effectively took over from the M1 Garand in the US forces during the 1950s and first half of the 1960s.

SPECIFICATIONS: **Springfield M1A Standard**

CALIBRE: 7.62 x 51 NATO

BARREL LENGTH: 56cm (22in)

WEIGHT: 4.2kg (9.2lb)

SIGHTS: adjustable aperture rear sight; front post; provision for scope

MECHANISM: gas operated

FEATURES: 10- or 20-round magazine; reliable action

The catalyst for the development of the M14 was a standardization of Western small arms to the 7.62 x 51 NATO cartridge. A quick glance at the receiver of the M14 speaks of its Garand ancestry, but the M14 had a selective-fire capability, although few soldiers found the full-auto mode practical when firing full-length rifle rounds.

Vietnam War service

The M14 went on to give service in the Vietnam War, but it was steadily replaced by the much lighter and more controllable 5.56mm (.22in) M16A1 rifle. This switch was a major source of controversy amongst the military, with many soldiers bitterly regretting the loss of the full-calibre firepower provided by the M14. Many soldiers felt that the 5.56mm (.22in) simply did not have the take-down power required for infantry combat. Production of the M14 has now ceased, but

the design lives on in Springfield's M21 military sniper rifle and their civilian M1A semi-auto series.

The standard M1A rifle is much like the original M14. It has a 56cm (22in) barrel, works on a gas-operated rotating-bolt mechanism, and takes its feed from a 10- or 20-round detachable box magazine. The 7.62mm (.308) rounds have a muzzle velocity of some 853m/sec (2800ft/sec), and the rifle is a practical option for hunting deer or other large game, although the gun has a substantial weight at 4.2kg (9.2lb) without a scope.

Military and match

The M1A is very popular format for civilian, law-enforcement and military use, so Springfield produced several different models. The National Match M1A and Super Match M1A, for example, are accurized versions that feature match-grade barrels and triggers, and other options such as stainless-steel barrels and fibreglass stocks.

The M1A Scout Squad has a shortened barrel and reduced overall dimensions and is designed for mounting the Aimpoint military sight on a forward optical sight base. Springfield also makes two SOCOM (Special Operations Command) models – the SOCOM II and SOCOM 16. The latter is a 41cm (16in) version of the M1A, while the SOCOM II is a very military-looking weapon featuring a high-efficiency muzzle brake.

The Springfield M1A is ideally suited to target shooting, it being more of a combat weapon than a hunting weapon. Various rail fittings allow the gun to take a scope.

Walther G22

$

The Walther G22 is a truly unusual looking gun. It uses state-of-the-art materials and a bullpup design to create a precision tool for hunting, plinking or target shooting.

SPECIFICATIONS: **Walther G22**
CALIBRE: .22 LR
BARREL LENGTH: 50.8cm (20in)
WEIGHT: 2.7kg (5.9lb)
SIGHTS: universal sight rail fitted
MECHANISM: blowback, magazine fed
FEATURES: bullpup mechanism

Walther G22s come in two colours: black, or military green (pictured above).

The Walther G22 is produced in one calibre – .22 Long Rifle. It is produced entirely out of steel and polymer (there is no wood to be seen), and the most immediately striking feature of the gun is its layout. The G22 is a bullpup gun, meaning that the action and magazine of the weapon are set behind the trigger. The reason for doing this is that the overall dimensions of the gun are reduced while the barrel can retain the length of a conventional gun's. The G22, for example, is 72cm (28in) in overall length but the barrel is 50.8cm (20in) long.

Accurate hunter

Longer barrels mean accurate shooting, and the G22 is certainly building a reputation for tight patterns. Fed from a 10-round magazine (a 13-round magazine

is also available), the G22 can perform with competition levels of accuracy between 100 and 200m (328 and 656ft).

Of course, this depends upon the sight. An open sight system is fitted, but a Weaver-style universal sight rail is fitted on the top handle, and a further mount is supplied at the front to take a laser sight. The inclusion of a laser mount is revealing.

The Carl Walther website places the G22 under the 'Defence' category, and the ability to fit highly effective sound suppressors have led to speculation about the gun's possible use in special forces hands. Whether that happens, the gun still offers plenty to entertain the civilian market.

Mounting rails underneath the G22's muzzle can take a variety of fittings and tools, including laser sights, combat torches and folding bipods.

Winchester Super X Rifle $

Although the Winchester Company's closure of its Connecticut production plant threatens the future of some gun lines, the Super X Rifle (SXR) is a brand-new semi-automatic weapon.

SPECIFICATIONS: Winchester Super X Rifle

CALIBRE: .30–06 Springfield, .300 Win Mag, .300 WSM, .270 WSM

BARREL LENGTH: 56cm (22in), 61cm (24in)

WEIGHT: up to 3.3kg (7.2lb)

SIGHTS: provision for scope

MECHANISM: gas operated

FEATURES: detachable trigger group; fast reloading; cross-bolt safety

The Winchester SXR can be fitted with telescopic sights for precision shooting.

The SXR is available in four calibres – .30–06 Springfield, .300 Win Mag, .300 WSM, and .270 WSM. Such calibres squarely put the SXR in the deer-hunting, large-game category. Its hunting application is suggested by the enlarged trigger guard, which is purposely designed for use with gloved hands. The trigger is a single-stage type, giving a crisp shot, and a cross-bolt safety allows a quick switch from safe mode to shot should a target present itself. The trigger group is also detachable, a useful feature if the gun has been subject to wet and mud and needs easy access for cleaning.

Winchester promotes the SXR on the basis of a very fast reload via its gas-operated system (company material claims that the reload 'is among the fastest on the planet'), and its hammer-forged barrel gives it good accuracy for those precision shots at distances of up to several hundred metres (yards). The bolt system is of the rotary type, giving a fast and secure lock prior to firing.

Features

The Super X has two different barrel lengths – 56cm (22in) and 61cm (24in). The overall length of the gun stands at 105cm (41.4in) and the weight is either 3.2kg (7lb) or 3.3kg (7.2lb) depending on the calibre and the barrel length. The length of pull is 36cm (14.1in).

The SXR is fed from a detachable box magazine, this fitting up into the walnut fore-end. The SXR is entering a competitive marketplace, but with good Winchester build quality and a price tag of around $800, its commercial performance looks promising.

Winchester promotes the Super X Rifle on the basis of its fast reloading, its removable trigger assembly (for ease of maintenance) and its 'bolt action accuracy'.

Glossary

Action – The working mechanism of a firearm, responsible for the main activities of loading, firing and ejecting. Action is also used sometimes in the same way as 'receiver'.

Blowback operated – A system used in automatic weapons, where the pressure on the cartridge case provides the energy to operate the loading and unloading cycle of the weapon when the gun is fired.

Bolt – The part of a rifle or semi-auto shotgun that pushes the cartridge into the chamber and locks it in place, and through which runs the firing pin.

Bore – The interior section of a gun's barrel.

Boxlock – A type of action in a break-open gun where all of the lockwork is contained within a box-like housing. Boxlocks are the most common type of double-barrelled shotgun mechanism, being relatively inexpensive to manufacture and extremely robust.

Breech – The rear part of a barrel into which a cartridge is inserted.

Centrefire – A cartridge that has the percussion cap located directly in the centre of the cartridge base.

Choke – The constriction, of various diameters, at the muzzle end of a smoothbore weapon that helps control the spread of the shot through the air. Chokes can be either fixed, meaning that the muzzle is built to the desired choke specification, or interchangeable, where the choke can

be altered by means of screw-in muzzle inserts.

Comb – The top of a gun stock, where the shooter's cheek sits when the gun is mounted.

Ejector – A system for throwing the spent cartridge cases from a gun.

Extractor – A system for lifting spent cartridge cases out of the chambers, making them easily removed by hand.

Fluted barrel – A barrel with longitudinal depressions cut into its surface, which reduce the overall weight of the barrel and improve cooling.

Fore-end – The front part of a stock, usually located under the barrel.

Free-floating – A barrel is free-floating if it is not in contact with the fore-end; this reduces barrel distortion and improves accuracy.

Furniture – External metal fittings on a gun, such as trigger guard, sling swivels etc.

Gas operated – An automatic weapon that uses burnt propellant gases to operate the cycle of loading and unloading.

Gauge – The calibre of a shotgun bore. The term relates to the number of lead balls the same diameter as the bore that it takes to make 1lb (0.45kg) in weight.

Hammer – In a long gun, the part of a gun that strikes the firing pin, driving it onto the percussion cap.

Lock – The system of securing a cartridge in the chamber to ensure that it is safe to fire.

Monobloc – The solid block at the end of some shotgun barrels into which the breech ends are machined.

Over-and-under – In a double-barrel shotgun, where the barrels are set one on top of the other in a vertical plane.

Receiver – The basic structure of a gun that houses the working parts and onto which the barrel and stock are assembled. Sometimes also called the 'action'.

Recoil operated – A gun that uses the forces of recoil to operate the loading and unloading cycle.
Rib – A metal platform running along shotgun barrels that acts as a sighting plane.

Rimfire – Cartridges that have the primer distributed around the rim of the cartridge head.

Sear – A part of the trigger mechanism that holds back the hammer, striker or firing pin in the cocked position until released.

Set trigger – A trigger that can be 'set' so that a light touch fires the gun.

Side-by-side – In a double-barrel shotgun, where the barrels are set side by side on a horizontal plane.

Sidelock – A shotgun mechanism which has the action mounted on removable sideplates.

Index